WAKING
FROM
SLEEP

Hay House Titles of Related Interest

YOU CAN HEAL YOUR LIFE, the movie,
starring Louise L. Hay & Friends
(available as a 1-DVD program and an expanded 2-DVD set)
Watch the trailer at: **www.LouiseHayMovie.com**

THE SHIFT, the movie,
starring Dr. Wayne W. Dyer
(available as a 1-DVD program and an expanded 2-DVD set)
Watch the trailer at: **www.DyerMovie.com**

***

AWAKENING TO THE SECRET CODE OF YOUR MIND:
Your Mind's Journey to Inner Peace,
by Dr. Darren R. Weissman

INSPIRATION DEFICIT DISORDER: The No-Pill Prescription
to End High Stress, Low Energy, and Bad Habits,
by Jonathan H. Ellerby, Ph.D.

UNLOCK THE SECRET MESSAGES OF YOUR BODY!
A 28-Day Jump-Start Program for Radiant Health and
Glorious Vitality, by Denise Linn

VISIONS, TRIPS, AND CROWDED ROOMS:
Who and What You See Before You Die, by David Kessler

WHY MEDITATE?, by Matthieu Ricard

All of the above are available at your local bookstore,
or may be ordered by visiting:

Hay House USA: **www.hayhouse.com**®
Hay House Australia: **www.hayhouse.com.au**
Hay House UK: **www.hayhouse.co.uk**
Hay House South Africa: **www.hayhouse.co.za**
Hay House India: **www.hayhouse.co.in**

WAKING
FROM
SLEEP

The Causes of Awakening Experiences
and How to Make Them Permanent

STEVE TAYLOR

HAY HOUSE, INC.
Carlsbad, California • New York City
London • Sydney • Johannesburg
Vancouver • Hong Kong • New Delhi

Published and distributed in the United States by: Hay House, Inc.: www.hayhouse.com • *Published and distributed in Australia by:* Hay House Australia Pty. Ltd.: www.hayhouse.com.au • *Published and distributed in the United Kingdom by:* Hay House UK, Ltd.: www.hayhouse.co.uk • *Published and distributed in the Republic of South Africa by:* Hay House SA (Pty), Ltd.: www.hayhouse.co.za • *Distributed in Canada by:* Raincoast: www.raincoast.com • *Published in India by:* Hay House Publishers India: www.hayhouse.co.in

Library of Congress Control Number: 2010922254

ISBN: 978-1-4019-2870-4
Digital ISBN: 978-1-4019-2948-0

13 12 11 10   4 3 2 1
1st edition, December 2010

Printed in the United States of America

To Pam

From the Editor: To our North American readers, please note that for the most part, we have maintained the British style of spelling, grammar, punctuation, and syntax of the original text in order to preserve the editorial intent of the author, who hails from the United Kingdom.

CONTENTS

ACKNOWLEDGEMENTS

This book has had a long life – in fact, I began developing its basic ideas and writing a first version as long ago as 1996. That was also when I first began to collect reports of awakening experiences. I would like to thank all of the friends, acquaintances, students and strangers who have provided the reports I have used in this book, including: Janice Hartley, Valerie Massey, Sandy Geddes, Paul Heaton, Liesbeth Coomans, Duncan Heath, Colin Stanley, Mark Sullivan, Mary Gant, Tony Wright, Richard Arkwright, Carrie Mitchell, Pamela Smith (my wife), Dave Brock, Melford Bramble, Kevin Hinchcliffe, and Tony Lomax and Ken Garrod at the Buddhist Society of Manchester. There I would also like to thank the spiritual teacher Russel Williams, who has been the source of many experiences of *satsang* for me over the years. Several of the experiences I've quoted were given me by my students at the University of Manchester CCE, whose names I unfortunately did not keep a record of. So, in lieu of personal thanks, I would like to offer collective gratitude to all of the students who attended my courses on the psychology of happiness between 2005 and 2009.

I am also grateful to Paul Marshall (author of *Mystical Encounters with the Natural World*), who closely read the manuscript and made many helpful suggestions, and to my agent Bill Gladstone, for his enthusiasm and help. Thanks also to Mike Daniels, Les Lancaster and everyone else involved in the transpersonal psychology courses at Liverpool John Moores University. But most of all, I'm grateful to my wife Pam, whom coincidentally I met the very same week I began this book, 13 years ago.

Steve Taylor

INTRODUCTION

I'm 22 years old. I left university a few months ago and have a temporary job at the local social security office, processing benefit claims from people who are too ill to work. Today I'm reading through the file of a 22-year-old girl who has died of brain cancer. I read the letters from her parents: the first one explains that she's had to leave her job and wants to claim sickness benefit; the second, a few weeks later, says that her condition has deteriorated quickly and she probably won't be returning to work. Then there is a final letter, from this morning, saying that she has died. The case shocks me, partly because the girl was my age and lived quite close to me. I feel as if I should know her but don't recognize the name. Reading the final letter from her parents is heartbreaking and I feel almost like crying. But at the same time it makes me realize how lucky I am to be alive myself. It could easily have been me; it's really just a matter of luck that it wasn't. It makes me realize that you can never take life for granted, that an illness or an accident can take you away at any moment, and because of that every moment is precious.

That feeling of freedom and gratitude is still inside me when I leave work. I usually catch the bus, but today it's warm and sunny and I decide to walk home. As I walk along the busy main road I look up at the sky, at the gigantic foaming white clouds with the smooth blue spaces between them and sunlight spraying across them. It seems so beautiful that I can't turn my attention away, and as I carry on looking the scene becomes even more beautiful. It seems to have taken on an extra dimension of reality: I can see more detail and perspective, the spaces between the clouds seem fuller and deeper, and the clouds themselves seem to have an intense presence that wasn't there before. The whole sky seems a fantastical landscape, full of bizarre shapes and beautiful colours. The white of the clouds and the blue of the sky are the purest and most perfect colours I have ever seen.

Now I have stopped walking and I'm so amazed by the beauty that I don't care that passing drivers must be looking at me and thinking I'm mad. There's a feeling of ecstasy building up inside me, as if the energy inside me is moving softly and slowly and intensifying. And now as I gaze at the scene something else happens: I can sense something *beneath* the clouds and the sky and the sunlight. The apparent separateness between them dissolves away. They are not separate things but expressions of the same force, a kind of ocean of radiant energy which underlies them and flows through them. They are all *one,* and the force that makes them one is so harmonious and benevolent that I feel that the world is a miraculously beautiful and meaningful place.

Three years later my exploits as a musician have led me to Germany, where I'm scraping a living from doing gigs with my band and giving a few English lessons each week. Our gigs often involve long periods of hanging around with nothing to do but drink beer and smoke cigarettes and then periods of over-excitement after we've finished playing when we try to unwind by talking to our 'fans' – especially the female ones – and drinking and smoking more. I used to meditate regularly and do *chi gung* exercises almost every day, but for the past year or so I haven't done either of them. I used to be inspired by books on mysticism – I used to carry a copy of the ancient Indian text, the Upanishads, around with me – but lately I seem to have lost interest in them as well.

On this particular night we don't have a gig, but I've been to one of the local bars for a few drinks as usual. The bars are always open into the early hours and I get to bed at about three in the morning, feeling slightly drunk. Just a couple of hours later I wake up, for no apparent reason. I should feel terrible, but I have a marvellous warm sense of well-being. I'm lying on my back, looking up at the ceiling. It's dark, but the darkness is different from normal. It's full of something, alive with something – a powerful harmonious force.

The darkness is so *thick* with this force that I feel that I can reach out and touch it. It's almost solid, as if the air is concentrated with 1,000 times more oxygen than normal.

But this force isn't just in my bedroom, it's everywhere – a kind of essence, something fundamental, which fills the whole of space and the whole of the universe. It feels like the heart of things, the source of everything that exists, and it fills me with a sense of calm euphoria, a sense that everything is well in the world, that there's nothing to worry about. No matter how messy and frustrating life can be, no matter how much trouble there is in the world, in some way all of that is just on the surface. Below the surface the whole universe is gently vibrating with warm radiance and is filled with harmony. And in some way I am a part of this force. There is no 'me' and no 'it'. I'm being carried along by it, out there in space, surfing on the waves of this ocean of bliss.

Now my unruly musician days are long behind me and I'm a semi-respectable member of society working as a lecturer, teacher and writer, and the father of two young children. We're on holiday in Anglesey, an island off the coast of north Wales. On the last night of the holiday I decide to explore some of the farmland around our bungalow. I climb over a gate I haven't noticed before because it is hidden by long grass and find myself looking down at a valley, with farmers' fields sloping as far as I can see and hundreds of sheep dotted over the hills.

We haven't had such a good week for weather, but this evening the sky is clear. I walk for a few minutes, and while I'm looking at the fields and the sky I have the same sense I had when I was walking home from work 16 years ago and which I've had regularly over the years since: suddenly, as if someone has pressed a switch, the scene becomes intensely real. The fields and the bushes and trees and the clouds seem to be powerfully *there*, even to have their own kind of identity, almost as if they're sentient beings. Seeing so much land in front of me with so much clear sky above it makes me think of the planet I'm on the surface of and that at this very moment it is spinning on its axis, away from the sun, and that's why it's starting to get dark.

I try to imagine my real situation: I see myself walking on an island surrounded by sea, with the bigger island of mainland Britain to the east, on the surface of a spherical planet moving through space, with the whole of the universe above and around me. And as I imagine this, I feel a sense of unity with the space above me. I look at the sky and can sense somehow that the space that fills it is the same space that fills my own being. What's inside me, as my own consciousness, is also out there. They are the same substance. My normal sense of duality – of being an 'I' inside my head, looking out at the world – is an illusion. The whole of the cosmos is one vast living unity which I'm a part of. In some sense I feel that the universe is inside me and that I am it.

These are three examples of the higher states of consciousness – or 'awakening experiences', as I prefer to call them – I've had throughout my life. I've chosen three fairly intense experiences; in fact, the second is probably the most intense one I've ever had. But I've had experiences of the same kind, if not always the same intensity, fairly regularly over the years.

I first remember having the experiences when I was 16. I grew up in an urban environment and sometimes at night I used to go to the playing fields of my school, the only place nearby where there was open space and quietness. I would wander around the fields in the darkness, feeling a sense of peace and wholeness and connection with the sky and the trees and fields around me. At that time I thought I was different, maybe even that there was something wrong with me, but within a few years I'd discovered that these experiences were far from unusual. When I studied literature at university I found that many poets had described visions of mystical radiance and unity, from explicitly religious poets such as Thomas Traherne and Henry Vaughan to romantic poets like Wordsworth and Shelley and mavericks like Walt Whitman and D. H. Lawrence.

Soon afterwards, I started to read books on spirituality and mysticism and found that people of every culture and every period of history had described such experiences. Awakening experiences seem to be universal. No matter what kind of culture a person comes from and no matter what their personal religious or philosophical beliefs are, they have essentially the same experiences. They might be interpreted slightly differently due to cultural differences, but they have occurred in essentially the same form all over the world throughout history. The vision of the world that Walt Whitman describes in *Leaves of Grass,* for example, is essentially the same as that of the Upanishads (the earliest of which were written down 2,500 years ago and probably originated centuries before then), of the third-century Greek philosopher Plotinus, of the medieval German mystic Meister Eckhart, and so on.

But these experiences certainly aren't confined to famous mystics and poets. Later I began to talk to friends and acquaintances about my own experiences and found that many of them had had them too, even people who didn't know anything about spirituality or mysticism. Later still, people I became friendly with at Buddhist groups told me about their experiences, and others contacted me through my website (usually in connection with my other books) to share theirs. A few years ago I began teaching courses on the psychology of happiness at the University of Manchester. During sessions on 'peak experiences' I asked my students to write a description of their highest, most ecstatic experiences and found that many of these were fully-fledged awakening experiences. Over the years I have collected over 150 examples of awakening experiences from friends, acquaintances and students, and I quote from these throughout this book.

In 2000 the British researcher Gordon Heald found that 29 per cent of 1,000 people had had an experience of 'a sacred presence in nature'.[1] Similarly, in 1974 the American researcher Andrew Greeley asked 1,460 people if they had ever had the experience of being 'very close to a powerful, spiritual force that seemed to lift you out of yourself'. Thirty-five per cent of them said they had, with 21 per cent saying they had had the experience several times and 12 per cent that it happened often.[2] There are many collections and studies of awakening experiences – such as Alister Hardy's *The Spiritual Nature of Man,* David Hay's *Exploring Inner Space,* Raynor Johnson's *Watcher on the Hills* or Edward Hoffman's *Visions of Innocence* – that illustrate how common the experiences are amongst 'ordinary' people.

Since the experiences are so common, it seems strange that we hear so little about them. Why did I spend so long thinking there was something wrong with me when in reality around a third or even two-thirds of the people around me had had similar experiences to mine?

The problem is that these experiences are slightly taboo. Like talking about sex in Victorian England, it's not socially acceptable to tell our friends or colleagues about these visions of oneness and harmony and feelings of bliss. We're afraid that we'll be thought of as 'weird' if we describe them, simply because we're not aware that many of the people we talk to are likely to have had the experiences too. We're afraid they won't know what we're talking about, when in reality they probably will.

THE 'SLEEP' OF OUR NORMAL CONSCIOUSNESS

Some materialistic scientists believe that awakening experiences are just 'tricks of the mind' caused by abnormal brain functioning. As a result, they claim they have no more validity than a hallucination or a dream and the vision of the world they give us is an illusion. But I believe that the reverse is true: these experiences are *more* real than our normal state. It's more accurate to see them as a kind of 'waking up' from the sleep of our normal state. Our normal consciousness is narrow and restricted and gives us a false and limited experience of reality. That's why, in awakening experiences, there is a sense that our consciousness has become wider and clearer and that we have gained access to a deeper and truer level of reality which is normally hidden from us.

In particular, my aim in this book is to try to explain *why* these experiences occur, to look at what *causes* them. The psychologist Abraham Maslow believed that awakening experiences (or 'peak experiences', as he termed them) occurred accidentally and there was nothing you could do to generate them. Other religious-minded authors believe that the experiences are given by the grace of God. But I don't believe that this is the case. Although some experiences may occur spontaneously, I believe that they have two basic sources, which I will describe in detail later.

This is important because once we understand why awakening experiences occur, it should become easier for us to have them. Rather than waiting for them, we should be able to make a conscious effort to generate them. And in the same way, once we understand the basic psychological 'mechanics' of awakening experiences, we should be able to understand what living in a state of *permanent* wakefulness would mean and how to go about trying to attain this.

You can think of our normal consciousness as a particular kind of 'mental structure'. In awakening experiences, the structure dissolves, but it usually reforms itself soon afterwards, like the limb of a newt regenerating after being cut off. That's why awakening experiences are usually temporary. But under certain circumstances, either through a long process of spiritual practise and development or through a sudden experience of detachment and liberation (often caused by intense suffering), the structure *permanently* dissolves away. The 'mould' of the structure is broken and so can't reform itself. There is a different structure in place instead. As a result, the person becomes permanently awakened.

I certainly don't want to underestimate the kind of effort needed to permanently transform your state of being. Many mystics struggled for years – even decades – to bring about a shift to a higher state of consciousness, subjecting themselves to severe disciplines and arduous spiritual practises. Spiritual paths such as Patanjali's eight-limbed path or the Eightfold Path of Buddhism demand great reserves of will-power and self-control, as well as a great deal of guidance from others who have followed them before. However, one of the central points of this book is that states of awakening are much closer to us than we might think. I'm going to show that, in a sense, higher states of consciousness are actually natural and normal, and that it is our 'normal' consciousness that is abnormal or, more strictly, *sub*-normal.

THE SCOPE OF THE BOOK

In the first section of the book we look at the vision of the world that our normal consciousness gives us and how most people take it for granted that it is the *true* picture of reality, so much so that our culture is dominated by a view of the world as an inanimate, mechanical place. Then we look at how awakening experiences transform this vision, moving from lower-intensity experiences – when our surroundings become more real, beautiful and alive – to the highest intensity of awakening, when the world dissolves into an ocean of pure spirit.

We then investigate the idea that higher states of consciousness – at least at a less intense level – may be normal to some peoples in the world. This may leave me open to accusations of romanticizing other cultures, but there is a great deal of evidence suggesting that peoples such as the Native Americans, the Australian Aborigines or the peoples of Polynesia had (and perhaps still have in some cases) a naturally 'spiritual' vision of the world. We also investigate the controversial idea that, in some respects, children may have a naturally 'awake' vision of the world too.

Following this, we investigate the two sources of awakening experiences and look at the different activities and situations that can trigger them, including fasting, sleep deprivation, drugs, sex, sports, meditation, the presence of an enlightened person, and so on. We also examine the paradox of why states of depression and despair are such a common trigger of awakening experiences and how encountering death can cause a permanent shift to an awakened state.

Finally, we turn to long-term development. We examine ancient spiritual paths and the methods which mystics and other spiritual adepts throughout history have used to transform themselves, looking at what 'spiritual development' means in terms of my explanation of awakening experiences. We also look at the connection between spiritual development and evolution. Then we look at where this leaves us in terms of our own life, what methods we should use and what lifestyle we should follow in order to move towards a permanent higher state of consciousness.

Waking up isn't just something we do for *ourselves*, for our own personal benefit or gratification. It *does* enhance our life massively, in the same way that being freed from prison or regaining full vision after being partially sighted enhances a person's life. But it isn't just a personal matter – as well as transforming our perception and our experience, waking up transforms our relationships and affects society as a whole, even the world as a whole. It's precisely because we're 'asleep' – because we perceive the world as a dreary, inanimate place and ourselves as separate, and because there's a fundamental psychological discord inside us all the time – that the world is filled with so much conflict and disorder. It's because we've been asleep for millennia that human history has been an endless saga of warfare, conflict and oppression. And it's because we're asleep now that we're so close to destroying the life-support systems of our planet and jeopardizing our future as a species (and that of many other species too). We need to wake up on behalf of the human race as a whole, on behalf of the world as a whole and on behalf of the whole evolutionary process that has taken life from the first single-celled amoeba to the astoundingly complex creatures with a hundred billion-celled brains such as us.

A NOTE ON TERMINOLOGY

Before we begin, I should clarify some of the terms I'm using. For me, the terms 'awakening experience' and 'higher state of consciousness' have exactly the same meaning. They both refer to a state of consciousness, or a state of being, in which our vision of the world and our relationship to it are transformed, an experience of clarity, revelation and joy in which we become aware of a deeper (or higher) level of reality, perceive a sense of harmony and meaning, and transcend our normal sense of separateness from the world. Although I use both terms regularly, I prefer 'awakening experience' to 'higher state of consciousness', as the latter sounds slightly clinical and is rather long and unwieldy.

I originally wanted to use the term 'spiritual experience', but soon found that this was confusing. When I began to ask people 'Have you ever had a spiritual experience?' I became aware of how many different interpretations of the word 'spiritual' there are. One person told me about a nightmarish vision of seeing her own dead body, while others gave me reports of psychic or paranormal experiences – strange dreams, out-of-body experiences, telepathic or clairvoyant experiences, or experiences of sensing an 'evil' presence. These experiences are certainly significant, but they aren't 'spiritual experiences' in the sense that I use the term.

I could perhaps have used the term 'mystical experience', but this wouldn't have been wholly accurate either. There are different intensities of awakening experience and what are usually described as 'mystical experiences' belong to the highest intensity. The term isn't therefore appropriate to describe lower-intensity awakening experiences. And in any case, 'mystical' is another confusing word. To my mind, a 'mystic' is a person who has managed to 'wake up' from their normal consciousness to some degree and so has a truer and more intense vision of reality and a new relationship to the world. But for other people, particularly sceptics and materialistic scientists, the term 'mystical' means going beyond the bounds of modern science or reason.

The experiences are sometimes described as – or at least included in the category of – 'religious experiences', but I think this is misleading too. That term can refer to a whole host of other experiences that have little in common with awakening experiences, such as visions of God, the Virgin Mary or the Devil, or believing that you've received help in response to prayer or that the Holy Spirit has healed you.

Moreover, awakening experiences in themselves are not religious. People who are religious often explain them in religious terms – for example, if they have a vision of a powerful radiant spirit-force pervading all things, they might believe that they have 'seen God' in some form. But this is only an interpretation based on pre-existing concepts. Many non-religious people have the same experience but don't explain it in those terms.

It's important to note that spirituality and religion aren't the same thing. Sometimes they merge, so that a person is spiritual and religious at the same time, like the most liberal and ecumenical Christians, Muslims or Jews. And it's true that certain aspects of the religious life, like prayer and fasting, give people access to spiritual experiences. But it's quite possible (and sadly very common) for people to be religious without being at all spiritual, for example fundamentalist Christians or Muslims.

And at the same time, it's possible for people to be spiritual without being religious. Many people feel a strong empathic connection to the cosmos (including other beings and nature) and a strong impulse to expand and intensify their consciousness without belonging to any religious tradition. In my view, this is one of the most significant developments of recent times – that so many people are having awakening experiences without explaining them in religious terms. As a result, we are beginning to see awakening experiences as natural and innate, as having their source inside us rather than arising from grace or God.[3]

The real significance of these experiences is that they are an 'awakening'. They give us a glimpse of the world of beauty, meaning and unity that lies beyond the normal human world of separation and suffering – a new world which it is possible for us to inhabit permanently.

1

THE VARIETIES OF AWAKENING EXPERIENCE

Before we look at awakening experiences, it makes sense to investigate the normal state we wake up *from*. Or to put it another way, if we want to investigate higher states of consciousness, we should first look at the normal state of consciousness they are higher *than*.

What is the reality that most people perceive as they go about their day-to-day lives? What does normal human consciousness tell us is the truth about our life and the world we are living in?

From the standpoint of normal consciousness, one of the most basic 'facts' about our existence is that we live in a state of isolation and separation. *You* are an entity inside your brain and your body which looks out at a world which is 'out there', like a person looking out of a window on to a street scene. You are 'in here', talking to yourself inside your head, with your own thoughts and feelings, one step removed from the world. Of course, you can interact with other people and tell them how you feel and what you think, but ultimately nobody will ever able to experience what it's like to be you or to know exactly what's in your head. Other people, and the world itself, will always be separate from you. You will always be, essentially, alone.

Experiencing this sense of separation can be very painful. Some people try to avoid it by spending as little time as possible alone and

1

by making sure that even if they are alone their attention is occupied by activities or distractions – for example, doing jobs around the house, watching television or surfing the internet. Other people try to escape this sense of aloneness by becoming a member of groups – football clubs, religious or political groups, gangs, fans of particular pop groups and so on. They gain a sense of belonging by becoming a part of something greater than themselves and conforming to the rules and conventions of the group.

Relationships enable us to 'bridge' our fundamental separateness, and distractions make us forget that it's there. However, there are always moments when we have to come back to ourselves – when we're on our own and can't find anything worth watching on TV, on a long train journey or flight, or lying in bed at night alone with our own thoughts. In fact, you could say that this is what loneliness basically is: the experience of our fundamental isolation, of being trapped inside ourselves with thoughts and feelings that we can't express to others.

Another obvious 'fact' about our experience from the standpoint of normal consciousness is that all the things we see in the world exist in separation from each other. Looking out of my window now, I see clouds in the sky, a few birds flying by, trees and bushes, chairs in the garden, clothes on the washing line, and the roofs of houses. From the standpoint of ordinary consciousness, it's obvious that all of these things are distinct and apart, with no connection between them. They are collections of particles with defined boundaries, separated by distance. And between them all is empty space, the space that we move through as we walk and that fills the sky above us and the universe beyond.

Normal consciousness sees all of these objects as inanimate too. What is a stone or a rock? What is the water in a river or the soil in the ground? They're just dead 'things' with no being of their own, made up of inert matter. And even though we describe trees and plants and other types of vegetation as 'alive' in a biochemical sense (because they're collections of cells and they can take in energy and reproduce), we still see them as basically inanimate. We certainly

2

don't consider them as alive in the same way that we are, in the sense of having a consciousness or being. And the empty space between all of these objects – it certainly isn't alive either. How could it be, since there's nothing *in* it, apart from chemicals?

As we'll see in the next chapter, there are some indigenous peoples in the world who don't see things in this way, who believe that even stones and rivers have their own kind of inner being. As a result they have great respect for natural phenomena and are reluctant to damage their environment. But our inability to sense the life of 'inanimate' things means that we lack this respect, and this has helped to generate the abuse of the environment that is now threatening to make us an extinct species.

In connection with this, another characteristic of our normal consciousness is what you could call its 'shadowy' vision of reality. Many anthropologists have told us that indigenous peoples have a much more intense perception of reality than we do. According to Stanley Diamond, for example, 'Among primitives the sense of reality is heightened to the point where it sometimes seems to blaze,'[1] while according to Morris Berman, early hunter-gatherer peoples had a 'heightened awareness' which also made their surroundings 'blaze' with intensity.[2] Berman suggests that these peoples didn't worship gods, because for them 'the aliveness of the world is all that needs to be worshipped'.[3] Children also appear to have a very intense vision of reality. To them, the world seems to be an incredibly bright, fresh and fascinating place. In the words of the developmental psychologist Alison Gopnik, they have 'infinite capacity for wonder'.[4]

For most adult westerners, however, the world seems much less real and intense. The buildings and streets, the trees and fields and the clouds and the sky around us are usually just half-real things we've seen thousands of times before, so familiar that we rarely pay any attention to them. How many people really *look* at clouds in the sky, at the trees they pass in the street, at the scenes they pass on the bus or the train, or even at the objects around them in a room? Young children do look at these things; it's almost impossible

3

for them to get bored, because every apparently mundane scene or object around them is so real and interesting that it has to be investigated. For them – and perhaps for indigenous peoples – life is an exhilarating experience. But most European or American adults sink into boredom if their minds aren't occupied by a distraction or activity.

This is part of the reason why most people suffer from what I call the 'taking for granted syndrome'. With our mind switched off to the is-ness of our experience, we take our health, our body, other people, the whole world and our life itself for granted. However, as we'll see soon, when we 'wake up' we begin to see the world as a strange and miraculous place, to appreciate the most mundane everyday phenomena and to feel grateful that we're alive.

The final judgement on our life, from the standpoint of our ordinary consciousness, is that it is meaningless. This world of empty space and inanimate objects certainly doesn't seem benevolent or to 'mean well' – it's just neutral, blankly indifferent. It doesn't matter to the world whether we are alive or not. We're born by accident, we run about its surface for a few decades, keeping ourselves alive with food and drink, working, sleeping and perhaps nurturing our children, and otherwise trying to keep ourselves amused and occupy our mind as best we can. And gradually our body decays until we die – at which point we (and all of our wealth and success and notoriety) disappear forever.

Since you're reading this book you no doubt already have an interest in self-development and spirituality, and it may be that you have already 'awakened' to a degree. So perhaps some of these characteristics don't apply to you. You may well have a sense of the life of the phenomena around you, of your connectedness to the world or that life is ultimately meaningful. But I believe it's valid to say that most people live in this basic state of 'sleep'.

And if this is how most people experience life, why shouldn't we believe it's the truth? As a materialist scientist might say, shouldn't we be brave enough to face up to bleak reality rather than use religion and superstition to deceive ourselves that life isn't as meaningless

4

as it seems? Shouldn't we just accept that we live in an inanimate, indifferent world where everything exists in separation and nothing that we do has any consequence?

Many of our scientists, philosophers and other intellectuals would agree that this is the 'truth' of the human predicament. Many modern scientists believe that life evolved accidentally, that human beings are nothing more than gene machines, that everything we think or feel is just the buzzing around of our brain cells and that there is no 'soul' or 'spirit' inside us which will survive the death of the body. This is the 'enlightened' view of the world that science has given us.

However, there's a giant fallacy at the heart of this view: the assumption that the consciousness through which we are aware of reality is perfect and objective, like a camera. We might admit that it's possible to look at the world in other states of consciousness – for example, in altered states induced by drugs, mental illness or 'spiritual experience'. But we assume that our everyday consciousness gives us a true and complete picture of the world.

But what if this isn't true? What if, rather than being objective, our normal consciousness is limited and blinkered and gives us what is in some ways a *false* picture of reality? What if we only see the world in this way because we are 'asleep'?

One major piece of evidence for this view is that, as I've suggested, many other peoples in the world have seen (and still do see) reality in a completely different way from us, not just in terms of their beliefs but in terms of their actual *experience* of life. These peoples have a different kind of *psyche* to ours, a different way of perceiving the world, and so perceive a different kind of reality (we will look at these peoples' experience of reality in more detail in Chapter 3). This suggests that our view of reality is not the absolute truth but a vision which is *relative* to us and moulded by our particular kind of psyche. This is similar to what the German philosopher Kant suggested: that our awareness of reality is filtered through the structures with which we perceive it. Our mind does not just observe reality, it co-creates it.

Another major piece of evidence comes from awakening experiences, in which this vision of the world and this experience of life are completely transformed.

LOW- TO MEDIUM-INTENSITY AWAKENING EXPERIENCES

Over the next two chapters we're going to go on a journey beyond our limited, ordinary 'sleep' consciousness into wider vistas of reality in which all of the characteristics we've just looked at are transformed. We're going to move through the whole continuum of awakening experiences, from the most basic to the most intense, looking at the different characteristics that unfold as they intensify.

In the most basic kind of awakening experience, our normal 'shadowy' vision of the world is transformed and we gain something of the intense vision of the world of children and some indigenous peoples. It's as if a new dimension of reality is added, as if the world switches from monochrome to colour. Things which normally don't seem beautiful or interesting at all, and which we don't normally pay attention to, suddenly seem to have a new kind of is-ness. They seem brighter, more colourful and more intricate, and to have more depth and perspective.

I describe this in the first and third experiences in the introduction: how the clouds seemed to take on an extra dimension of reality and how, in the third experience, all the natural world around me seemed to be powerfully *there*. I often have this experience after meditation. If I've had a good practise and have managed to quiet my chattering mind, I find that even household objects seem to possess a new is-ness. I might drink a cup of tea and really *see* the painting on the cup, or really *see* the patterns on my carpet, or find myself staring at the beautiful patterns of sunlight on the kitchen floor, or watching the patterns of splashing water and bubbles when I do the washing-up.

The great writer on mysticism Evelyn Underhill refers to this as 'a clarity of vision, a heightening of physical perception',[5] while

William James, author of *The Varieties of Religious Experience*, describes how, in mystical experiences, 'an appearance of newness beautifies every object'.[6] James illustrates this with a report from an evangelist named Billy Bray, describing his conversion experience: 'Everything looked new to me, the people, the fields, the cattle, the trees. I was like a new man in a new world.'[7] Here one of my students describes how the world became incredibly real and beautiful to her while she was walking along a beach:

> *The sun was setting and I was watching it go down. I felt*
> *everything in the world was here, at this moment. The*
> *sunlight was so incredibly bright and pure and beautiful.*
> *The blue of the sky was the smoothest and purest blue I've*
> *ever seen. I could see everything about the clouds, as if they*
> *had a whole new dimension. It seemed so simple and so*
> *right. I felt how easy it would be to be happy.*

While here an experience given to the Religious Experience Research Unit at Oxford University describes the same intensification of perception:

> *The phenomenon invariably occurs out of doors, more*
> *often than not when I am alone, although it has occurred*
> *when I have been in the company of others. It is generally*
> *prefaced by a general feeling of 'gladness to be alive'. I*
> *am never aware of how long this feeling persists, but after*
> *a period I am conscious of an awakening of my senses.*
> *Everything becomes suddenly more clearly defined; sights,*
> *sounds, and smells take on a whole new meaning.*[8]

At a slightly higher degree of intensity, awakening experiences – in addition to this sense of is-ness – bring a sense of how things are *alive*. Things which normally seem inanimate come to life. Objects which normally only have a one-dimensional surface reality have a new kind of depth, a new kind of *being*. In William Wordsworth's

7

phrase, we 'see into the life of things'. This is clear from the following description of a higher state of consciousness induced by the drug mescaline:

> Every object in my field of vision took on a curious and intense kind of existence of its own … everything appeared to have an 'inside' – to exist as I existed, having inwardness, a kind of individual life, and every object, seen under this aspect, appeared exceedingly beautiful… Everything was *urgent* with life… All things seemed to glow with a light that came from within them.[9]

This sense of 'aliveness' is often accompanied by a vision of *radiance*, a brilliant light shining from everything. A friend told me he had this experience while going home from his Buddhist centre after meditating:

> *It was as though I had a new kind of vision. The sky and the trees seemed alive. The trees seemed almost conscious, as if they were intelligent beings overlooking and observing the street scenes. And there was a light that seemed to shine. The cars and the houses seemed to lose their solidness [sic] and be somehow glowing.*

Similarly, here a woman describes an experience she had at the age of eight. She was in the garden, looking at a tree full of white blossom and at the meadow and the sunrise beyond it and listening to the singing of a blackbird:

> *As I looked at this, someone or something said to me, 'That is beautiful,' and immediately the whole scene lit up as though a bright light had been turned on, irradiating [sic] everything. The meadow was a more vivid green, the pear tree glowed and the blackbird's song was more loud and sweet.*[10]

At this intensity, awakening experiences also reveal to us that the world isn't the empty and indifferent place it appears to our ordinary consciousness. There's a sense of *meaning*, a sense of an atmosphere of harmony and benevolence. We have the beginning of a sense that all is well, that in some strange way the world, far from being the coldly indifferent place that science tells us it is, does 'mean well' by us and is a benign place. No matter what problems fill our life and how full of violence and injustice the world is, there's a sense that in some strange way everything *is* good, that the world is somehow perfect.

In *Walden* – his account of the year he spent living alone in the woods – Henry David Thoreau describes how he felt this sense of harmony and benevolence. He remarks that he never felt lonely in the woods or hankered for human company, simply because he never felt alone. There was, he writes,

> *an infinite and unaccountable friendliness all at once like*
> *an atmosphere sustaining me… Every little pine needle*
> *expanded and swelled with sympathy and befriended me. I*
> *was so distinctly made aware of the presence of something*
> *kindred to me … that I thought no place could ever be*
> *strange to me again.*[11]

In a similar way, a person gave me an account of an awakening experience she had while walking through a ruined cathedral: 'I had a feeling that everything was perfect as it was. There was no need to worry. Everything was in harmony. The world was a wonderful place.'

INNER TRANSFORMATION

So far we've been looking at changes of *vision*, of the way that we perceive the world. But awakening experiences also change us *inside*.

In our normal state of being we're never far away from inner discontent, with worries and desires gnawing away at our mind. However, in awakening experiences a sense of well-being fills us. We feel that there's a new kind of power or energy running through us, an energy which can be still and intense and fill us with a glow of serenity or be wild and powerful and fill us with ecstasy. There's a feeling of being exalted, of being *lifted up* by this power.

There may also be a sense of freedom, which is partly the result of being free from the normal worries and concerns which fill our mind. The ego-mind that generates all our worries fades away, taking all its anxiety with it and leaving only the deep river of peace which was flowing underneath our mental turmoil all along. As a result, reports of awakening experiences often include phrases like '[there was] a feeling of absolute bliss ... a feeling of intoxication, so great was the happiness', 'a sense of lightness, exhilaration and power' and 'I was filled with a great surge of joy.'[12]

Here one of my students describes a feeling of harmony and inner well-being she felt while swimming in a friend's lake in Canada:

> *I felt as though I was the only person there, the only person in the world. I swam out as far as I could to the middle of the lake and just looked around, treading water. I could see no houses, no people, no cars or roads. I could hear no noise, just my arms splashing. I felt completely alone, but part of everything. I felt at peace. All my troubles disappeared and I felt in harmony with nature. It only lasted a few minutes but I remember the sense of calmness and stillness and it soothes me now.*

This sense of well-being can also express itself as love – intense feelings of love for the people you are with at that moment, for the whole human race and for the whole world. Once a Christian minister named Rev. Leslie Whitehead was on a train when the whole compartment flooded with light. Like the person walking through the ruined cathedral, he felt 'that all was well for mankind… All men were shining glorious beings who in the end would enter incredible joy.' He went on to describe how he 'never felt more exalted. A most curious but overwhelming sense possessed me and, filled with ecstasy … I loved everybody in that compartment. I would have died for any one of the people in that compartment.'[13]

A sense of inner joy and love is a prominent part of the following experience too, which occurred when the person was driving. At a certain point she felt that she was 'directed' to look at the sky:

One small cloud is hanging there. Suddenly it explodes with light. It is outlined in brilliant silver – radiating gold and pink. I cannot describe the beauty and otherworldliness of the colours. At the same time I am filled with such love that I would die happily in this moment. Such joy![14]

And alongside this feeling of love, there is a sense of compassion for other people, other living beings or the world as a whole. The walls of the ego begin to melt away as we move beyond separateness and so begin to experience a 'shared sense of being' with other people. We begin to realize our common identity with them and so become able to 'feel with' them. We feel their joys and sufferings as our own.

MEDIUM- TO HIGH-INTENSITY AWAKENING EXPERIENCES

So far, then, awakening experiences contradict ordinary consciousness in three ways. First, the world is no longer an unreal and inanimate place; instead everything is intensely real and alive. Second, the world is no longer empty and indifferent to us; it's full of meaning and harmony and pervaded with benevolence. And third, we no longer feel a sense of inner discontent; instead we feel a sense of inner peace and joy.

As we move into high-intensity awakening experiences, all of these characteristics intensify and new characteristics are added to them. At roughly a medium intensity, for example, our sense that things are alive and our sense of meaning and radiance coalesce into a vision of what the Upanishads refer to as *brahman* and what Native American groups have called the 'Great Spirit' or 'Life Master'. We become aware of the presence of a spirit-force in the world, pervading all things and the spaces between things. We realize that it's this spirit-force that makes so-called 'inanimate objects' alive and that this is the source of the harmony and the radiance we can see everywhere. We can't see the sun on a cloudy day, but we can still see its light and feel something of its warmth, and, in the same way, with low-intensity awakening experiences we're aware of the *effects* of *brahman*, even if we can't see or sense the source itself. But with a medium-intensity experience and above, we become aware that the radiance and harmony we can sense emanate from an ocean of spirit which fills the whole universe and is the essence of reality. We realize that in reality there is no empty space, because all space is filled with spirit.

In a way there's nothing particularly esoteric about this 'spirit-force'. It's simply an energy which is present everywhere in the universe, a fundamental force which pervades all space and all matter. It seems to be at the core of everything, a kind of underlying ocean of energy which the universe has arisen from and somehow 'floats' on top of. As we'll see in Chapter 3, most if not all of the world's indigenous peoples appear to have accepted it as an everyday reality and to have sensed it as easily as we can smell a flower or see the sky.

Normally we aren't able to perceive it. Our senses seem to be 'switched off' to it. However, in awakening experiences this spirit becomes an obvious reality. I describe my awareness of it in the first passage in the introduction – how I became aware of an 'ocean of radiant energy' underlying the sky, the clouds and the sunlight. Similarly, one man described an awakening experience he had while sitting on a mountain top, waiting for friends. Suddenly his vision was transformed and he was aware of an 'immensely powerful benign force' pervading his surroundings.[15]

Here another man describes how he is always aware of what he describes as a 'sweet, cool presence' around him, which seems to intensify or weaken in different circumstances:

> *I find the presence strongly in old churches, some old*
> *houses, in wild countryside, music and a few people. About*
> *three times it has intensified into what I suppose could be*
> *called a mystical experience – a pinkish golden light which*
> *was in everything, was love and made everything look*
> *beautiful, even council houses and a corporation bus.*[16]

Visions of this spirit-force have inspired many beautiful passages of poetry, one of the most famous of which is the passage from 'Tintern Abbey' where Wordsworth describes his sense of 'something far more deeply interfused':

> **Whose dwelling is the light of setting suns,**
> **And the round ocean and the living air,**
> **And the blue sky and in the mind of man:**
> **A motion and a spirit, that impels**
> **All thinking things, all objects of all thought,**
> **And rolls through all things.**[17]

With a poetry just as beautiful, the Chandogya Upanishad describes *brahman* as 'an invisible and subtle essence [which] is the Spirit of the universe',[18] while the Mundaka Upanishad states, 'Spirit is everywhere, upon the right, upon the left, above, below, behind, in front. What is the world but Spirit?'[19]

It's the presence of this force that gives us a sense of the sacredness of the world. With spirit pervading them, all things become divine.

When people with religious beliefs have this experience, they usually interpret it in theistic terms. They associate spirit-force with God and see it as the energy or radiance of His being pouring out into His creation. The thirteenth-century Christian mystic Angela de Foligno, for example, described a vision of all-pervading spirit in the following way:

> *The eyes of my soul were opened, and I beheld the plenitude of God, whereby I did comprehend the whole world, both here and beyond the sea, and the abyss and all things else; and therein I beheld naught save the divine Power in a manner assuredly indescribable, so that through excess of marvelling the soul cried with a loud voice, saying: 'This world is full of God!'*[20]

Here a man describes an intense awareness of all-pervading spirit he experienced as a child, also interpreting it in theistic terms. He was walking through a passageway when he looked up and was struck by the contrast of an old brick wall standing against the blue of the sky:

> *For some reason I immediately thought of God – being out there, up there, in the dazzling blue sky. In the very next instant I was overwhelmed by the awareness that God was also in the bricks, and everywhere. In everything that I saw, everything that I sensed and everything that I touched I felt that God surrounded me, and though I surely wouldn't have verbalized it at the time in these words, I knew that God was good, He was love.*[21]

Sometimes when religious people have awakening experiences, they find that they have to radically revise their concept of God. For example, one theology student who experienced a higher state of consciousness after taking LSD described how, rather than seeing 'him' as an anthropomorphic entity, he was now aware that 'God is a very present force that flows through everything in existence.'[22] Similarly, another person describes how, during an awakening experience, he became aware of 'power at the same time within and

14

outside me', and as a result he no longer thought of God 'in the anthropomorphic sense that I used to'.[23]

On the other hand, some people find awakening experiences difficult to reconcile with religious beliefs. Their vision of spirit may be too far away from the traditional concept of God as a controlling, autonomous entity. The person above who became aware of an 'immensely powerful benign force' while sitting on top of a mountain goes on to describe how he began to find conventional religious false and 'second hand' after the experience, and stopped going to church.[24]

BEYOND SEPARATENESS

This awareness of spirit as a force pervading everything is closely linked to the awareness of the *oneness* of all things. Spirit-force *makes* all things one. It folds the whole world into oneness by pervading all things and the spaces between them. We realize that the underlying nature of all seemingly separate things is one and the same; the seeming difference is just on the surface, like peaks of the same mountain which seem separate when the ridges between them are covered by cloud. In high-intensity awakening experiences this whole massive underlying dimension opens out and we realize that normally we are just aware of the surface reality of things. We become aware that, say, a tree and a river – or you and I – are only different in the way that two waves of the sea appear to be separate and distinct. In reality they – and we – are part of the same ocean of being. And just as there is no real distinction between seemingly separate things, so there is no real distinction between (seemingly) empty space and matter. The boundaries between solidity and emptiness fade away. In a sense, there is no empty space any more, because, like all matter, all space is filled with spirit-force.

The sense of compassion and love I mentioned a few pages ago is the first glimmer of this oneness manifesting itself. At this low intensity, we begin to feel a *connection* with other people; the boundaries of the ego become softer, but remain intact. But at a higher intensity, we don't just feel connection but *oneness*. In the words of one person who had an intense awakening experience after meditating, 'There was a perception of oneness, all was a manifestation of Being. Through all the objects in the room [there] glowed a radiance.'[25]

Alongside this, we transcend the second type of separateness which is a part of our ordinary experience: the seeming duality between ourselves and the world, our sense of being an 'I' locked away inside our heads, detached from a world which is 'out there'. The boundary between our own self and the world dissolves away and we realize that we're part of the world, that in a sense we *are* everything. We know that the essence of our being is the essence of everything else; the spirit-force which fills the universe is inside us, as the most subtle and the purest energy of our being. In Hindu terms, the *atman*, our own deepest spiritual self, is one with *brahman*. In the famous phrase from the Chandogya Upanishad, 'Thou art that.'

This experience of oneness is one of the most common features of awakening experiences. It can manifest itself as a sense of oneness with other people or animals. We've seen that low-intensity experiences sometimes feature a 'shared sense of being' with other people, bringing an intense love and compassion for them. And at a higher intensity, this becomes an experience of actually *becoming* other beings, so that we can sense what they are feeling.

The novelist and poet D. H. Lawrence appeared to possess this ability as a normal state, which is why his writings are so amazingly perceptive and vivid. In his book of poems, *Birds, Beasts and Flowers*, for example, he seems to actually *become* the animals and plants and to know exactly how they experience the world.

A friend of mine had a similar experience of oneness at a stressful time in her life when she was on the point of separating from her husband. On the recommendation of a psychologist, she went for a long walk along the beach to think things through:

*I ran out to Hillbury Island and I had an amazing
experience where I was at one with the seabirds. It was
absolutely beautiful and fantastic. There was definitely a
feeling of oneness, a really strong feeling of affinity with the
birds. The sun was coming down in shafts of light from the
clouds and it was all just beautiful.*

And with no boundaries, she had the ability – like D. H. Lawrence –
to know what other people and animals were feeling:

*I walked back from the island and there was an old man
walking his dog and I could really* feel *the love that he
had for his dog and the dog had for him. I could feel other
people's emotions. There was a runaway horse and I
caught him. I held him and was really conscious of how he
was anxious and how he calmed down slowly.*

Occasionally this sense of oneness can be specifically with other
human beings. Here, for example, a student was in a waiting room at
a train station with 20 or so strangers when, for no apparent reason,
he became aware of a 'mysterious current of force' sweeping through
the room:

*I looked at the faces of those around me and they seemed
to be suffused with an inner radiance. I experienced in
that moment a sense of profoundest kinship with each and
every person there… I lost all sense of personal identity
then. These people were no longer strangers to me. I knew
them all. We were no longer separate individuals, each
enclosed in his own private world, divided by all the
barriers of social convention and personal exclusiveness.
We were one with each other and with the Life which we all
lived in common.*[26]

Most frequently, though, this experience of oneness is more general. We don't just become one with other beings, but with all living and non-living things and with the world – or the universe – as a whole. Here, for example, an acquaintance of mine describes an awakening experience she had one morning. She had been attending the meetings of a Buddhist group for some time and had recently had a constant feeling of calmness inside:

> *I was driving to work, with the feeling of calm and my mind open to the senses occurring around me, when I had a life-changing experience. I suddenly knew Who I was. The duality disappeared and I became. I became everything around me, the air, the trees, the slip road, just everything.*

At this level, the inner changes which awakening experiences bring intensify too. The sense of inner well-being reaches the point where we feel an incredible sense of ecstasy or bliss – the 'extraordinary joy' which the person describes above. This isn't a joy *because of* something, it's just there, a natural condition of being, radiating from the spiritual essence inside us in the same way that the harmony and 'aliveness' of the world radiate from *brahman*.

And in connection with this, another inner change which takes place at this level is a kind of identity shift. Through making contact with a deeper part of ourselves, the spiritual essence of our being, we become aware that this is who we *really* are. In the words of my acquaintance, 'I suddenly knew Who I was.' We realize that the ego-self which we always thought was our true self – the chattering 'I' with its never-ending worries and desires – is only a kind of limited and false shadow self, a sort of impostor which has taken over our psyche. Now we become a much more stable, deep-rooted and expansive self, which can't be damaged by rejection and doesn't constantly hanker for attention and is free of the anxieties that oppress the ego.

2

BEYOND THE WORLD OF FORM: HIGH-INTENSITY AWAKENING EXPERIENCES

The experiences we've looked at so far may make it seem as if awakening experiences just happen to individuals when they're on their own, meditating or walking in natural surroundings. This does seem to be true in most cases – a 1987 Gallup survey found that 60 per cent of spiritual experiences occurred when people were alone.[1] But it's important to remember that awakening experiences can be communal too. When I began to ask my students to write descriptions of their most powerful peak experiences, several of them described experiences they'd had while watching dance or theatrical performances. The following experience occurred while a person was watching a performance of Turkish Dervishes, for example:

The theatre fell silent – no babies crying, no movement or sounds from the audience, only the gentle swishing sounds of white skirts twirling and the soft sounds of felt gliding on the stage. There was a feeling of intense peace and calm, happiness and tranquillity. Nothing else mattered in the

*world and outside the theatre. We all felt as one – it was a
mesmerizing experience and unforgettable.*

Performers often experience this sense of oneness too, within their
own group and occasionally with their audience. A folk musician
told me that he sometimes experienced moments when 'the band
becomes much more than me and the other members. We become
one, and whatever we do, we do it together naturally and it's
always exactly right. It's as if we're telepathic and it feels like being
transported to another realm.' And here is the experience of a friend
of mine who used to be a morris dancer:

*We were dancing outside on a beautiful day, surrounded
by the hills. As we were dancing I started to feel as if it
wasn't me who was doing it any more. I didn't have to
think. It was just dancing me, and it was the best I'd ever
danced. I felt as though I was just a channel for the music.
Everything fell into place with the other members of the
group. We weren't individuals any more, we were a whole
body of six people. There was no division between us. I felt
an expansion of awareness into space. I was dancing in
the space in the middle of the hills. I was part of this vast
background.*

Since these are group activities, it's natural that they should
strongly feature a sense of oneness with other people – the other
members of the audience or the group itself. And it's striking that
both the musician and the dancer found that their performance was
transformed by the experience. On the one hand, they both felt that
these were moments of peak performance, when everything they
did was naturally and spontaneously perfect. And at the same time, it
was as if *they* weren't doing the performing any more, that they were
only channels for something which was working through them.

In a similar way, it's not uncommon for those providing care
and service for others, such as voluntary workers, community or

charity workers, counsellors or even teachers, to have experiences of transcending individuality. They may feel a sense of oneness with the person or people they're caring for. As one counsellor explained, describing his experience of working with a particular client, 'There was a blending of souls. It was a like a third dimension of communication, on a different plane altogether. We didn't need to speak to each other because we knew what each other was thinking. There was an intense vibrancy. It was electrifying.'

This sense of oneness can expand further too. The caregiver may feel that they're not only connecting to another person but also to a transpersonal dimension, a shared network of consciousness beyond human individuality. The psychiatrist Arthur Deikman interviewed 24 caregivers and found that most of them frequently had such experiences. A doctor who set up an organization providing care for cancer patients described it as 'a sense of connection that you have to something beyond the moment… It's like seeing both of you as part of a much larger process that has no beginning and no end.'[2] Similarly, a man who set up an organization to give care to AIDS sufferers described it as 'an extension of self… You're serving something greater and deeper than the person in front of you.'[3]

Sometimes the caregivers Deikman interviewed even experienced this connection as a tangible energy moving between them and the people they were serving. They described a 'flow' or 'current' between them and the person, or a 'literal electric charge that was passing back and forth between us'.[4]

These experiences also show that awakening experiences can occur when we're being *active*. As with solitude, most of them *do* happen when we're relatively inactive, for example walking in the countryside, meditating, listening to music or simply relaxing. But they can occur when we're busy too. In fact, many awakening experiences are *caused* by activities. As we'll see in Chapter 6, some sports can be powerful triggers of awakening experiences, particularly fairly sedate and rhythmic activities like running or swimming. Like the dancer and musician above, the experience often affects an athlete's performance too – they are likely to be 'in the zone', to run faster and more easily than ever before and to feel as if it's not necessarily *they* who are making the effort to run. As we'll also see, there are many reports of awakening experiences occurring during and after sex too. Naturally, these are often 'communal' awakening experiences, when a person feels as if their own identity has dissolved away and they have become one with their lover.[5]

BEYOND TIME

Another important feature of awakening experiences is the different perception of time they bring. In ordinary consciousness we experience time in a linear way, as a river of moments which flow by and disappear into the past, never to return again. This adds to the sense of *angst* that is part of our normal condition. We feel that time is always against us, always threatening to take away our happiness by turning the present into past, slowly eating away at our good looks, our health and ambitions and gradually moving us closer to our inevitable death. But in higher states of consciousness this 'linearity' of time fades away. Particularly with medium- to high-intensity experiences, time seems to expand massively and the distinctions between the past, present and future seem to fade away. Linear time dissolves into panoramic open space.

This often happens in higher states of consciousness induced by drugs. As Aldous Huxley noted in *The Doors of Perception*, his report of his own drug-induced mystical experiences, psychedelic drugs like LSD and mescaline can 'telescope aeons of blissful experience into one hour'.[6] A correspondent from Belgium gave me a report of a mescaline experience in which:

Time has disappeared completely... The 'concept' of
time as such seems ridiculous. I can shift time forwards,
backwards, to the left, to the right, up and down. I am time.
I live my whole life and more in a fraction of a second...
Everything is blended in an everlasting moment.

In one of my own awakening experiences, which I describe in my book *Making Time,* I was standing on a beach alone, watching the waves and the seagulls flying, when suddenly the present seemed to merge with the past. I felt as if I was there thousands of years ago – or more strictly that thousands of years ago was *that moment.*[7]

Similarly, an acquaintance had an awakening experience when he was walking through a wood one winter afternoon, looking up at the trees above him. Suddenly the trees seemed to 'open out into a vision of eternity' and everything around him seemed to have massive significance. He had the sense that he was immortal, that 'death didn't mean anything', and felt that he was beyond time:

> *An eternal state of consciousness seemed to be there in that very simple event... The recognition that took place was that now was eternal. The importance of the moment itself somehow defeated death by being outside time.*

'INGOING' AWAKENING EXPERIENCES

So far we've been looking at different intensities of awakening experience, but there's a different *type* we should consider as well. Almost all of the experiences we've looked at so far have been, to borrow a term from the scholar of mysticism Evelyn Underhill, 'outgoing'. That is, they have all been experiences of perception and vision, of seeing the world in a different way and experiencing a different kind of relationship with it, perceiving it as intensely real and beautiful, pervaded with harmony and radiance, and seeing the oneness of phenomena or experiencing a sense of unity with the world. But awakening experiences can also be 'ingoing'. This is when they're not focused *outside* on the world but *inside*, within our own being. These usually occur during meditation, when we're hovering between sleep and wakefulness or just relaxing with our eyes closed, i.e. in situations where our senses are closed down to the external world (or at least when sensory input is reduced) and our awareness is mainly occupied with our own consciousness. (The philosopher Walter Stace made a similar distinction to this with his concepts of 'extrovertive' and 'introvertive' mystical experiences.)

Ingoing awakening experiences have different intensities too. If you practise meditation, you probably have a low-intensity ingoing experience fairly regularly. Once you've slowed down your chattering mind to some degree, you should begin to feel a pleasant glow of inner well-being and a sense of peace and freedom. This is the same basic sense of well-being that outgoing experiences bring.

At a slightly higher intensity, you might feel that your consciousness has expanded, that the black space inside your mind which is normally so cramped has opened up. There seem to be new vistas of space around you and you feel a sense of freedom. You might experience the 'identity shift' that I mentioned at the end of the last chapter. In fact, this shift to a deeper and truer self is a more common feature of ingoing than outgoing experiences, simply because the self – rather than the world – is the whole focus of the experience. Our normal ego-self is sustained by 'thought-chatter', and so when the chattering stops, it dissolves away, like a balloon without air. Then the *atman* reveals itself underneath, like a clear blue sky beneath clouds, and we realize that the sense of well-being we feel is emanating from this true self, like heat and light emanating from the sun.

At this point, you might also experience what the philosopher Robert Forman calls the 'pure consciousness event'. Our consciousness becomes 'pure' when our mind is completely empty and silent. We move beyond the normal boundaries of the self and experience the oneness of the cosmos. We don't become one with *the world*, as we do in outgoing experiences, but one with *an energy*. The energy of our own consciousness seems to flow into the spiritual energy of the whole universe.

I had this kind of experience just a fortnight before writing this. I was lying in bed at night, feeling relaxed and drowsy, but instead of going to sleep I seemed to slip into a different realm of consciousness. There seemed to be an enormous space around me, as if I had walked out of a room into an open landscape. All through the space there was a powerful atmosphere of serenity and peace, which seemed to be gently vibrating. I felt very serene and blissful too – in fact, it was impossible to differentiate myself from the 'space' around me. I didn't know whether this space was inside me or whether I was outside myself. I couldn't say where I ended and it began. I still had a sense of being an 'I', but there was no sense of individuality or separation. I also had the feeling of 'all is well' that outgoing experiences usually bring, the feeling that D. H. Lawrence described as 'a great reassurance, a deep calm in the heart'.[8]

Here a friend of mine describes a powerful ingoing awakening experience he had while meditating at a Buddhist centre:

> *While I was meditating I felt as though my body was becoming transparent. I felt that I didn't have a body any more. There was no separation, no 'in here' and 'out there' – it was all just one energy. It was like being immersed in water. There was no me any more. No inside and outside. It was all one.*

Here a person describes a similar ingoing experience, which occurred when he was sitting down with his eyes closed, listening to a symphony by Brahms:

> *I must have become completely relaxed, for I became aware of a feeling of 'expansion' and seemed to be beyond the boundary of my physical self. Then an intense feeling of 'light' and 'love' uplifted and enfolded me. It was so wonderful and gave me such an emotional release that tears streamed down my cheeks. For several days I seemed to bathe in its glow, and when it subsided I was free from my fears.[9]*

These experiences have very similar characteristics to outgoing experiences: transcending separateness, a glow of inner well-being, a strong feeling of love, an awareness of an all-pervading atmosphere of harmony and even a sensation of light. There are obviously some small differences between ingoing and outgoing experiences. For example, since they don't involve perception of the world, ingoing experiences obviously can't feature 'external' characteristics like the sense of the 'aliveness' and oneness of different objects. And it's logical that they should feature 'inward' characteristics, like the sense of well-being or of becoming a deeper self, more strongly. But despite this, it seems clear that they aren't two different *kinds* of experience but two variations of the same one.

BEYOND THE WORLD OF FORM – ABSOLUTE WAKEFULNESS

Some of the experiences we've looked at – such as the last I quoted, or Angela de Foligno's – are so powerful and revelatory that it's difficult to imagine that there could be anything 'higher' than them. Anyone lucky enough to have such an experience would certainly be changed for life and feel that they had seen the 'ultimate reality' of the world. Nevertheless, there is level of awakening beyond this.

Yoga philosophy refers to a mystical state of consciousness as *samadhi* (literally, 'ecstasy') and makes a distinction between *savikalpa samadhi* and *nirvikalpa samadhi*. The former literally means 'ecstasy tied to a particular form' and the latter means 'formless ecstasy'. The experience of seeing the world as the manifestation of spirit and realizing that you are a part of the ocean of spirit is *savikalpa samadhi,* since there's still a self that is perceiving the world and a self that feels a sense of unity with it. But in *nirvikalpa samadhi,* which Yoga philosophy suggests is the highest possible form of consciousness, there is no consciousness of being a self. We expand beyond the boundaries of our normal self until our awareness of being an 'I' completely falls away. We don't just become *one with* absolute reality, we *become* it.

Nirvikalpa samadhi means going beyond the world of form altogether. The material world dissolves away; the world of objects and natural phenomena is 'drowned' in an ocean of pure spirit-force. It's as if we have entered into the absolute essence of reality, the 'ground' of pure spirit, *brahman* in its pure form, which underlies everything and pervades everything. We realize that this ground of pure spirit is the source of all things, that the world is its manifestation, that its energy 'pours out' into the world and that the nature of this energy is bliss and love. There is no time, only an eternal now, and there is no form, only spirit.

Of course, this isn't just an Indian concept. The ancient philosopher Plotinus referred to the pure spiritual essence of reality as 'The One' and had four experiences of oneness with it in his life, so his disciple Porphyry tells us. The great medieval German mystic Meister Eckhart called it 'the Godhead', the unconditioned source from which the whole world – including God Himself – flows out.

As awakening experiences become more intense, they also become less common. In a 1987 survey of mystical experiences by David Hay and G. Heald, 21 per cent of people said that they had sensed 'a sacred presence in nature', while only 5 per cent said they had had a sense of 'the unity of all things'.[10] This makes sense, since the latter is a characteristic that occurs at high-intensity awakening experiences. And since this experience of becoming one with absolute reality is the highest-intensity awakening experience, it is also the least common.

As it is the highest intensity of awakening, we might call this state 'absolute wakefulness'. The second experience I describe in the introduction is the only experience I've had of this state. I found that passage extremely difficult to write, simply because the state is so far beyond our normal experience that it's impossible to describe accurately. Our everyday language of subjects and verbs and objects isn't subtle enough to convey a state in which there are no subjects and objects and no solid 'things'.

In fact, some spiritual traditions make no attempt to describe the experience. In the Upanishads this ultimate reality is described as 'undefinable, unthinkable, indescribable'.[11] The Kena Upanishad states that spirit is 'beyond knowledge'.[12] In Christian mysticism, there is also a recognition that the human mind – and its language – can never understand or capture this absolute reality of God. As Meister Eckhart wrote, 'Why dost thou prate of God? Whatever thou sayest of him is untrue.'[13] Or, in the words of St Augustine, 'There is in the mind no knowledge of God except the knowledge that it does not know Him.'[14]

Fortunately, however, some people have attempted to describe their experiences of absolute wakefulness. One of the best descriptions I've come across was given by the English author and mystic Paul Brunton. In the 1920s he travelled around India, searching for spiritual wisdom. After some unsatisfactory experiences, he visited one of the most revered Indian mystics of the last century, Ramana Maharshi. Here he describes what happened when he was meditating with Ramana one evening:

> *Finally it happens. Thought is extinguished like a snuffed*
> *candle. The intellect withdraws into its real ground,*
> *that is, consciousness working unhindered by thoughts. I*
> *perceive … that the mind takes its rise in a transcendental*
> *source. The brain has passed into complete suspension,*
> *as it does in deep sleep, yet there is not the slightest loss of*
> *consciousness… Self still exists, but it is a changed, radiant*
> *self. For something that is far superior to the unimportant*
> *personality which was I, some deeper diviner being rises*
> *into consciousness and* becomes *me. With it arrives an*
> *amazing sense of absolute freedom, for thought is like a*
> *loom shuttle, which is always going to and fro, and to be*
> *freed from its tyrannical motion is to step out of prison into*
> *the open air.*

So far Brunton is describing what we could call a medium-intensity ingoing experience which includes some of the characteristics we looked at above, such as a shift to a more genuine identity and a sense of freedom. But the experience intensifies until he reaches a state beyond all form and all concepts, where he merges with the divine 'ground' of reality:

> *I find myself outside the rim of world consciousness. The planet which has so far harboured me disappears. I am in the midst of an ocean of blazing light. The latter, I feel rather than think, is the primeval stuff out of which worlds are created, the first state of matter. It stretches away into untellable infinite space, incredibly alive.* [15]

Although absolute wakefulness might originate from an 'ingoing' process such as meditation, at this level the terms 'ingoing' and 'outgoing' aren't relevant, since the concepts of 'inner' and 'outer' cease to have any meaning. As Evelyn Underhill noted, although the two types of experience might seem to be different, 'In that consummation of love which Ruysbroeck has called "the peace of the summits" they meet.' [16]

Absolute wakefulness can certainly arise from 'outgoing' situations too. Here, for example, is the experience of the nineteenth-century Indian mystic Ramakrishna. He was depressed and frustrated because, despite all his prayer and meditation, he felt he wasn't getting any nearer to the divine. In a moment of despair he picked up a sword, intending to kill himself, and suddenly experienced a vision of – and became one with – pure spirit:

> *Houses, doors, temples and everything else vanished altogether; as if there was nothing anywhere! And what I saw was an infinite shoreless sea of light; a sea that was consciousness. However far and in whatever direction I looked, I saw shining waves, one after another, coming towards me.* [17]

As Paul Brunton's experience shows, at this level the radiance or bright light which we perceive at lower levels can intensify to the point of being blindingly bright or even appearing as fire. This was also the case with the experience of 'cosmic consciousness' described by the author of the famous book of that name, Richard M. Bucke. This experience also came from an 'outgoing' situation, when he was being driven to his lodging in a hansom cab after spending the evening discussing poetry and philosophy with friends:

> *All at once, without warning of any kind, I found myself wrapped in a flame-coloured cloud. For an instant I thought of fire, an immense conflagration somewhere close by in that great city; the next instant I knew that that fire was in myself. Directly afterwards there came upon me a sense of exultation, of immense joyousness, accompanied or immediately followed by an intellectual illumination quite impossible to describe. Among other things, I did not merely come to believe, but I saw that the universe is not composed of dead matter, but is, on the contrary, a living Presence: entirely alive; I became conscious in myself of eternal life... I saw that all men are immortal; that the cosmic order is such that without any peradventure all things work together for the good of each and all; that the foundation principle of the world, of all the worlds, is what we call love, and that the happiness of each and all is in the long run absolutely certain.[18]*

At this point of 'absolute wakefulness' we make contact with the ultimate reality of the universe and attain our complete fulfilment as human beings.

REALITY ACCORDING TO AWAKENING EXPERIENCES

From the standpoint of awakening experiences, then, all of the 'truths' that our normal consciousness, together with modern materialistic science, tells us about ourselves and the world appear to be lies, or at best partial truths.

Awakening experiences tell us it's false that we're separate entities, that the world and other people are 'out there' while we're 'in here'. They tell us that in reality there is no separation, that we are one with the world and with all other beings. The same spiritual essence that fills the entire universe is inside us. The 'ground' of our being is also the 'ground' of everything that exists. We only experience separation because we're out of touch with the spiritual essence of our being.

In the same way, the separateness we perceive between different objects is an illusion, since this spiritual essence brings them all into oneness. Separateness is only superficial – all things have the same underlying identity. Imagine if there were a flood and all but the highest part of a tree disappeared underwater, so that all you could see was a few branches sticking out. At first you might assume that you were looking at a number of separate sticks, without realizing that they were all connected as a part of the same entity.

Awakening experiences also tell us that our normal sense that the world around us is basically inanimate is wrong. Everything – rocks, rivers, trees, plants, the whole Earth itself and even the sky – is alive. Everything has its own being, its own consciousness. As well as their surface exterior reality – the one we see in normal consciousness – all things have an interior, a subjective dimension. This is the spiritual essence (or energy) which flows through all things and through the whole universe. There is no such thing as inert matter – all matter is alive. Every atom is pervaded with spiritual energy.

In a similar way, awakening experiences tell us that there is no such thing as empty space. In a normal state of consciousness we might look up at the night sky and be frightened by the seemingly vast emptiness of the universe, an eternity of cold black space dotted with stray fragments of matter. But if you look up at the night sky in a *higher* state of consciousness, you will see a different vision: an eternity of black space which is radiant and alive, pervaded with spirit.

Awakening experiences also tell us that our normal 'shadowy' vision of the world is false. The world is not the dreary, uninteresting place it seems to us in normal consciousness. In reality everything around us is intensely real and beautiful. The world is so exhilaratingly vibrant and fascinating and colourful that if this were our normal vision we would never be bored for one moment ever again. Even the most mundane everyday things such as garden weeds, pieces of gravel or man-made objects like chairs and the roofs of houses seem to be intricate and interesting. Awakening experiences tell us that the fresh perception of children is more real than our adult perception. They suggest that something has *gone wrong* with our vision of the world, that in the process of developing into adults we have 'filtered out' this bright and intense reality.

As we've seen, the experiences also tell us that our normal view of time is false. In the same way that the normal material world of space and solidity dissolves away, our normal linear view of time also fades away. There is no longer a present or a future. Everything that has ever happened and everything that will ever happen exists in an 'eternal now'.

In this state of consciousness we experience life in a completely new way. The 'human condition' is not bleak and miserable but joyful and meaningful. The world is no longer coldly indifferent towards us; instead, there is an atmosphere of harmony and benevolence. In awakening experiences there *does* seem to be a meaning to life. This meaning isn't something which you can express as a formula or a statement, it's just something which is *there*, which you can see and feel all around you, which tells you that it's somehow *right* to be alive in the world and that – in some strange way – everything is perfect.

Awakening experiences tell us that – absurd though this may sound – the fundamental reality of the universe is *bliss*. The spiritual energy that fills the universe has the quality of bliss in the same way that, say, water has the quality of wetness. And since that awakening energy is the essence of *our* being too, bliss is also *our* basic nature.

Awakening experiences contradict modern science by telling us that life is something more than a chemical process and that our own consciousness is something more than the result of the buzzing of neurons. They make us realize that there is something essential inside us which transcends the matter of our body and brain. And as an extension of this, the experiences make us aware that our consciousness will not cease to exist when we die. Particularly at the higher intensities, there is an awareness that the essence of our being is non-material and indestructible and that we are therefore, in a sense, immortal. The spiritual energy that fills the universe is infinite and eternal. And since that energy is the essence our being, we are infinite and eternal too. In the words of Meister Eckhart, 'I am unborn, and following the way of my unborn being I can never die... I have always been, I am now, and shall remain eternally.'[19]

In *The Republic,* Plato suggests that most of us see the world as if we're imprisoned in a dark cave, looking at the shadows on the wall and believing that they're real. And this is exactly what awakening experiences suggest: that our normal 'reality' is a constricted grey shadow world, filtered through our limited ordinary consciousness. In awakening experiences we turn away from the shadows and towards the light.

However, you might argue that this could easily be turned the other way around. What is there to say that this 'awakened' consciousness is more valid than our ordinary consciousness? It's all very well to have a vision of the unity of all things or to see the whole world pervaded with spirit, you might say, but why should we believe that this vision of the world is true? In fact, since ordinary consciousness is our normal state, it's surely logical to assume that it's more correct than higher states of consciousness. Higher states happen in exceptional circumstances, so it surely makes more sense to see them as aberrations. Why shouldn't we simply see them as illusions created by a malfunctioning brain?

It's this question of the validity of awakening experiences that we're going to examine in the next chapter.

3

THE VALIDITY
OF AWAKENING
EXPERIENCES

As you'd expect, many scientists do see higher states of consciousness as aberrations. Materialist scientists usually see our consciousness as the product of the brain – the buzzing around of millions of neurons – and so inevitably see higher states of consciousness as the result of brain activity. More specifically, they see them as the result of *unusual* levels of activity in different parts of the brain. For example, some neuroscientists have speculated that they can be caused by stimulation of the frontal lobes or a higher level of activity in the parasympathetic half of the nervous system.[1] In other words, awakening experiences are thought to occur when the normal functioning of the brain is impaired in some way. They are seen in the same light as states of psychosis or hypnosis, as distortions of our normal and 'correct' perception of the world caused by neurological abnormalities. (We'll look at neurological explanations of awakening experiences in more detail in the next chapter.)

QUANTUM PHYSICS

Ironically, one possible reason for taking the opposite view and being open to the possibility that awakening experiences give us a wider and truer picture of reality actually comes from within modern science. The 'awakened' vision of the world may be completely contrary to the worldview of mainstream science, but it's by no means contrary to what modern physics tells us about reality.

Quantum physics has shown that the tiniest particles of matter break all of the rules that operate in our everyday macrocosmic world. In the quantum world, there is no separation. Particles are not discrete entities which can only affect each other through physical contact. Once they have interacted with each other they are forever connected, no matter how far apart they might be. They will always be affected collectively by what happens to any of them individually. If a particle is split in two, the resulting particles always behave as if they're still one, spinning together in perfect harmony and balancing each other's random fluctuations.

The issue of what a particle *is* is also far from straightforward. It may appear to be a hard, solid entity like a tiny billiard ball, but in reality it's a whirl of energy which is manifesting itself as a particle at that particular moment. At other moments, it can appear as a wave. And this is one aspect that can be affected by a human observer.

Another way in which the observer affects the quantum world is through the methods that they use to measure it. As Heisenberg's uncertainty principle pointed out, you can never know both the exact position and the momentum of a particle at the same time. The more specifically you try to measure its momentum, the less accurately you'll be able to measure its position. Until you measure it, a particle is never in a specific place or a specific state. (This is what physicists call *superposition*.)

This interpretation of quantum physics suggests that in the sub-atomic world – as with the 'spiritual world' – there is no separation between our own consciousness and the world 'out there'. The traditional idea of the 'objective' scientist who stands apart from their experiments, observing and recording results with complete detachment, is a myth. In the quantum world, the observer always interacts, changing the behaviour of particles through the acts of observation and measurement. As one of the founders of quantum physics, Pascual Jordan, put it, 'Observations not only disturb what has to be measured, they produce it.'[2] This can't be otherwise, since the consciousness with which we observe the world is also *in* the objects that we observe.

At the subatomic level, the concept of time is unclear too. As with high-intensity awakening experiences, the boundaries between past, present and future may sometimes blur. As Heisenberg put it, 'In elementary particles space and time are strangely blurred in such a way that one can no longer define correctly the concepts of earlier and later... When experimenting within very small space–time domains, one should be aware that process could run in a timely reverse order.'[3] In other words, in the quantum world the normal forward flow of events sometimes runs backwards. According to Heisenberg, when an explosion takes place inside an atomic nucleus, it can be *followed* by the cause of the explosion, rather than the cause happening first.

Quantum physics also suggests that there's no such thing as empty space, because every point in the universe is full of 'zero-point energy' (also referred to as the 'electromagnetic quantum background'). Physicists have called this the 'ground' reality of the universe, an underlying sea of energy pervading everything, which we can't directly sense because it's present in everything.[4] In recent decades this zero-point energy has been used to explain some of the most puzzling phenomena of quantum physics, such as the stability of atoms, wave/particle duality and even gravity.[5] Although I wouldn't like to say – and perhaps nobody can for sure – whether this energy *is* the same as the all-pervading spirit-force we sense in awakening experiences, it does have some clear parallels with it.

One of the puzzling things about this is why these findings have had so little impact on the general worldview of modern science. Many scientists (particularly non-physicists) still hold to the strictly Newtonian view of reality, as if quantum physics had never happened. Although they may be aware of some of the vagaries of subatomic particles, in practise they still treat the world as if it's made up of solid particles that are separate from one another and can only interact by physically touching or moving each other. They still think that consciousness is produced by the brain and is completely separate from everything it observes. And they still believe that the world is ultimately explicable, that it obeys rational principles which will eventually be understood.

Many scientists deal with the 'anomalies' of quantum physics by separating them off from macrocosmic reality, treating the subatomic world as a completely different realm where different rules apply. But this is a fallacy, of course – the subatomic world is *this* world, only at a sub-microscopic scale, and what's true at that level is also true at *this* level. As the scientists Nadeau and Kafatos have written, 'We can no longer rationalize [quantum] strangeness away by presuming that it applies only to the quantum world.'[6] Other materialistic scientists tell themselves that although the subatomic world may *seem* strange, one day someone will come up with a rational explanation for all its weirdness. But this is like believing that one day a schizophrenic person will be discovered to be sane, once we understand the logic of their seemingly irrational behaviour.

And even if you aren't willing to accept that the similarities between the quantum and everyday world are more than parallels, quantum physics at least makes it clear that the common-sense view of the world is extremely deceptive and that there's much more to reality than mainstream materialistic science tells us. It at least suggests that, as Kant argued, we don't have access to reality in its pure state. The world we perceive is filtered through and created by our mind. We live our life under the assumption that the world as we see it is reality, and in the macrocosmic realm this works out well. But when we look into the quantum world we begin to see hints of a different, much more complex reality, like people who are locked inside a room which they think is the whole world but then find a small crack between the bricks through which they can just pick out details of strange new colours and shapes.

REVELATIONS

There are two other, perhaps more substantial, reasons for doubting the objectivity of our normal vision of the world and for believing that awakening experiences are a kind of 'waking up' from our normal consciousness.

The first is the subjective feeling of *revelation* that the experiences bring. They always have a sense of 'So this is the way things *really* are!' There is the feeling that we have 'woken up' in some way, transcended limitations, that we are now seeing a truer and clearer picture of the world, that we're aware of more reality than normal. It's as if a fog has cleared and we can now see the whole of the landscape. In comparison, our normal vision of the world seems narrow and blinkered. In the words of the eleventh-century Sufi mystic Al-Ghazali, this is a state 'whose relation to your waking consciousness is analogous to the relation of the latter to dreaming. In comparison with this state your waking consciousness would be like dreaming!'[7]

Richard M. Bucke felt this very powerfully with his experience of 'cosmic consciousness'. He was convinced that he had seen the ultimate truth of the universe, since, as he wrote, 'I had attained to a point of view from which I saw that it must be true.' Similarly, a person who had an awakening experience while reading an Indian spiritual text wrote that 'I *knew* with unshakeable conviction that I had been in touch with Reality in those few minutes.'[8]

Because of this, awakening experiences usually have what William James called a 'noetic' quality. That is, the person who has such an experience feels that they have gained new knowledge, knowledge that their normal consciousness was too limited to see. As James put it:

[Mystical experiences] are states of insight into depths of truth unplumbed by the discursive intellect. They are illuminations, revelations, full of significance and

*importance ... as a rule they carry with them a curious
sense of authority for after-time.*[9]

In reports of awakening experiences, this noetic quality is expressed
in phrases like 'I was beginning to understand the true meaning of
the whole universe',[10] 'I was transported into what I can only term
"reality"'[11] and 'I had an intense feeling ... of *knowing* in a quite
different way from intellectual knowledge. Knowing with all my
being what is meant by the concept of God is love.'[12]

Sometimes we may find it almost impossible to describe
– or intellectually understand – *what* we know, but still have the
conviction that an incredibly powerful and meaningful new reality
has been revealed to us. Here, for example, a person describes an
experience they had while they were alone on a beach:

*I remember that it was a cool, clean, fresh, calm, blue,
radiant day, and that I stood by the shore, my feet not in
the waves. And now – as then – I find it difficult to explain
what did happen. I expect that the easiest thing is to say
that suddenly SOMETHING WAS. My whole soul was cleft
clean by it, as a silk veil slit by a shining sword. And I
knew. I do not know now what I knew. I remember, I didn't
even then... But whatever it was I knew, it was something
that made ENORMOUS SENSE. And it was final... Then
joy abounded in all of me. Or rather, I abounded in joy, I
seemed to have no nature, and yet my whole nature was
adrift in this immense joy, as a speck of dust is seen to
dance in a great golden shaft of sunlight.*[13]

A scientist might argue that all of this tells us nothing, since these
are just subjective feelings and can't be scientifically validated. But
the sheer strength of this sense of revelation and insight can't be
dismissed lightly.

There is no reason why awakening experiences *should* carry
this kind of authority. After all, the perceptual distortions that come

from other 'altered' states of consciousness usually don't have this revelatory quality. In fact, this is one of the essential differences between altered and higher states of consciousness. Altered states such as trances, dream states, hallucinations, psychotic states, etc. don't bring a heightened state of awareness. In fact, they usually distort or occlude our normal awareness. (Although in a sense, of course, awakening experiences are a type of altered state of consciousness too, since they involve a shift out of our normal consciousness.) A dream might seem real while you're having it, but as soon as you wake you realize it was illusory. A person who experiences perceptual distortions as a result of schizophrenia – e.g. hearing voices, seeing hallucinations – might also feel that they're real at the time, but once they return to a normal state they will usually have no doubt that they were illusions. However, when we return to a normal state from awakening experiences, we never think of them as illusions. The revelations they bring have a massive impact which never diminishes, even after decades, and even though the experiences themselves usually last no longer than a few minutes.

One woman had an awakening experience when she was 15 or 16, when the room flooded with light and 'for a minute by clock time I was immersed in this, and I had a sense that in some unutterable way the universe was all right'. She noted that the experience 'affected me for the rest of my life. I have lost all fear of death.'[14]

One friend of mine, the author and publisher Colin Stanley, had a powerful awakening experience when he was meditating by staring at a candle flame. Suddenly the light exploded, filling his head with a brilliant white light. He felt 'a surge of joy and security (as if nothing could ever harm me) and a feeling of timelessness which (sounds like a contradiction) seemed to contain all of time'. This was nearly 40 years ago and he has never had a similar experience since, but in his words, 'That tiny glimpse of my potential as a human being has had a huge impact on my life and work.'

It's because of this 'revelatory' quality that people are able to remember awakening experiences so clearly. As we've seen many times already, people are able to recall them with amazing vividness and detail decades after they occurred. Dreams and hallucinations quickly fade from the memory, but because awakening experiences give us a truer and more intense vision of reality, they are imprinted on our memory.

In other words, to adapt the metaphor I used at the end of the previous section, we're like people who've grown so used to being locked in a room that they've started to assume it's the whole world. But in awakening experiences the walls of the room dissolve away and we find ourselves in a spacious new world, brighter and richer and more beautiful than we could ever have imagined. And this world is self-evidently wider and truer than our normal constricted reality in the same way that a panoramic view of a landscape is wider and truer than a view through a small window.

PRIMAL WAKEFULNESS

The third reason for believing that awakening experiences may give us a truer picture of the reality than our normal consciousness comes from the idea that what we think of as a 'higher' state of consciousness may in some sense be a *normal* state of consciousness – normal, that is, to indigenous or primal peoples.

By 'indigenous or primal peoples', I mean the original inhabitants of North and South America and Australia, traditional African peoples and the tribal peoples of Oceania (including Polynesia, Melanesia and Micronesia), together with more scattered groups such as the tribal peoples of Borneo, of the forests and hills of India, the Andaman Islands or northern Europe and Siberia (such as the Laplanders). Essentially, I'm talking about all peoples outside the European and Asian landmass (and a few isolated peoples within it), who lived in small tribes, mostly living from hunting and gathering (although some of them used horticulture too), with very little technology.

Unfortunately in many cases it's probably more appropriate to speak of these cultures in the past tense than in the present. A few cultures in very isolated places – such as the tribal peoples of the Andaman Islands or parts of Borneo or Africa – still live something close to their original way of life, but the vast majority have been disrupted to some degree (and in most cases a severe degree) by contact with European culture. That's why, in most of the examples I provide over the next few pages, I rely on the reports of anthropologists from earlier decades, who had contact with these peoples when their cultures were more 'pristine'. However, in some cases I will use the present tense, where I'm speaking of the contemporary indigenous peoples who still live their natural way of life.

PERCEPTUAL INTENSITY AND LIFE

One of the reasons why many people are reluctant to accept the validity of awakening experiences is because we assume that our normal vision of the world is objectively true and gives us a correct picture of reality. Similarly, we tend to assume that all people in the world experience reality in the same basic way, that all other peoples have the same vision of the world as we do. Different peoples might have different beliefs about gods and the afterlife, of course, or different views of how the world works and what causes different events, but we assume that they perceive the same basic reality as we do as they go about their lives. It doesn't matter whether it's seen by a person from England, India or Africa or a member of an Amazon tribe – or a person who lived 5,000 or even 50,000 years ago – a sunset is always the same sunset, stones are always just stones and a river is always a river. When we look at the sky or at a tree we surely see the same things as other peoples do.

But this isn't the case. Judging from their own pronouncements and the reports of anthropologists, many indigenous peoples perceived a different reality from us.

We've seen that two of the most basic characteristics of awakening experiences are a fresher and more intense perception and a sense of the phenomena around us being alive. And it seems that, generally, indigenous peoples experience(d) these constantly, as part of their normal state. We've already quoted the anthropologist Stanley Diamond's view that indigenous peoples have a heightened sense of reality. In a similar way, the psychologist Heinz Werner described indigenous peoples' perceptions as 'vivid and sensuous', with a 'sensuousness, fullness of detail ... colour and vivacity of ... image' which has faded away from our vision.[15]

As a result, to indigenous peoples there are no such things as 'inanimate objects'. This is one of the reasons why they had a more reverential attitude to nature than Eurasian peoples: they sensed that even rocks, the soil and rivers had a being or consciousness of their own. Whereas European or Asian peoples tend to see these things as nothing more than one-dimensional objects which they're entitled to use for their own devices, indigenous peoples *felt* that the natural phenomena around them were alive and so treated them with respect. As the anthropologist Tim Ingold writes, to indigenous hunter-gatherer peoples, the environment is 'saturated with personal powers of one kind of another. It is alive.' As a result, says Ingold, hunger-gatherers seek to maintain a harmonious relationship with the environment, 'treating the country, the animals and plants that dwell in it with due consideration and respect, doing all one can to minimise damage and disturbance'.[16] Or, as the Cherokee Native American scholar Rebecca Adamson points out, for indigenous peoples 'the environment is perceived as a sensate, conscious entity suffused with spiritual powers through which the human understanding is only realized in perfect humility before the sacred whole'.[17] The Hopi use the term *Novoitti* for the concept of living in harmony with nature, while the Tlingit (also of North America) call it *Shogan*.

As with awakening experiences, indigenous peoples' sense of the 'aliveness' of the world goes together with a sense that natural phenomena have their own *being* too, a subjectivity beneath their surface reality. This is what the Aboriginal Australians refer to as the 'Dreaming' of things. As the anthropologist Robert Lawlor notes, to them, 'Every distinguishable energy, form or substance has both an objective and a subjective expression.'[18] Aborigines have complained that the problem with European Australians is that they can only perceive the surface reality of the world and can't enter its interior life. As one Aboriginal elder stated, 'Unless whiteman learns to enter the dreaming of the countryside, the plants, and animals before he uses or eats them, he will become sick and insane and destroy himself.'[19]

EVERYDAY AWARENESS OF 'SPIRIT-FORCE'

We've seen that one of the characteristics of awakening experiences – at a medium intensity and above – is an awareness of an all-pervading spirit-force. It's this force that makes all things alive, fills the air with an atmosphere of harmony and benevolence and brings seemingly separate things into oneness. And it's very significant that, while we only become aware of this force at a higher level of consciousness, for most (if not all) of the world's indigenous peoples it was apparently an everyday reality.

One of the strange things about the religious practises of indigenous peoples was that they usually weren't based around the worship of gods. When European colonists first had contact with them and for some time afterwards, the concept of gods had little or no significance to them. They had no deities who presided over certain localities or certain aspects of life, and they didn't pray, make sacrifices to gods or have temples.

Rather than the worship of gods, primal peoples' religious practises were based on their awareness of – and their reverence for – what certain Native American groups called the Great Spirit or the Life Master: that is, a universal spirit-force. I've been collecting examples of this from anthropological and religious books for years and have now lost count of the number I have. To give just a few examples, in America, the Hopi called spirit-force *maasauu,* the Pawnee called it *tirawa* and the Lakota called it *wakan-tanka* (literally, the 'force that moves all things'). The Ainu of Japan call it *ramut,* while in parts of New Guinea it was called *imunu.* In Africa the Nuer called it *kwoth* and the Mbuti call it *pepo.* The Ufaina Indians (of the Amazon rainforest) called it *fufaka.*

All of these concepts refer to an impersonal force which pervades all space and all objects and beings. The early German anthropologist R. Neuhaus, speaking of the indigenous peoples of New Guinea, used the term 'soulstuff', while the British missionary J. H. Holmes translated *imunu* as 'universal soul'. Holmes described it as 'the soul of things... It was intangible, but like air, wind, it could manifest its presence.'[20] This is clearly something very similar to – if not the same as – what the Upanishads call *brahman,* or the 'immensely powerful benign force' or 'sweet, cool presence' which is usually seen at medium-intensity awakening experiences. The anthropologist Gordon Munro described the Ainu's concept of *ramut* as a force which is 'all-pervading and indestructible' and compared it with Wordsworth's description of 'A motion and a spirit, that impels / All thinking things, all objects of all thought / And rolls through all things.'[21] Later in the poem Wordsworth describes it as 'something far more deeply interfused, whose dwelling is the light of setting suns'. And this is very close to this description of spirit-force given by a member of the Pawnee tribe:

We do not think of Tirawa as a person. We think of Tirawa as [a power which is] in everything and ... moves upon the darkness, the night, and causes her to bring forth the dawn. It is the breath of the newborn dawn.[22]

THE WORLD AS A MEANINGFUL PLACE

Another characteristic of awakening experiences I mentioned is the sense of the world as a meaningful and benevolent place, and indigenous peoples appear to naturally sense this too. Like Henry David Thoreau, they seem to have had the sense that the world around them – including animals and plants – was kindred to them and also 'meant well' by them. One of the Cherokee, Jingme Darham, spoke of how 'we are taught from childhood that the animals and even the trees and plants ... are our brothers and sisters',[23] while another Native American, Thomas Yellowtail, spoke of the 'sacred support that was always present for traditional Indians', a sense of meaning which was always present and made you feel that 'you were participating in a sacred life and you knew who you were and carried a sense of the sacred within you'.[24]

When European colonists first made contact with Native Americans and Aboriginal Australians, they often assumed that they weren't religious, because they didn't have special places of worship or specific religious leaders. But these peoples didn't need 'religion' because the sacred was around them all the time, in everything. As the elder of the Australian Yuin tribe, Guboo Ted Thomas, says, 'Sacredness, power and energy emanate from nature.'[25] Whereas we experience our surroundings as empty space filled with lifeless material objects, for indigenous peoples everything shone with this sacredness and meaning. Or, as the theologian Laurtenti Magesa notes, to traditional African peoples a rock is not an inanimate object but an entity which 'incorporates, shows and for that reason is, in fact, some supernatural quality of the divine'.[26]

As I mentioned in relation to awakening experiences, it's impossible to separate this sense of the sacred and the sense of the 'aliveness' and inner life of phenomena from indigenous peoples' awareness of spirit-force. All things are alive and have an interior because of the spirit-force inside them. And the harmony, meaning and sacredness that they perceive are the *qualities* of spirit-force. *Brahman* (or *wakan-tanka* or *pepo*) radiates these qualities in the same way that the sun radiates light and heat. What Thomas Yellowtail calls 'the sacred' and what Ted Thomas refers to as 'sacredness, power and energy' *is* the spiritual force that radiates through the world.

RELATEDNESS

So far we've looked at most of the characteristics of low- to medium-intensity awakening experiences and found that indigenous peoples possess all of these as their *normal* state. What we experience as a higher state of consciousness appears to be an everyday reality to them.

We've also seen that another characteristic of awakening experiences – and another effect of all-pervading spirit-force – is a transcendence of separation, both amongst the phenomena around us and between us and our surroundings. With spirit-force pervading them, the seeming separateness of things fades away, in the same way that the seeming separateness of a group of rocks disappears when the sea level falls. Indigenous peoples don't seem to experience this as *oneness* but, at a lower intensity, as a strong sense that everything is interconnected and related. As the Indigenous American philosopher Vine Deloria says, the 'fundamental premise [that] undergirds all Indian tribal religions' is that 'all things are related'.[27] Or, as an African theologian, Charles Nyamiti, writes of the traditional African worldview, 'The universe is conceived as a sort of organic whole composed of supra-sensible or mystical correlations or participations.'[28] In other words, there is no separateness – phenomena can't be understood on their own, but only in relation to each other and as a part of the whole.

Similarly, it seems that, while they don't experience the kind of sharp duality between themselves and the world that is our normal state, indigenous peoples don't experience the kind of union with the cosmos described by mystics. For them this oneness manifests at a lower intensity, as a strong sense of *bondedness* with the natural world, an awareness that they are part of the web of creation (and one which is no more important than any other). As Tim Ingold writes of the Batek Negritos of Malaysia, for example, 'They see themselves as involved in an intimate relationship of interdependence with the plants, animals and *hala'* [spirits] (including the deities) which inhabit their world.'[29] Or, as Chief Oren Lyons of the Onondaga tribe puts it, Native Americans 'believe in a higher power. We believe in a great authority. We believe that we're hooked together. The way that we are intertwined, the way that we live with one another, all of this one being.'[30]

In many cases, this manifests itself as deep attachment to their own land. Many primal peoples feel that their own identity is actually bound up in their land and that they cannot exist independently of it. The indigenous inhabitants of the Fiji islands, for example, had a belief that every generation had an obligation to take care of the land on behalf of the spirits of their dead ancestors and of the generations to come. And, as the native Fijian anthropologist A. Ravuva wrote, to them their land 'is an extension of the concept of self. To most Fijians, the idea of parting with one's *varna* or land is tantamount to parting with one's own life.'[31] Or, as one contemporary Sioux, George Barta, writes, 'We believe that land and people are one. We believe that only people with an integral relationship to the land can survive.'[32] It's therefore not so surprising that some contemporary indigenous peoples – such as the U'wa people of Colombia or the Kaiowa of Brazil – have threatened to commit collective suicide if their land is taken from them. As one Kaiowa chief has said: 'We *are* the land.'[33]

WELL-BEING

Finally, we saw that another characteristic of awakening experiences was a sense of inner well-being, peace or joy. If indigenous peoples were naturally 'awake', we'd expect them to experience this well-being too. However, since happiness is such a subjective state – and since even if it exists, we can't say for sure what has caused it – it's very difficult to draw any conclusions about this. Perhaps the most we can say is that the reports of anthropologists *suggest* that these peoples possessed a natural contentment and serenity. The American anthropologist Edward T. Hall lived on reservations with the Navaho and Hopi Native Americans in the 1920s and described them as being so inwardly content that they would wait for hours for appointments without showing any signs of irritation or impatience, while European-Americans who were waiting with them would be seething with frustration. The English anthropologist Colin Turnbull lived with the pygmies of the forests of central Africa during the 1950s and described them as living in complete harmony with each other and their environment. To them, life was 'a wonderful thing full of joy and happiness and free of care'.[34] Similarly, Elman R. Service wrote that the Copper Inuit of northern Canada 'display a buoyant light-heartedness, a good-humoured optimism which has delighted foreigners who have lived with them'.[35]

As I pointed out in *The Fall*, our normal inner discontent is the root cause of much our pathological behaviour as human beings, such as our compulsive restlessness, materialism and status-seeking. And it's perhaps significant that most indigenous peoples didn't suffer from these problems. For example, indigenous peoples didn't seem to have had any problem being inactive. Anthropologists have discovered that, rather than struggling to survive, most traditional hunter-gatherer peoples only hunt or gather food for two or three hours a day, leaving the rest of the time free for leisure activities. Many Europeans thought Native Americans were lazy because they would only work when they needed to. Once they had accumulated enough food they would stop for weeks or months and be happy to 'do nothing'. In addition, as I show in *The Fall*, indigenous peoples are generally non-materialistic and egalitarian, and show little desire to accumulate either possessions or power. For example, hunter-gatherer tribes don't have a concept of individual ownership of land, while people only have a bare minimum of possessions. There are no different classes or castes and women have completely equal status to men. Perhaps, then, indigenous peoples' lack of these characteristics is also evidence that their normal inner state was one of well-being.

Of course, this seeming contentment could have had other causes – their less stressful lives, a more natural and beautiful environment, less loneliness and less social oppression – but it's certainly the kind of inner well-being we would expect people who are naturally 'awake' to possess.

A CONSTANT STATE OF WAKEFULNESS

This experience of the world is so different from our normal consciousness that it's almost impossible for us to imagine. And in the same way, our materialistic model of the world – with its assumption that matter is inanimate and living beings are nothing more than complex collections of particles – would be incomprehensible to indigenous peoples. So would modern philosophies like existentialism or deconstructionism, which presume that life is fundamentally meaningless and that 'meaning' is only constructed by the human mind. The indifferent, inanimate and empty world that we inhabit is literally a different reality from indigenous peoples' world of meaning, harmony and sacredness. It's not surprising that many of them thought Europeans were insane. A Native American chief told the psychologist Carl Jung that the white people he saw were always tense and unhappy-looking and in a state of constant wanting. 'They are always seeking something,' the chief said. 'They are always uneasy and restless. We don't know what they want. We think they are mad.'[36]

But of course, in a way we *can* imagine what this experience of the world is like, because many of us have glimpsed it ourselves in awakening experiences. Judging by the reports of anthropologists and indigenous peoples themselves, it seems that their normal state of consciousness was what we experience as a 'higher' state of consciousness. The permanently heightened state of consciousness which the mystic strives so hard to attain was – at least to a certain level – the natural birthright of indigenous peoples. Or, as Stanley Diamond put it, 'The experience of primitive and mystic converge, for mysticism is no more than reality perceived at its ultimate pitch.'[37]

However, as I've suggested, indigenous peoples' normal state of consciousness doesn't appear to reach the *highest* intensities of awakening. Their normal state seems to be one of medium-intensity wakefulness, with a natural awareness of spirit-force pervading the world but not an experience of oneness with phenomena. There's no evidence to suggest that they normally experienced the blazing spiritual 'ground' of reality either, which is a characteristic of high-intensity awakening experiences.

Of course, this doesn't mean that they *didn't* experience high-intensity wakefulness. In fact, the highest intensities of awakening would presumably be more accessible to them, in the same way that Mount Everest is more accessible to a person at base camp at the foot of the mountain than to a person at sea level. As we'll see later, many of the ceremonial activities of indigenous peoples – such as drumming, dancing, ingesting sacred psychedelic plants and going on vision quests – were designed for the purpose of reaching a higher-than-normal intensity of wakefulness.

WHAT WENT WRONG?

All of this begs the question of why *we* don't experience this naturally awakened state. Have we lost something which was once normal to us as well? Did something go wrong in our development?

It's beyond the scope of this book to go into this question in detail, but I do believe that this is the case. As I suggested in *The Fall*, the fundamental difference between most modern Eurasian peoples (that is, European, Middle Eastern and Asian peoples) and the world's indigenous peoples is our stronger and sharper 'ego structure'. Our sense of being an 'I' inside our heads is stronger than theirs. Whereas we see ourselves as individuals, separate from the world around us and from each other, indigenous peoples don't separate their identity from their community or from their land. They are not self-sufficient and self-contained individual beings. As the anthropologist George B. Silberbauer wrote of the G/wi people of the Kalahari Desert in Africa, for example, 'Identity was more group-referenced than individual. That is, a person would identify herself or himself with reference to kin or some other group,'[38] while according to Spike Boydell, the indigenous peoples of Fiji have a concept of 'the self-embedded-in-community [which] contrasts with the western value of individualism with its idea of the self as separate and separating from others'.[39]

This strong ego structure has given us some massive benefits, such as greater powers of abstract thought (when we analyse, deliberate and plan) and greater conceptual knowledge (e.g. knowledge of the laws of nature, of the structure of matter and of the universe itself). It has also given us more personal autonomy, leading to more control over our own life. But in a sense the ego has become *over*developed. Its boundaries have become too strong and its self-reflective ability has mutated into the chaotic thought-chatter that runs through our mind whenever our attention isn't occupied. In *The Fall* I showed how this overdeveloped ego is the root cause of many of our social pathologies, including warfare, male domination, social inequality and oppression, and hostility to the body and to sex. And one of its most severe disadvantages has been the loss of the 'natural spirituality' of indigenous peoples.

It's possible to explain this in terms of 'mental' or 'psychic' energy – that is, the energy that is used by our mind, through our mental and psychological functioning. Our strong ego structure needs a great deal of energy in order to function, in the same way that a massive house with dozens of room requires – and uses up – a lot of electricity. In particular, our constant thought-chatter uses up a lot of energy. As the modern-day American mystic Bernadette Roberts puts it, 'The continual movement [of thoughts] inward and outward, back and forward ... consumes an untold amount of energy that is otherwise left free when the mind is restricted to the now-moment.'[40] The actual *structure* of the ego requires a lot of energy to be maintained too, in the same way that the physical structures of the body, such as our bones and internal organs, need a constant input of energy to maintain themselves. There has to be some input of energy just to keep such a powerful structure intact and in place. (We'll look at this energy in a lot more detail in Chapter 5.)

All of this means that with the ego 'gobbling up' so much of our mental energy, there's very little available for us to use in perceiving the world around us. Indigenous peoples' weaker ego structure requires much less energy and so there's always energy left free to put into perception, into attending to their surroundings and taking in the reality, beauty and meaning of their experience.

In fact, we seem to have developed a psychological mechanism specifically for the purpose of reducing the psychic energy we use up through perception. In our mind there is a 'desensitizing mechanism' which turns the is-ness of our surroundings to familiarity, as a way of conserving energy. This is what happens when we 'get used to' things – when we move into a new flat on a busy road, for example, and are disturbed by the noise to begin with but stop noticing it after a few weeks. Or when we go into a smoky room: at first we feel as though we can hardly stand it, but after 15 minutes or so, it doesn't seem to bother us any more. Or think about how a new prisoner might feel during his first week in prison: he might be overwhelmed by the noise and overcrowding and new faces, and hate his tiny cell and his bed. But after a while – perhaps a few weeks – this mechanism 'edits out' the reality of these experiences, desensitizes him to them, so that he begins to feel more comfortable.

This mechanism acts on *all* our perceptions. It edits out the reality of *all* our experience. It makes the world dreary to us so that we don't need to pay attention to it, in order to ensure that the ego always has enough energy to meet its requirements.

For indigenous peoples this mechanism doesn't seem to function, at least not to the same degree. They don't need it, because their weaker egos don't require such a large input of energy. But for us, it means that the fantastically real world they perceive is a shadow reality. The desensitizing mechanism switches our attention off to the life, harmony and oneness of the world and the all-pervading spirit-force that generates those qualities. In other words, it's largely responsible for our normal state of sleep.

Our strong ego structure is also the reason why we don't have the sense of connection to the world that indigenous peoples experience. Our strong ego creates a sense of duality and separation. It gives us the illusion that we are each an isolated entity, alone inside our body with our own thoughts and feelings, disconnected from the world 'out there' and the people and animals and plants that make up that world. The boundaries of our ego are fixed and firm, 'walling us off' from the world around us so that we can't experience the kinship and shared sense of being that indigenous peoples felt towards other beings and their land.

This is also part of the reason why we lost the natural happiness of indigenous peoples. Duality and separation create a basic sense of anxiety within our mind. At the same time, the thought-chatter of our ego creates a constant disturbance inside us, so that our being is never still or peaceful. And since our mind is tinged with anxiety already (as a result of duality and separation), our thought-chatter is often negatively based, creating worries and problems. And finally, as we'll see later, the energy of our being has a natural quality of happiness. But when the ego develops and monopolizes the energy of our being, we lose touch with this natural well-being.

CHILDHOOD WAKEFULNESS

Even as individuals, we haven't always been asleep. Another reason for seeing wakefulness as natural is that all of us once experienced it – or at least elements of it – in our own life, as a young child.

Human beings are not born with egos. According to the developmental psychologist Jean Piaget, babies don't begin to develop a sense of self until around the age of six months. From that point, the ego develops very slowly, becoming stronger as we move through childhood towards adolescence and becoming fully formed as a structure in the late teens. And because of their weak ego structure, children – particularly young children – experience some elements of wakefulness.

Many poets and authors have remembered their childhood as a time of bliss and heightened awareness. Most famously, William Wordsworth describes his as a time when the world was 'apparelled in celestial light' with 'the glory and the freshness of a dream',[41] while another mystic poet, Thomas Traherne, described his childhood as a state of constant ecstasy, when 'all appeared new, and strange at first, inexpressibly rare and delightful and beautiful'.[42]

This is more than just romanticism. I've already suggested that children are awake to the is-ness and radiance of reality. Anyone who has young children will surely have been struck by the intensity of their perception. In fact, this is one of the best things about having children: they teach you to see wonder in the world again. They have an insatiable curiosity and are amazed and fascinated by all kinds of 'mundane' things which most adults take for granted and scarcely pay attention to. Their experience seems much more real than ours and the world appears a much brighter, more colourful, complex and beautiful place to them.

Many developmental psychologists have noted this. The psychologist Ernest Schachtel believed that children perceived the world around them with a powerful directness and immediacy, completely open to its is-ness, unclouded by familiarity or concepts. (He called this 'allocentric perception'.) However, as we become adults, what Schachtel called 'secondary autocentricity' begins to take over. The is-ness of objects becomes less important as we start to view them in terms of their usefulness to us and to see them though a veil of familiarity.[43] As a result, we lose what the developmental psychologist Jane Loevinger described as the child's 'enjoyment of the sensuous encounter with the world'.[44] Alison Gopnik puts it more directly: 'I believe that babies and young children are actually more conscious and more vividly aware of their external world and internal life, than adults are... I think that, for babies, every day is first love in Paris.'[45]

Researchers such as Edward Hoffman and Edward Robinson have collected many examples of adults recalling spiritual feelings and visions during childhood (I've quoted from their collections already). Some people recalled having such feelings when they were as young as three, although they were most common between the ages of five and 15.[46] And throughout their collections, many people recalled the kind of perceptual intensity described by Gopnik. One person described having a 'clear awareness, almost like a radar'[47] and having 'a more direct relationship with flowers, trees and animals'.[48] Another used the description by the Victorian author John Ruskin, who wrote that as a child he had 'a continual perception of sanctity in the whole of nature – from the slightest thing to the vastest'.[49]

Several people described a sense that trees, flowers and other natural phenomena were alive, that they were sentient beings with whom they could communicate. A 69-year-old minister remembered how, as a child growing up on the coast of Nova Scotia, he had a 'strong sense of the numinous – and warmth and peace – that accompanied some of nature's moods',[50] while a German woman told Hoffman how, as a child, she was always aware that nature was alive and had a 'definite soul'. She would hug the old maple tree in her backyard and feel that it was speaking to her, that 'its branches and leaves were like arms hugging and touching me'. And, as she goes on:

Not only the trees would speak to me, but also the plants, streams, and even the stones. In the Harz Mountains we would often picnic next to a certain brook. In those years there were few tourists, and I'd frequently sit for hours without moving and listen to its sound. When I would find an especially beautiful rock on the road, I would take it, feel it, observe it, smell it, taste it, and listen to its voice.[51]

It's important to note that these people aren't describing temporary *experiences,* but an awareness that they experienced constantly as their normal childhood state.

These descriptions hint at a further characteristic of awakening experiences: the sense that the world is meaningful and harmonious, filled with a benign atmosphere, in contrast to the seemingly empty and indifferent cosmos, filled with nothing apart from empty space and matter, that most adults perceive.

Children have this awakened vision for the same reason that indigenous peoples do: because the desensitizing mechanism I described above doesn't function for them either. Since children – especially young children – don't have a strong ego structure, there is no need for it to do its energy-conserving job. As a result, young children's perceptions are never automatic. They are always 'energized', always fresh and intense.

And as with indigenous peoples, perhaps children's natural spirituality also expresses itself through their inner well-being. To a large extent, children – especially younger children – seem to be naturally happy. Of course, every child experiences discontent frequently, when they're tired, insecure or when their desires are frustrated. Some children also suffer trauma and abuse at the hands of their carers or others, making them withdrawn and disturbed. But most parents and teachers would surely agree that, in general, young children have a deep well of natural happiness inside them, which makes being with them a massive pleasure. They may experience brief storms of upset or anger, but they always quickly return to a foundation of natural happiness. They're free from most of the mental turmoil adults suffer from: anxiety about the future, guilt about the past, boredom and indifference to the world, dissatisfaction with their lives, and so on. Young children respond to everything (and everyone) with the same openness and excitement. They appear to be in touch with the reservoir of inner well-being I described above, which radiates naturally from the energy of our being. The philosopher Michael Washburn describes this state very vividly. According to him, children are 'bathed in the water of life. Ripples and waves of delicious energy move through the infant's body, filling it with delight. When its needs are satisfied and it is otherwise content, [it] experiences a sea of dynamic plenitude, blissful fullness.'[52]

HIGH-INTENSITY AWAKENING EXPERIENCES IN CHILDHOOD

I'm certainly not trying to say that children are fully fledged mystics or that they're 'enlightened'. I've suggested that native peoples' normal state is one of medium-intensity wakefulness, and perhaps children's normal state is one of *low*-intensity wakefulness. In Chapter 1, I showed that with medium-intensity awakening experiences we have an awareness of *brahman,* or spirit-force, pervading the whole world, revealing itself as the source of the life, beauty and harmony you perceive. This awareness is sometimes a constant part of a childhood experience, as the above descriptions of nature as 'numinous' or with a 'definite soul' suggest. However, it isn't as common or as strong as the other characteristics. And the characteristics of high-intensity awakening experiences – e.g. an awareness of the oneness of the world, or transcending the world of form – certainly don't appear to be a feature of the child's normal state.

Children certainly can have temporary experiences of these, though. This shouldn't seem surprising: if children are naturally awake at a lower intensity, then – like indigenous peoples – they should have fairly easy access to higher intensities of wakefulness. And indeed, experiences of becoming one with other phenomena or the cosmos as a whole – which I classed as a medium- to high-intensity characteristic – appear to happen to children quite frequently. One person told Edward Robinson how at the age of 'barely three', they became 'part of the flowers, and stones, and dusty earth. I could feel the dandelions pulsating in the sunlight, and experienced a timeless unity with all life.'[53] Another person told Robinson how, at the age of four or five, he 'felt a unity with the world around me ... absorption in something far greater than myself of which I was at the same time a part and glad and grateful to be so... I and the world seemed to dissolve into a new vastly more significant reality which had hitherto been only vaguely sensed.'[54] Similarly, a person told Edward Hoffman how, in the fourth grade, she would have days when 'I would feel a tremendous connectedness to everything and everyone. Everything was one, I could see the connection between all things.'[55] Finally, a man who grew up on farmland in North Carolina recalls how he would spend hours staring at small patches of ground and often had the sense that 'Plants and animals radiated an aura of aliveness, and I often felt that I was simply part of a great Whole.'[56]

It's not surprising that children have such experiences frequently when you consider that their ego is less developed as a structure. This means that they don't experience the same sense of separation from the world as adults. Whereas our strong ego creates a sense of duality, for children this boundary is less defined. As a result, these 'self-boundaries' may often fade away altogether, bringing a sense of connection or oneness with the world.

However, one of the differences between childhood and adult awakening experiences is that children very seldom appear to experience the *highest* form of awakening – absolute wakefulness, when we transcend matter and time and dissolve into an ocean of pure consciousness. This experience seems to be even rarer amongst children than it is amongst adults. (I will discuss the reasons for this later, when we look into the causes of awakening experiences.)

Another difference is that childhood spiritual states or experiences are almost always 'outgoing'. Childhood wakefulness is usually an experience of vision and perception, rather than the kind of 'ingoing' experiences adults sometimes have during meditation or relaxation. This makes sense when you consider that children live in a constant state of *extraversion*. Their attention is always focused externally. They don't yet have the stable sense of self that would allow them to withdraw their senses from the world and rest their attention purely without their own consciousness.[57]

THE LOSS OF CHILDHOOD WAKEFULNESS

After describing how 'Heaven lies about us in our infancy', Wordsworth describes how 'shades of the prison-house begin to close' until eventually the divine vision of childhood disappears: '...the Man perceives it die away, / And fade into the common light of day.'[58] The philosopher Ernest Becker wrote that, as we grow into adulthood, we repress our vision of 'the primary miraculousness of creation' until 'By the time we leave childhood, we have closed it off, changed it, and no longer perceive the world as it is to raw experience.'[59]

And we lose this natural low-intensity wakefulness for the same reason that we lost the natural wakefulness of native peoples, only in terms of our own individual development rather than that of our species: because, as we become adults, our ego structure becomes more developed. As the ego boundaries become stronger, we gradually 'Fall' into separateness. And at the same time, what you could call a 'redistribution of energy' occurs. The energy that used to be left free for perception of the world's is-ness and radiance is diverted to the ego. The desensitizing mechanism starts to operate, as a way of conserving energy for the ego. As a result, our perceptions become automatic, and the world which was once so full of wonder becomes a shadowy, half-real place. This is the point when, as individuals, we fall asleep.

And as the adult ego develops, the natural well-being of the child slowly fades away, to be replaced by anxiety and discontent. Duality and separation create anxiety, thought-chatter creates disturbance and negativity, and as the ego monopolizes our psychic energy, we lose touch with the reservoir of natural well-being inside us.

I'm certainly not saying that childhood is an ideal state which we should return to. There are, of course, many ways in which our development from childhood to adulthood is a massive progression: the ability to think logically and abstractly, plan the future, organize our life, control our impulses, and so on. All of these are the positive aspects of the ego and life would be very difficult without them. But these benefits have a massive shadow side. As we grow up, a kind of 'developmental malfunction' occurs. Rather than developing to a healthy and integrated point, the ego becomes *over*developed. Its boundaries become too sharp and it becomes too strong and dominant.

These, then, are further reasons – after the evidence of quantum physics and the revelatory quality of awakening experiences – for believing that awakening experiences are more authentic than ordinary consciousness and give us a truer and wider vision of reality: that wakefulness is natural both to indigenous peoples and to young children. The natural wakefulness of many indigenous peoples suggests that what we experience as a higher state of consciousness was once normal to all human beings and is, in a sense, our *natural* state of consciousness. Our 'normal' consciousness may be a kind of degeneration from a fuller and more intense kind of consciousness that was once normal to all human beings. That normal state has become a higher state which we can only have glimpses of from time to time. We have fallen into a sleep and wake up so rarely that we have begun to assume that this sleep is something completely natural and normal. Our development as individuals suggests something similar – that wakefulness was natural to us as children and is a state which we gradually lose as we develop towards adulthood.

The really important point about all this, though, is that if we know why we lost this natural spiritual state – both as individuals and as a species – then we should be able to see how to *regain* it. In this book I hope to show you how we can find a way to do this, so that this state can become our normal state of consciousness once again.

4

DISRUPTING THE
EQUILIBRIUM

Perhaps deep down we sense that our normal consciousness isn't natural to us. Sometimes we feel a strong instinctive resistance to it, a desire to transcend its narrowness and its shadowy vision and to experience a more intense perception of the world. In Plato's metaphor, we're usually content to just look at the shadows on the wall of the cave, but occasionally a deep instinct for light and space stirs inside us, an ancient memory of the way we used to live, and we feel the need to turn towards the light.

This is probably part of the reason why it's so important for us to go away on holiday every so often. We don't just go away to relax and enjoy ourselves, but also to put ourselves into unfamiliar environments and to have fresh and new experiences. We live for the most part in environments that have become completely familiar to us and (although this depends to some extent on how we choose to live) our life consists of experiences that we have had many times before and that are also therefore completely familiar to us. But when we go on holiday this changes. In an unfamiliar environment such as a foreign country, the desensitizing mechanism in our mind doesn't work, at least not straight away. It hasn't had the chance to turn our perceptions to familiarity. As a result, on holiday we often experience the fresh, 'first-time' vision of children or the intense perception of indigenous peoples. As Alison Gopnik remarks, 'As adults when we are faced with the unfamiliar, when we fall in love with someone new, or when we travel to a new place, our consciousness of what is around us and inside us suddenly becomes far more vivid and intense.'[1] In this sense, strange though it may sound, the experience of unfamiliarity can be a low-intensity awakening experience equivalent to those moments of heightened perception when the world around us seems to take on an extra dimension of reality.

The desire to take drugs may also come – at least in part – from this instinct to transcend our normal consciousness. Probably the main reasons why people take drugs are to escape from mental suffering – such as boredom, loneliness, depression or residual psychological pain from past experiences – or to enjoy the feelings of well-being they bring, caused by chemical changes in the body (such as increasing the brain's production of endorphins). But another reason is because of the intensified perception they can generate. This is undoubtedly true of drugs like LSD and magic mushrooms, which can have a very powerful 'mystical' effect (although even with these drugs, a lot of people take them for hedonistic rather than 'mystical' reasons). But even our one socially sanctioned drug, alcohol, can sometimes have a transcendent effect and give us a fresh and intense perception of the world. As William James noted, 'The sway of alcohol over mankind is unquestionably due to its power to stimulate the mystical faculties of human nature, usually crushed to earth by the cold facts and dry criticisms of the sober hour.'[2]

Most of us seem to be satisfied with occasional glimpses of a more intense reality, like city dwellers who need to go out into the countryside every so often to get a 'fix' of nature. We are content to be asleep as long as we wake up briefly from time to time. However, a small number of people feel such a strong dissatisfaction with their normal consciousness that the desire for transcendence completely dominates their lives. These people have a powerful sense that something isn't right about the way they are, that they aren't existing in the state they should be in and that the world as they see it is not the world as it is. They know that they are asleep and feel a powerful instinct to wake up. In previous centuries these people would have become hermits and monks, withdrawing from the everyday human world so that they could completely devote themselves to the struggle to attain a fuller and higher kind of consciousness. Nowadays they might be people who dedicate their lives to paths of awakening like Yoga or Buddhism, who practise consciousness-raising activities like meditation, hatha yoga or *chi gung*, and who try to make their everyday lives a source of spiritual development by serving other people or being mindful of their experience.

EXPLANATIONS FOR AWAKENING EXPERIENCES

The question we need to look at now is *why* awakening experiences occur. Why is it that the limits of our normal consciousness sometimes fall away, giving us access to a world of is-ness, beauty and meaning which is normally hidden from us? This question is crucially important, since if we can identify what actually happens in awakening experiences then we will be able to see what living in a permanently awakened state would entail.

Neuroscientists generally believe that awakening experiences are 'all in the brain'. According to neuroscientists such as Michael Persinger and V. S. Ramachandran, they are the result of stimulation of the temporal lobes of the brain.[3] Persinger has even claimed to induce mystical experiences with a 'helmet' – now called the 'Shakti helmet' and available to buy – which stimulates a person's frontal lobes with magnetic fields.[4]

Another theory, put forward by the American scientist Andrew Newberg, suggests that mystical experiences of oneness come when the part of our brain that is responsible for our awareness of boundaries (the posterior superior parietal lobe) is less active than normal. Newberg also suggests that mystical feelings are linked to the autonomic nervous system, which controls our bodily organs. The autonomic nervous system has two halves: the parasympathetic (which slows down the activity of our organs) and the sympathetic (which speeds them up). According to Newberg, the kind of serene feelings which meditators often experience are linked to an over-active parasympathetic half, while the feelings of ecstasy which may come through dancing, chanting or taking drugs are linked to an overactive sympathetic half. (In fairness to Newberg, he doesn't actually say that these states *cause* spiritual experiences, just that they *correlate* with them, although others have interpreted his theories in this way.)[5]

However, on closer inspection the kind of experiences that Persinger and Ramachandran managed to induce by stimulating the temporal lobes are not what we mean by awakening experiences. What they're talking about are what are usually called 'religious experiences', or 'mystical experiences' in the common, pejorative sense of the term – that is, paranormal or irrational phenomena that can't be substantiated by science. Ramachandran, for example, claims that stimulating people's temporal lobes generates visions of UFOs, shamanic-type journeys to other worlds or supposed regressions to previous lives. Persinger's helmet often produces what he calls a 'sensed presence' – that is, the person wearing the helmet feels that they're not alone, that there is somebody or something behind them, or that they're being watched. The helmet also induces visions of bright geometrical patterns and awakens powerful childhood memories. But apart from the strong feelings of well-being and a feeling of alertness, these reports don't include any of the characteristics of awakening experiences that we've discussed.

In any case, the fact that awakening experiences appear to be associated with certain brain states doesn't necessarily mean that the brain states *produce* the experiences. It could be the other way round – increased electrical activity in the frontal lobes or less activity in the posterior superior parietal lobe could just as easily be the *results* of higher states of consciousness rather than causes of them.

Another materialistic explanation of spiritual experiences has been put forward by the eminent British scientist Robert Winston, who suggests that the sense of peace and well-being they bring may be caused by higher levels of the neurotransmitter dopamine. Winston suggests that particularly 'spiritual' or religious people may simply be people who have a naturally high level of dopamine in their brain.[6] But this doesn't really prove anything, since it may be spiritual experiences themselves that make dopamine levels rise. If I see a tiger, there will probably be a rush of adrenaline inside my body, but nobody would suggest that the adrenaline came before the tiger and created my encounter with it.

At the same time there is the difficulty of explaining subjective experience in purely objective terms. In the same way that they try to account for awakening experiences in terms of brain activity, many scientists attempt to explain consciousness itself – our sense of being an 'I' in our heads – purely in terms of the brain. In their view, all of the millions of neurons in the brain work together to produce consciousness in the same way that all of the electronic circuitry inside this box in front of me works together to produce a computer which can store vast amounts of information and perform incredibly complex tasks.

This might seem to be the logical explanation, but there are some serious problems with it. Despite decades of intensive research, neuroscientists have not been able to suggest how the brain produces consciousness, or even identify which parts of the brain it's associated with. The consensus now is that it doesn't come from any one area but is somehow generated by the brain as a whole.

There is also the puzzle of near-death experiences, when people's brains completely shut down for a time and are clinically dead, and yet their consciousness continues. In the words of the Dutch cardiologist and near-death experience researcher Dr Pim van Lommel, although they have a complete absence of brain activity, 'These people are not only conscious; their consciousness is even more expansive than ever.'[7] And if consciousness can continue when the brain is dead, it can't purely be generated by the brain.

Telepathic experiences also argue against a straightforward link between the brain and consciousness. In my opinion, the work of researchers such as Dean Radin and Rupert Sheldrake leaves little doubt that telepathy exists, for both human beings and animals. And if I can detect and respond to another person's actions or thoughts without perceiving or directly communicating with them, then my consciousness expands beyond my brain, which suggests that it isn't solely produced by the brain's neurons.[8]

In recent years, many philosophers have also cast doubt on the idea that consciousness is produced by the brain. Since the brain is just a physical thing, a lump of matter, to say that it can give rise to our consciousness is, as the English philosopher Colin McGinn puts it graphically, like saying that 'numbers emerge from biscuits or ethics from rhubarb'.[9] To assert that the 'water' of the brain can produce the 'wine' of consciousness is, McGinn says, to believe in a miracle.

Another British philosopher, Galen Strawson, believes that there is a fundamental gulf between matter and conscious experience which makes it impossible for the latter to emerge from the former. In contrast to a liquid, where you can see how molecules can work together to produce something different from themselves, there is nothing about the brain which seems to work together to generate conscious experience.[10]

As an alternative explanation, philosophers have begun to suggest that consciousness has no cause because it is an *a priori* reality, a fundamental property of the universe. The Australian philosopher David Chalmers, for instance, suggests that consciousness should be seen as 'as a fundamental feature of the world, alongside mass, charge, and space-time'.[11] Physicists do not attempt to search for a cause of these phenomena; they see them as 'ground realities' without a cause, and Chalmers suggests that we should view consciousness in the same way.

In a similar way, Strawson believes that the only logical solution to the 'consciousness problem' is to assume that *all* matter as conscious. Since there is no way in which consciousness can emerge from physical elements, no matter how complex their interactions, we must assume that all physical elements were 'conscious' in some sense to begin with.[12]

And as far as higher states of consciousness are concerned, the point is that if it's so problematic to explain consciousness itself in terms of the brain, then it's surely problematic to try to explain awakening experiences in terms of different patterns of brain activity.

PSYCHOLOGICAL EXPLANATIONS

Aside from these attempts to explain higher states of consciousness in terms of brain activity, psychological explanations have been put forward. In 1927 the French spiritual seeker Romain Rolland wrote to Sigmund Freud, describing what he called the 'oceanic feeling' of being connected to the cosmos, a part of something eternal and boundless. Freud didn't see this as a valid experience and explained it away as a regression to early childhood, when a child is still at its mother's breast and its ego has yet to differentiate itself from the external world. Similarly, a few years before Freud, the American psychoanalyst Cavendish Moxon suggested that mystical experiences were a regression to an even earlier state, to the womb. They were 'nothing less than a return to the intra-uterine condition' and the 'God' which mystics felt that they became one with was 'a projected image of the narcissistic ego ... a regression to the mother'.[13]

Other early psychologists were even more disparaging towards mystical experiences, seeing them as a kind of mental disorder. For example, in 1925 the American psychologist James Henry Leuba suggested they were a combination of hysteria and neurasthenia, with symptoms of neurosis, hallucinations and hypersensitivity.[14] Even as late as 1976, a report of the 'Group for the Advancement of Psychiatry' concluded that mystical experiences were a kind of psychosis caused by a loss of the normal 'healthy' ego boundaries, which brought 'delusions' of a fantasy universe in which problems did not exist.[15]

However, other psychologists – usually with a 'transpersonal' bent – have put forward less reductive explanations. Although he deals with *altered* states of consciousness rather than specifically with *higher* states, the eminent American psychologist Charles Tart suggests an explanation which has some similarities with the one I'm going to put forward. He believes that states of consciousness are the result of the interaction of a large number of neurological and psychological processes – such as attention, perception, cognition and emotions – and that if any one process is altered sufficiently, an overall consciousness shift may result. In other words, if you give intensified attention to an object (in meditation, for example), or if you have an intense emotional experience (such as being in love), this will cause a shift to an 'altered' state of consciousness.[16]

In a similar way, the psychologist A. M. Ludwig suggests that altered states can be caused by any type of extreme psychological or chemical change, such as a high or low level of stimulation, a high or a low level of alertness, or significant changes to body chemistry.[17]

My view, however, is that higher states of consciousness have two basic causes. As I mentioned earlier, I don't believe that *all* awakening experiences have an identifiable cause – some of them do seem to happen spontaneously (although it's also possible, of course, that they have causes which just aren't readily apparent). But I believe that the majority of them can be traced back to two basic sources. In 1971, another American psychologist who investigated mysticism, Roland Fischer, made an important distinction between two different types of mystical experience, which other authors have followed. As he saw it, mystical experiences can be either 'high-arousal' active or ecstatic experiences, or 'low-arousal' passive and serene experiences. High-arousal experiences can come from drugs, dancing, fasting and breath control, while low-arousal experiences usually come from meditation and relaxation.[18] (This is the same distinction that Andrew Newberg makes between the sympathetic and the parasympathetic halves of the nervous system.) My explanation of awakening experiences fits closely into these categories.

In the rest of this chapter we're going to examine the first basic source of awakening experiences: disrupting the biochemical homoeostasis of our brain and body.

DISORDERING THE SENSES

The nineteenth-century French poet Arthur Rimbaud had such a powerful resistance to our normal consciousness that he spent his whole life trying to transcend it.

Rimbaud is one of the strangest figures in the history of literature. At the age of 15, he started writing poems which were amazing for their technical brilliance and imagery. At this time, after being a quiet and well-behaved child, he began to rebel against the quiet bourgeois life of his home town. He started smoking and drinking, stopped cutting his hair and washing, stayed away from school and went out of his way to be offensive and uncouth. He made three attempts to run away in six months and was eventually arrested for vagrancy after sleeping rough in Paris and going without food for days.

By this time Rimbaud was obsessed with the idea of becoming a *voyeur*, or visionary. He had a strong sense that 'ordinary' reality was only part of the story and that the world was full of unknown realities which, as he wrote, our 'pale reason' hid from us. In May 1871 (still only 16) he wrote his famous *Lettre du Voyant* to his schoolteacher Izambard, in which he set out his method of 'awakening' the mind and breaking through to these unknown regions. 'The poet becomes a visionary,' he writes, 'by a long, immense and reasoned disordering of all the senses,' as a result of which he becomes 'the Supreme Sage ... for he arrives at the unknown'. According to him, this 'disordering of the senses' means disrupting the workings of the mind with sleep deprivation, alcohol, drugs, sickness, solitude and sex. At the end of the process the poet will emerge as the prototype of a new human being, with a new language which is 'of the soul, for the soul, encompassing everything'.[19]

Rimbaud wasn't just being theoretical; he did everything he could to become a *voyeur* himself. He tried to keep his mind awake by living like an ascetic, ignoring his physical needs and subjecting himself to pain and discomfort. He smoked hashish, drank absinthe and attempted to practise magic and alchemy. He also experimented sexually, particularly with his homosexual lover, the older poet Verlaine. He began to see his poetry as a way of disabling the ordinary conscious mind and breaking through to higher realms of reality.

He appears to have had some success. He certainly experienced altered states of consciousness which gave him intoxicating hallucinatory visions in which, as he writes, 'I saw quite clearly a mosque instead of a factory, a phalanx of drums made by angels, coaches on the roads of heaven, a drawing room at the bottom of a lake.'[20] But he also appears to have experienced ecstatic states which gave him mystical insights. In his long autobiographical prose poem *A Season in Hell,* his final work, he speaks of 'a minute of awakening that gave me the vision of purity'.[21]

However, after three years of attempting to disorder his senses in this way, Rimbaud realized he could go no further. In *A Season in Hell* he speaks of being 'brought back down to earth, with a duty to find and a gnarled reality to embrace!'[22] He even doubted the validity of his visions, believing that they were illusions and that he had 'fed myself on lies'. At the age of only 19, full of self-disgust and a sense of futility, he abandoned his attempts to become a visionary. And since for him poetry was closely linked to his attempts to disrupt the equilibrium, both as a method and as a creative result, one of the world's shortest and strangest literary careers came to end too.

After this, Rimbaud tried to keep himself 'awake' in a different way – by continually exposing himself to new environments and experiences. For the next 18 years, until his death at the age of 37, he wandered the Earth 'with wind in the soles of his shoes', as his lover Verlaine wrote, trying to keep one step ahead of the desensitizing mechanism and to maintain the perceptual intensity of a low-level state of awakening.

In my early twenties I had a friend who also had a powerful instinctive desire to break free of the limits of ordinary consciousness. Another friend put me in touch with him after he'd heard him giving an impromptu speech in a pub, telling the assembled drinkers that they were suffocating with dullness and needed to make their lives more colourful and exhilarating. Samuel thought of himself as a kind of prophet with a mission to wake everybody up and in order to do this he knew that he had to be awake himself. When I got to know him he was 24 and had spent the last few years travelling around Europe doing different jobs in different towns and never spending longer than a few months in the same place. Like Rimbaud, he was trying to keep himself awake by never allowing the desensitizing mechanism to edit out reality.

Also like Rimbaud, Samuel spent a lot of time trying to disorder his senses. He did almost everything Rimbaud recommended in his *Lettre du Voyant* and many other things besides. He smoked cannabis, took magic mushrooms and deprived himself of sleep and food. He even inflicted pain on himself, like the Christian ascetics who wore hair shirts and belts of nails. Once I went round to see him and noticed with a shock that he had a series of bright red circular marks down his forearm, some with scabs on. When I asked him what had happened, he said, 'Cigarette burns – they give you an electric shock of pain that really makes you alert and makes your senses sharp.' He was determined to do absolutely anything to stop his mind from slipping into the mould of ordinary consciousness, so that he could retain his 'awake' vision of the world.

I was only friendly with Samuel for six months, before he moved to London. Shortly after arriving there on the coach, he had all his possessions stolen while he was in a phone box (he had left his bags outside the box). He didn't have any friends to stay with there and ended up sleeping rough in the middle of winter. He went to see a doctor to get some help; the doctor saw the cigarette burns on his arms and referred him to a psychiatrist. The psychiatrist saw some signs of psychological abnormality and sectioned him. I visited him in London a few weeks after he'd been released from the psychiatric hospital and he seemed like a different person. His energy and intensity had gone; he was docile and drowsy and overweight from the heavy tranquillizing drugs he was being given.

DISRUPTING HOMOEOSTASIS

What is really important here is the methods which Rimbaud and my friend Samuel used to try to transcend normal consciousness. They had both stumbled on a very simple truth and one way in which it is actually very easy to generate higher states of consciousness. The human organism has a certain normal, optimum way of functioning which, if everything goes according to plan, we experience throughout our whole life. This is what biologists call homoeostasis – a state of equilibrium in which everything inside us functions the way it's supposed to. Homoeostasis means having the right body temperature, the right levels of blood sugar, the right amount of salt concentration, the regular level of brain chemicals, and so on. Maintaining homoeostasis is both involuntary and voluntary. To a large extent the autonomic nervous system does it for us by regulating our breathing, digesting food for us, sweating and shivering, and so on. But we have to do our bit by eating when we're hungry (and eating appropriate foods), sleeping when we need to, steering clear of extreme temperatures or altitude, avoiding pain and injury, and so on. If we don't manage to do this for some reason, we're liable to get ill or even to die, especially if we remain out of homoeostasis for a long period.

But the strange thing is that when we're out of homoeostasis there is the possibility that we may experience a higher state of consciousness. This is a loophole which human beings have made use of throughout history.

FASTING

This is why there has always been a link between fasting and spirituality, for example. A prolonged lack of food can loosen the hold that ordinary consciousness has over us and bring us closer to an awakened vision of the world. Fasting can put us out of homoeostasis by causing physiological changes such as a lower level of blood glucose, higher levels of insulin and a lower body temperature.

A friend of mine had the only awakening experience of his life when he was hitch-hiking through France, making his way back to England, and had run out of money. He'd been sleeping rough on beaches and in motorway service stations and hadn't had a proper meal for days. The experience he described was probably the result of his hunger, together with a lack of sleep:

I was looking at the sky and suddenly the sun appeared from behind some clouds. It was the most beautiful thing I've ever seen in my life. Light flooded everywhere. It was like a Van Gogh painting. The clouds were incredibly real and beautiful and everything seemed alive.

Native peoples often fast and deprive themselves of sleep as preparation for rituals, dance and vision quests, using physical deprivation as a way of 'purifying' themselves. The vision quest was a spiritual exercise used by some Native American peoples as a way of building up spiritual power and communicating with spirits. The person would go to a solitary spot – often the top of a mountain – and stay there for up to four days, fasting and exposing themselves to the elements (usually wearing almost no clothes, even if the weather was cold). They would try to attain a state of complete attentiveness to their surroundings, since sacred powers might try to communicate with them at any moment. As a result, they might experience a higher state of consciousness (that is, higher than their normal low-level higher state), with strong feelings of peace and a sense of connection to the natural world, and also be given special knowledge, such as a message or a new song or dance, by spirits.[23]

In ancient Greece and, at a later time, throughout the Middle East and the Roman Empire, a large number of esoteric cults existed outside conventional religions. These 'mystery cults' were usually centred on particular gods, but rather than just worshipping them, the participants aimed to become one with them or to be possessed by them. They fasted and went without sleep before ceremonies and used a variety of other methods of disrupting homoeostasis during them: they would take drugs, beat themselves and dance frenziedly, so that they might be – in the words of the ancient philosopher Proclus, who observed the mysteries at first hand – 'filled with divine awe ... assimilate themselves to the holy symbols, leave their own identity, become at home with the gods, and experience divine possession'.[24] The mystery cults also staged 'sacred dramas' that re-enacted myths involving their gods, so that they could experience – in the words of the scholar of mysticism W. F. Otto – 'a sublimation to a higher existence, a transformation of [their] being'.[25]

For conventional religions like Christianity and Islam, fasting was – and still is, particularly in Islam – seen as a way of weakening 'the flesh' so that the spirit can become stronger and as a way of opening yourself to divine revelation. Moses fasted for 40 days before God appeared to him and gave him the Ten Commandments, just as Jesus fasted for 40 days in the wilderness before beginning his work as a messiah. Other major biblical figures like Ezra, Daniel and Elijah describe fasting too, to gain God's protection or his revelations.[26] Fasting used to be widely practised by ordinary Christians too. In ancient times, Lent was similar to the Muslim Ramadan and most Christians would fast every day until the evening. From the Middle Ages, however, Lent became more relaxed and people would usually only abstain from certain foods, like dairy products or meat.

Of course, millions of Muslims still follow a strict fast during the holy month of Ramadan. This has several purposes. It's seen as an opportunity to experience the hunger that poor people experience in order to become more empathic and charitable towards them. It's a way of learning to value food and drink and other pleasures rather than taking them for granted, and a way of strengthening bonds between families and communities. However, it's also recognized that fasting creates a more spiritual state of being and that, as a result, Ramadan is the time when Muslims are closest to God.

This obviously doesn't mean that everyone who goes without food is likely to feel more spiritual. Being hungry is usually just a miserable and painful experience. To have any awakening effect, it seems that fasting usually has to be done voluntarily, in the context of a religious or spiritual tradition, although, as my friend's experience at the beginning of this section shows, this isn't always the case.

SLEEP DEPRIVATION

The same is true of sleep deprivation. In nearly all cases, going without sleep for long periods is a very uncomfortable experience and doesn't have any psychological effects apart from making us more anxious and irritable. In fact, prolonged sleep deprivation can cause serious psychotic symptoms. As the psychologist Ian Oswald found when he studied a group of people who went without sleep for five nights, it can cause symptoms identical to schizophrenia, with visual hallucinations and acute paranoia.[27]

However, sleep deprivation also puts us out of homoeostasis. It causes physiological changes such as higher blood pressure, a depressed immune system and hormonal and metabolic changes. As a result, it can occasionally give rise to a higher state of consciousness. This was why the mystery initiates and native peoples went without sleep before ceremonies and rituals.

This paradoxical 'awakening' effect of sleep deprivation is clear from the following report, given me by a nurse who had been working night shifts without sleeping properly during the day. On the last morning she was 'so tired that I was absolutely loaded with energy' and decided to walk home instead of getting the bus:

*It was a really nice morning, clear blue sky, about April,
and I wanted to appreciate a bit of fresh air. I was walking
down a long lane that had fields on either side of it. I
walked past this tree and looked up and the sun was
shining behind it. The leaves were out, and each leaf looked
as though it was coming out of the tree at me. They were all
really vivid, glowing, shining, and I felt a feeling of ecstasy.
Each leaf looked as though it was growing. It was quite
amazing. I've never seen anything as beautiful ever again.*

The author and researcher Tony Wright has practised prolonged sleep deprivation for many years. He believes that lack of sleep makes the left side of the brain less dominant and so enables the more creative and intuitive right brain to take over. During his first trial, when he stayed awake for 80 hours, he experienced an 'extraordinary change of perception' which led to an experience of 'all-encompassing religious bliss'. As he described it to me:

*It turned my whole world around... It was almost like being
born again, like seeing it all with new eyes, a completely
different vision of reality... Everything was familiar but
richer; things looked more intense, with more depths of
colour. And it just seemed to expand, the intensity seemed
to slowly build up and turned into an incredibly euphoric
profoundly insightful experience... There was no fear or
panic, just wonder. It was an insight into the mechanisms
of the human psyche, and into the innate being-ness of the
universe. It lasted for around 20 minutes but the feeling of
well-being lingered inside me for hours afterwards.*[28]

ASCETICISM

It seems, therefore, that there is a strong connection between states of physical deprivation and awakening experiences. When the body's needs and instincts are contravened – usually purposely but sometimes accidentally – there is a chance that we may experience higher states of consciousness.

Pain is usually desperately unpleasant too, of course, but it can also be used as a way of inducing awakening experiences. We can see this in the long tradition of asceticism, for instance, which runs through all of the world's religions and spiritual traditions. An ascetic is someone who deliberately denies their body's needs and inflicts pain and discomfort on themselves, either through fasting and abstaining from sensual pleasures and comforts or by physically beating or injuring themselves. This sounds like masochism, and for some ascetics it probably was. It's also likely that some were motivated by morbid self-hatred and neurotic feelings of guilt towards sex and other bodily processes, which made them want to punish themselves.

The practises some of them used were gruesome in the extreme. The early Christian saint Simeon Stylites only ate once a week, wore a rope of palm leaves twisted around his body, went completely without food or drink during Lent and spent the latter part of his life at the top of a 67-foot-high pillar with an iron collar around his neck. The fourteenth-century German mystic Henry de Suso went even further: he spent years wearing a hair shirt and an iron chain, as well as a leather belt containing 150 inward-facing sharp brass nails. He didn't shelter from the cold in winter and never allowed himself to touch or scratch any part of his body except his hands and feet. After 16 years of torturing himself in this way, he took the extra measure of making himself a cross with 30 needles and nails on it, which he carried on his back all day and all night. And in the Muslim world there is the example of the Sufi mystic Shibli, who took a bundle of sticks with him into his cellar every day, with which he would beat himself whenever he found his attention wandering from contemplation of Allah. At the end of the day he would dash his hands and feet against the wall.

It's easy to see why asceticism is often seen as an expression of the anti-physical ideology of Christianity, the belief that the 'flesh' is corrupt and evil and has to be punished. But it's likely that, at least to some extent, the ascetics were using pain and discomfort as a way of 'disrupting the equilibrium' and transcending ordinary consciousness.

This isn't the only purpose of asceticism, though. As a 'spiritual technology' it has both long-term and short-term aims. And especially with milder forms of asceticism (where the emphasis was on discipline and denial rather than actual pain), its long-term aim was to 'tame' the physical desires, so that they no longer dominated people and monopolized their energy and attention. As we'll see later (in Chapter 9), this process of 'mortification' can feature as part of the struggle to move towards a permanently awakened state.

DRUGS

It goes without saying that inflicting pain on yourself or forcing yourself to go without sleep or food is hardly an ideal way of transcending ordinary consciousness. Although some ascetics apparently managed to continue torturing themselves for years, even decades, there's obviously a very high risk of seriously injuring yourself or dying of self-neglect. Aside from the famous ascetics like St Simeon and Henry de Suso, there were probably many others who followed similar practises but didn't live long enough to gain any recognition. As a short-term spiritual technology, asceticism is fairly futile anyway; you might gain a brief glimpse of a higher reality but this only lasts as long as the chemical changes that the pain and suffering have produced inside you. Your body always returns to homoeostasis and you always return to your constricted normal consciousness.

There must be an easier way of disrupting the equilibrium than fasting, sleep deprivation or pain – and there is. If you know that all an ascetic is really doing by torturing themselves is changing their normal chemistry, then surely, you might say, it'd be more sensible to interfere with this chemistry directly – by taking drugs, for example, which would give the same effect but wouldn't involve any self-harm.

This is exactly what the great novelist and scholar of mysticism Aldous Huxley recommended. Huxley also believed that ordinary consciousness is a kind of sleep. As he saw it, the human brain is designed to reduce and restrict our awareness of reality. This is a survival mechanism, since if we were awake to the is-ness and wonder of the world all the time, we would find it impossible to concentrate on the business of everyday life.

Huxley believed that mystical experiences occur when chemical changes inhibit the functioning of the 'reducing valve' which keeps our awareness of reality down to the 'measly trickle of consciousness' which we need for survival purposes. After discussing the practise of asceticism, he wrote:

> *For an aspiring mystic to revert, in the present state of knowledge, to prolonged fasting and violent self-flagellation would be as senseless as it would be for an aspiring cook to behave like Charles Lamb's Chinaman, who burned down the house in order to roast a pig. Knowing as he does (or at least can know, if he so desires) what are the chemical conditions of transcendental experience, the aspiring mystic should turn for technical help to the specialists – in pharmacology, in biochemistry, in physiology and neurology, in psychology and psychiatry and parapsychology.*[29]

Human beings have always used drugs as a means of intensifying or altering consciousness. The ancient peoples of Europe apparently smoked opium and cannabis 6,000 years ago, 2,000 years later the early Indo-European conquerors of India worshipped their drink soma, which most scholars believe was made from magic mushrooms; and later still the initiates of the Greek Eleusinian mysteries used a psychoactive drink called *kykeon*. Indigenous peoples often use drugs too: the indigenous tribes of North America ingested sacred plants such as fly-agaric mushrooms and peyote, those of the Amazon use ayahuasca, and the Australian Aborigines have a powerful form of tobacco called *pituri*.[30]

Some drugs don't appear to have any real transcendent properties. Although they obviously alter our normal chemical balance and so put us out of homoeostasis, some sedatives or depressants, such as heroin, barbiturates and tranquillizers, rarely, if ever, seem to bring intensified perception or mystical vision. In a way this is logical, since these drugs depress the central nervous system, causing feelings of numbness and detachment. Rather than heightening awareness, they decrease it.

Drugs like cannabis and alcohol may sometimes have transcendent properties – cannabis was, for example, used by the religious adepts of ancient India and by the Sufi mystics of Islam – but they're more likely to bring altered states of consciousness rather than higher ones.

By far the most powerful in terms of their transcendental effects are psychedelic drugs such as mescaline, ayahuasca, LSD or magic mushrooms. These drugs certainly don't always bring higher states of consciousness – they frequently just generate altered states, with hallucinations, perceptual disturbances and visionary journeys, and occasionally they can create psychotic states of mind as well, as with the classic LSD 'bad trip' – but in the right circumstances, and the right state of mind, these drugs can, it seems, take our mind out of the mould of ordinary consciousness and give us access to wider and more intense realities.

In two different 1960s studies of the effects of LSD, 40 per cent and 90 per cent of people involved felt that, as a result of the experience, they now had 'a greater awareness of God, or a higher power or an ultimate reality'. At the same time, 66 per cent and 81 per cent described it as 'an experience of great beauty' and 32 per cent and 85 per cent felt that they had had a religious experience. (The wide discrepancy is due to the fact that the second group of experiments took place in a more supportive setting in which the participants were encouraged to listen to music and surrounded by works of art, flowers and beautiful furniture.)[31]

Once LSD was banned in the United States in 1967, research into drug-induced mystical experiences ground to a halt. However, in 2006 a new study into the effects of psilocybin – the active ingredient in magic mushrooms – was carried out at Johns Hopkins University in the United States. Of 36 volunteers who were given the drug, more than 60 per cent described characteristics of mystical experiences and just over a third said that it was the most important spiritual experience of their lives, as significant as the birth of their first child.[32]

One of the most common effects of psychedelic drugs (especially at a fairly low dose) is a heightening of perception, which I described as the most basic characteristic of awakening experiences in Chapter 1. Psychedelics seem to stop the desensitizing mechanism working and so cause what Roland Fischer described as 'amplification of sensing, knowing and attending' and a 'torrential flood of inner sensations'.[33] (The desensitizing mechanism is, I believe, the 'reducing valve' or filter which Huxley describes, even though he doesn't describe it in exactly the same terms.)

In my younger years, I took magic mushrooms several times and LSD twice. Apart from one terrible LSD experience, when all my perceptions became distorted and waves of anxiety and paranoia constantly swept through me, I had low- to medium-intensity awakening experiences every time. All my surroundings had more colour, depth and presence – and became animate. Once I looked at a group of large stones and could feel an energy emanating from them. I felt that they were somehow 'vibrating' with life and even had a kind of intelligence. I could somehow sense the *age* of the stones too, the fact that they had been there for thousands of years. I was tired and wanted to sit down and – absurd though it sounds – I felt that I had to ask one of them, so I said, 'I'd like to sit down on you if that's all right?' To just sit down without asking would have seemed disrespectful, I felt. (There are shades here of native peoples' respectful attitude to nature and of the Aborigines talking aloud to natural phenomena.)

Once, during my other LSD experience, a brilliant otherworldly radiance lit up the whole of the sky and melted across the landscape, making everything so bright and so beautiful that I couldn't stop staring for what seemed like an eternity.

Similarly, here an acquaintance of mine describes how magic mushrooms transformed his vision of his surroundings:

> *Everything I looked at – trees and stones and blades of grass – seemed to have a powerful presence... They seemed to have personalities or souls. At the same time they were all interconnected. I looked at a meadow which was full of wild plants and bushes and weeds, and in some way – which I can't really describe – everything in it was one. They were all separate on one level but on another they were all just one thing. I lay down on the grass and looked around and when I sat up I felt like I was one of the blades of grass.*

This has most of the characteristics of what we would call a medium-intensity awakening experience: heightened perception, a sense of the life and the 'interiority' of things, a sense that all things are part of a whole, and a loss of the sense of duality between a person and their environment.

As we've seen, at a slightly higher intensity of awakening, this perception of a 'shared sense of being' intensifies to the point where individuality and multiplicity dissolve away completely. William James experimented with nitrous oxide and was in no doubt that the vision of the world it gave him was the same as that of the mystics, writing, 'It is as if the opposites of the world, whose contradictoriness and conflict make all our difficulties and troubles, were melted into a unity.'[34]

The Russian philosopher P. D. Ouspensky made similar experiments with nitrous oxide and had similar results. As he wrote:

In this new world which surrounded me there was nothing
separate. Nothing that had no connection with other
things or me personally... All things were dependent on one
another, all things lived in one another. I felt that separate
existence of anything – including myself – was a fiction,
something non-existent, impossible.[35]

Another characteristic of Ouspensky's experience was a massively expanded sense of time. His companion was speaking to him and he felt that so much time was elapsing between each word that it was impossible to follow his meaning. As he wrote, 'I felt I had lived through so much during that time that we should never be able to understand one another again, that I had gone too far from him.'[36] We've seen that this expanded sense of time is a common characteristic of all awakening experiences, and it seems to be a particularly strong feature of drug-induced experiences. Many people experience this under the influence of ayahuasca, for instance. When the novelist Henry Shukman drank ayahuasca he found that 'If something lasted for a minute it was eternity,'[37] while according to the Israeli researcher Benny Shanon, when a person is intoxicated by ayahuasca, 'It may seem that time has altogether stopped, or that temporal distinctions are no longer relevant.'[38]

OTHER 'SPIRITUAL TECHNOLOGIES'

Another way of disrupting homoeostasis and possibly inducing a higher state of consciousness is by altering our normal breathing patterns. Normally we breathe in and out at the same rate and keep a balance of carbon dioxide and oxygen levels inside us. But if we breathe in more quickly and deeply than usual (as in hyperventilation), we build up a higher-than-usual concentration of oxygen, and if we breathe out more quickly and deeply than usual (which is called *hypo*ventilation), we build up a higher-than-usual concentration of carbon dioxide. Both of these are non-homoeostatic states and both of them can, it seems (although by no means always), give rise to mystical experiences.

Studies of people who suffer from hyperventilation as a condition have found that they occasionally have mystical feelings and visions. As two of them told Dr L. C. Lum (who interviewed them for his paper 'Hyperventilation and Anxiety States'): 'The room suddenly seemed to be flooded with sunlight and I felt a wonderful glow surrounding me'; 'It was a beautiful feeling. There was this beautiful light and I felt warm and uplifted.'[39]

In view of this, it's not surprising that indigenous peoples have made use of breathing techniques as a spiritual technology. Native American groups like the Salish, the Algonquians and Kiowa used hyperventilation and hypoventilation as spiritual technologies.[40] And as the psychedelic pioneer Ralph Metzner notes, native peoples such as the Inuit practise a rapid and rhythmic kind of chanting, which they call 'throat music', which induces hyperventilation.[41]

Chanting is an important part of some spiritual traditions too. Buddhist monks endlessly chant sections of religious texts, the Sufis make a practise of repeating the name of God or phrases such as 'Glory to Allah' or 'There is no God but Allah,' and in a similar way members of the Eastern Orthodox Church repeat the 'Jesus Prayer' to themselves. The main purpose of this chanting is meditative – that is, it serves the same purpose as a mantra in meditation, acting as a focusing device to divert a person's attention away from thought-chatter and so allowing the mind to quiet and slow down. But it's tempting to suggest that part of the appeal – and the power – of this chanting comes from the fact that it also has a homoeostasis-disrupting effect. As Huxley pointed out in an appendix to *Heaven and Hell,* when you sing or chant you tend to breathe out more than you breathe in, which results in a build-up of carbon dioxide inside you, a state of hypoventilation which may gave rise to mystical experience.

Breathing exercises are an important stage of the Hindu path of Yoga, where they're seen as a way of regulating life-energy and preparing for the practise of meditation. But again, it's tempting to suggest that part of the appeal of the breath-control (*pranayama*) exercises is their power to induce temporary mystical feelings and visions. Amongst the various *pranayama* exercises there is, for instance, a breath-control technique called *kevali-kumbhaka*, the aim of which is simply to hold the breath for as long as possible. This would quickly produce a state of hypoventilation, which would potentially induce a higher state of consciousness.

Another common spiritual technology is dancing. Long spells of dancing cause physiological changes such as a higher body temperature, a faster heart rate and faster and heavier breathing, which would certainly disrupt homoeostasis and possibly lead to higher states of consciousness. As we've seen, the initiates of the ancient Greek and Roman mystery cults would dance frenziedly as a part of their effort to 'become at home with the gods, and experience divine possession'. Many Native American groups used – and still use – dancing as a spiritual technology too. In the Sun dance of the Lakota Indians, for instance, people fast and dance for days at a time, moving around a pole which symbolizes the centre of the world. Some dancers use pain as a further way of disrupting homoeostasis, piercing their chests and tying themselves to the centre pole, dancing and chanting and singing for hours until the skin rips free. Similarly, the Whirling Dervishes of the Sufi tradition use dancing as a way of inducing the state that they call *fana,* or 'passing away'. After fasting for several hours, they slowly rotate themselves for 15 minutes, build up speed over the next 30 minutes and then begin the actual whirling, which lasts until they lose their balance and fall over. At this stage the Dervish should 'pass away' from the familiar world to a transcendent spiritual one. Then the 'unwhirling' begins, when the Dervish lies down on his stomach for at least 15 minutes and tries to remain passive and quiet.

Extremes of temperature have also been used for their homoeostasis-disrupting effect. The native peoples of the Arctic region, for instance, often experience a spontaneous shamanic trance which, as Mircea Eliade suggests, is brought on by the extreme cold of the climate, together with darkness, solitude and a lack of vitamins.[42] While at the other extreme, Native American groups such as the Lakota use a 'sweat lodge' – a kind of sauna – as a way of purifying themselves before rituals, hunts or vision quests. The lodge is a small and simple wooden dome which is made airtight with blankets and animal hides. Heated rocks are placed in a hole in the centre and water is poured on them to create steam. We've seen that methods of disrupting the equilibrium are often used together – such as fasting at the same time as going without sleep, or fasting while dancing – and the Lakota also fast before they go into the lodge and chant while they're inside.

Henry de Suso might also have been making use of this spiritual technology when he didn't take any protection against the harsh cold of the German winter. Perhaps some of the Christian Desert Fathers of the third to fifth centuries (of whom St Simeon Stylites was one) did this too, leaving the shelter of villages and towns and exposing themselves to the blazing heat of the deserts of the Middle East.

ILLNESS

The most common kind of homoeostasis disruption we experience is when we are ill, when our organism isn't functioning properly or is being invaded by bacteria or viruses. So does that mean that we have awakening experiences when we are ill?

This doesn't appear to happen very often. We've seen that homoeostasis disruption usually needs to be done consciously to generate awakening experiences and it's not likely that anyone would want to – or even be able to – consciously make themselves ill. And perhaps the other reason for this is that when we're ill our energy levels are very low. So much of our organism's energy is devoted to fighting the illness that there's probably little available to 'fuel' or support higher states of consciousness.

However, there are certainly some cases of illness inducing awakening experiences. As with drugs, certain illnesses are more likely to cause awakening experiences than others. And the condition that is *most* likely to trigger awakening experiences, it seems, is temporal lobe epilepsy. As early as 1875, the German psychologist P. Samt noted that some of his epileptic patients believed that they were in heaven. Some believed that the doctors treating them were divine beings, as a result of which Samt called this phenomenon 'God nomenclature'.[43]

The author Karen Armstrong, a former nun, described an awakening experience that occurred just before her first epileptic seizure. She was walking through the ticket barrier at an Underground station when a strange scent and taste and a flickering light assaulted her senses. She felt frightened at first and held a railing to steady herself. And then she received what she called 'the greatest gift of all':

Suddenly, at last, all the conflicting pieces of the pattern seemed to fuse into a meaningful whole. I had entered a new dimension of pure joy, fulfilment and peace: the world seemed transfigured and its ultimate significance – so obvious and yet quite inexpressible – was revealed. This was God.[44]

The Russian novelist Dostoyevsky had many high-intensity awakening experiences both before and at the onset of his epileptic seizures. He describes one in his novel *The Idiot*, through the voice of his character Myshkin:

His mind and his heart were flooded with extraordinary light; all his uneasiness, all his doubts, all his anxieties were relived at once; they were all merged in a lofty calm, full of serene, harmonious joy and hope. But these moments, these flashes, were only the prelude of that final second (it was never more than a second) with which the fit began. That second was of course, unendurable ... the acme of harmony and beauty ... a feeling unknown and undivined

until then, of completeness, of proportion, or reconciliation
and of ecstatic devotional merging in the highest synthesis
of life.

   'At that moment I seem somehow to understand the
extraordinary saying that there shall be no more time.' [45]

This experience features almost every characteristic of high-level awakening experiences: a vision of 'extraordinary light', a sense of joy, harmony and of the complete 'rightness' of the universe, timelessness and an experience of becoming one with the universe.

   There is also evidence that some of the major religious figures in history had revelations and visions induced by epilepsy. Because of his own experiences, Dostoyevsky was convinced that the prophet Mohammed suffered from epilepsy too. 'Mohammad assures us in this Koran that he had seen Paradise,' Dostoyevsky noted. 'He did not lie. He had indeed been in Paradise – during an attack of epilepsy, from which he suffered, as I do.' [46] In the Bible, both Luke and Paul mention that St Paul suffered from an unknown 'bodily weakness', and Paul's own description of his Road to Damascus experience – when he was blinded by a bright light and heard the voice of Jesus – is suggestive of an epileptic fit. Similarly, neurologists have suggested that Joan of Arc had symptoms of temporal lobe epilepsy (TLE) which gave rise to mystical experiences in which she was blinded by bright light, saw visions of angels and felt that the secrets of the universe were being revealed to her. [47]

   Some scientists have seen the awakening experiences of TLE patients as evidence that mystical experiences are caused by the changes to the brain. This link is at the heart of Michael Persinger's suggestion that mystical experiences are caused by stimulation of the temporal lobes (referred to close to the beginning of this chapter). However, just because they're linked, it doesn't necessarily follow that temporal lobe seizures actually *produce* the mystical experiences. We could just as easily see seizures as sudden and dramatic disruptions to homoeostasis which make awakening experiences much more likely.

Other brain conditions can induce powerful mystical experiences too. One recent example is the story of the scientist Jill Bolte-Taylor, who had an experience of *nirvikalpa samadhi* while having a stroke. As she got up one morning, a blood vessel exploded in the left hemisphere of her brain. Over the next few hours, her brain deteriorated until she lost the ability to walk, talk, read and write, and became – as she puts it – 'an infant in a woman's body'. But while this was happening she was experiencing the formless spiritual ground of reality. As she describes it:

> *I could no longer define the boundaries of my body. I couldn't define where I began and where I ended. Because the atoms and molecules of my arm blended with the atoms and molecules of the wall. All I could detect was this energy… My left hemisphere brain chatter went totally silent, just [as though] somebody [had taken] a remote control and pressed the mute button. At first I was shocked to find myself inside a silent mind. But I was immediately captivated by the magnificence of the energy around me… I felt enormous and expansive. I felt at one with all the energy that was and it was beautiful there…*
>
> *My spirit soared free like a great whale gliding through a sea of silent euphoria. Nirvana, I found nirvana…*[48]

Aside from these brain conditions, infectious diseases may also occasionally have an awakening effect. The anthropologist Raymond Prince suggested that for prehistoric human beings, infectious diseases, together with starvation and exhaustion, were even more important than hallucinogenic plants as a source of transcendental experience. As he notes, most of the micro-organisms that cause infectious diseases are plants and fungi, or closely linked to them, and so can be psychoactive in the same way that psychedelic plants are. He suggests that infectious diseases like smallpox, typhoid or pneumonia can sometimes generate transcendent states, while non-infectious ones such as diphtheria, tetanus or cholera generally don't.[49]

Indeed, there are cases of religious figures having powerful revelations whilst seriously ill with infectious diseases. For example, the British nineteenth-century Catholic leader Cardinal Newman was suffering an almost fatal attack of typhoid (or possibly gastric) fever, when he 'had a most consoling and overpowering thought of God's electing love and seemed to feel I was His'.[50] Similarly, one of England's greatest mystics, Julian of Norwich, came close to death at the age of 30. While she was gravely ill she had a series of 16 'showings', some of them visions of Jesus and others more general mystical visions of God as an endless source of bliss and love, when she learned that 'He is in all things', that 'tender love completely surrounds us, never to leave us' and was 'so happy spiritually that I felt completely at peace and relaxed: nothing on earth could have disturbed me'.[51]

HOW DOES HOMOEOSTASIS DISRUPTION GENERATE AWAKENING EXPERIENCES?

The question of *why* all of these different varieties of homoeostasis disruption can lead to awakening experiences is difficult to answer exactly. It seems clear, though, that our ordinary consciousness and homoeostasis are closely interlinked. The most likely explanation is that in some way our normal homeostatic functioning mediates or helps to regulate our ordinary consciousness, so that when it is disrupted, ordinary consciousness is disrupted too. After all, as far as survival is concerned, ordinary consciousness is our optimum state, so it seems logical that in some way our physiological functioning should work to maintain it.

Perhaps we should think of ordinary consciousness as a kind of mould or pattern which our mind has been set into. To some extent this mould is held in place by our physiological functioning. But it is very fragile, so that all it takes is a slight change in our physiology – enough to put us out of homoeostasis – to dislodge it. The exact chemical nature of the physiological change doesn't seem to matter

– it can be a higher or lower level of oxygen, carbon dioxide, blood glucose, insulin, blood pressure, and so on. *Any* change can – if it's done consciously and in a religious or spiritual context – give rise to a higher state of consciousness.

However, we need to be careful about distinguishing between altered states of consciousness and higher states. In general, homoeostasis disruption is more likely to produce altered states than higher ones, and states of extreme hunger, tiredness and pain are more likely to produce delusional and psychotic states, with hallucinations and perceptual distortions. Awakening experiences are most likely to occur when 'spiritual technologies' are used voluntarily, especially within a religious or spiritual setting. Psychedelic drugs appear to be the most reliable way of inducing higher states through non-homoeostasis, but even they only generate them when the circumstances are right. As Roger Walsh notes, they 'can induce genuine mystical experiences, but only sometimes, in some people, under some circumstances'.[52]

ARE THESE STATES GENUINE AWAKENING EXPERIENCES?

Some people have doubted whether drug-induced higher states of consciousness are genuinely 'spiritual'. Religious scholars tend to believe that mystical experiences are related to – and even caused by – God, and don't accept that they can be induced 'artificially'.[53] However, if we compare the experiences we've looked at in this chapter with the characteristics of awakening experiences in Chapter 1, it's hard to see why they shouldn't be considered 'genuine'. In states of homoeostasis disruption (or 'HD states' for short), we experience heightened perception, can sense that things are alive, can see a radiance emanating from the world, have a sense of the meaningfulness and benevolence of the world, are aware of all-pervading spiritual force and of the unity of everything, and so on.

This is clearly the same wider reality that other, more spontaneous awakening experiences reveal. As Walter Stace wrote of the drug experience, 'It's not a matter of it being similar to mystical experience; it *is* mystical experience.'[54]

However, this doesn't mean that the experiences are identical in every way. There are, I believe, a few significant differences between HD states and more spontaneous awakening experiences.

I became aware of one of these differences in my own experiments with magic mushrooms. Once, after taking them, I was staring at a group of trees which looked amazingly vivid and alive, and was mesmerized by their intricacy and beauty. But at the same time I felt that something was slightly wrong. 'All of this may be beautiful,' I told myself, 'but there's something missing.' I realized that I wasn't feeling anything *inside*. Unlike the awakening experiences I'd had spontaneously or as a result of meditation, there was no sense of joy or even well-being inside me, only a kind of blankness. And I realized that this was true of all of my drug experiences: even though they gave me mystical vision, they didn't bring a serene glow of well-being, a sense of exaltation or ecstasy, or feelings of love or of making contact with my spiritual essence.

This seems to be true of HD states in general. In Chapter 1 we heard people speak of being 'filled with ecstasy', being 'filled with such love that I could die happily' or experiencing 'a feeling of absolute bliss'. In spontaneous awakening experiences – or at least ones which *seem* spontaneous – these feelings always go hand in hand with the 'external' visions of radiance and non-duality. But drug experiences and other HD states don't seem to feature this well-being to the same degree.

Similarly, we've seen that one of the characteristics of awakening experiences is a sense of becoming a deeper and truer self, the real self rather than the shadow self of the ego. In my own experience and from the accounts I've read, HD states generally don't feature this characteristic either, at least not to anything like the same degree. They don't appear to cause this identity shift, this sense of making connection to the 'ground' of your being.

The term 'entheogens' has been used for psychedelic drugs – literally, 'revealers of the god within'. But since they generally *don't* appear to give us contact with our spiritual essence or allow us to experience the bliss and love it radiates, this term is perhaps misleading. Drugs can certainly help us to see *brahman* in the world, but in general they don't give us such ready access to the *atman* inside. It would perhaps be more appropriate to call them '*ex*theogens' – revealers of the god *outside*.

Because of this, I don't think it's accurate to call HD states *spiritual* experiences. The word 'spiritual' has an interior meaning – it refers to the 'spirit' inside us, the life-energy that constitutes our being. And so the term 'spiritual experiences' should have an inner meaning too and refer to an inner change, a change that happens *to* our 'spirit' or life-energy. Since HD experiences don't involve this inner dimension to any strong degree, it would be misleading to use this term to describe them.

THE DISADVANTAGES OF HD STATES

In this way, HD states don't give us quite as *full* an experience as other types of awakening. They still seem almost too good to be true, though. It seems so easy: if you want to take your mind out of the mould of your normal sleep consciousness and perceive a wider and more intense reality, all you need to do is to throw a spanner into the works of your organism in some way, throw it off balance so that – at least for the time it takes to correct itself – you can experience freedom.

However, there are some serious drawbacks to HD states. For one thing, making an ongoing effort to keep your mind awake in this way would be dangerous to your health, and probably kill you if you went on with it for too long. Too many drugs, or too much pain or physical deprivation, could easily lead to permanent physical damage.

And there's also the potential danger to your *mind*. Especially with drugs, there's the danger of not being prepared for the intensified awareness they bring. Rather than being slowly prised open, the door to a new world is ripped off its hinges. As a result, we might be overwhelmed by the sheer strangeness and intensity of this world, especially if we don't have any foreknowledge of mystical experiences and so can't interpret or understand what's happening.

Even Aldous Huxley became aware of this danger when he took mescaline: looking at a chair which seemed to him 'like the last judgement', he suddenly felt a sense of panic, that this was somehow going too far, and experienced 'the fear of being overwhelmed, of disintegrating under a pressure of reality greater than a mind, accustomed to living most of the time in a cosy world of symbols, could possibly bear'.[55] Fortunately, Huxley understood enough of what was happening to turn his attention away and his experience of this schizophrenic 'hell' was only momentary. But this was easy for him: he was 60 years old, with a strong, well-integrated personality and a full understanding of the mechanics of the experience he was undergoing. We could easily imagine that somebody who didn't have such a strong ego structure and didn't understand what was happening *would* be liable to disintegrate under the pressure of this reality. And their psychic equilibrium might be permanently disturbed.

Or, in a similar way, the sheer force of the experience might erode the ego structure away and lead to schizophrenia or psychosis. Drug experiences (and other HD states) produce a powerful blast which immobilizes the ego, and if this blast is regularly repeated, the ego structure may dissolve and never be able to reform itself. These were the effects suffered by the so-called 'acid casualties' of the 1960s, such as the musicians Syd Barrett, Peter Green and Brian Wilson.

In a sense, HD experiences are only really a short-cut too. It's as if we've stumbled on a defect in the mechanisms of consciousness, a kind of legal clause which gives us a quick way of escaping ordinary consciousness, and are exploiting it. You could compare it to schoolchildren tricking their teacher into leaving the room so they can enjoy a few minutes of freedom – but the teacher always comes back again, of course, and then everything goes back to normal.

This is why there's always something *futile* about the experiences, as Rimbaud seems to have eventually realized. Just as it's ultimately useless to try to keep your mind awake by chasing after unfamiliar experiences (moving from one place to the next because the 'familiarity mechanism' keeps turning the experiences to unreality), so you can't defeat your organism's natural tendency to return to homoeostasis and – in the process – to also return to ordinary consciousness. In the end, you're always going to be back where you started.

In terms of attaining a *permanently* awakened state, therefore, there's obviously no way that HD states can help us. They can't permanently change our consciousness in such a way that we become enlightened – although they might change it in such a way that we become schizophrenic. The best we can say of them is that they give us 'peek' experiences into higher realities. These certainly can be useful, though: they might come as a bolt out of the blue, breaking through the familiar taken-for-granted world and making us aware that higher realms of reality do exist. For some people, their first experiences of LSD, magic mushrooms or mescaline might have the same effect as experiencing flashes of normal vision would have on a man who'd been partially blind all his life without realizing it. The powerful transcendent reality they've been exposed to might also bring about a change in their personality, at least over the following months, and perhaps even years. It might make them more humble, less materialistic or egotistical, and give them a sense of security or hope. This is presumably why, two months after the 2006 study of psilocybin that I described earlier, most participants said their moods, attitudes and behaviour had become more positive. Psychological tests showed that they had a significantly higher level of well-being compared to other volunteers who were given a placebo at the same session.

Similarly, in the famous 'Good Friday Experiment' at Harvard University in 1965, the psychologist Walter Pankhe gave ten members of a group of 20 theological students doses of psilocybin. (It was a double-blind experiment, so the students didn't know whether they were receiving the drug or a placebo.) All ten had more intense 'mystical' feelings and perceptions than the others, including several powerful experiences comparable to those of great Christian mystics. In a follow-up study six months later, eight out of the ten students said that the experience had had a powerful long-term effect, deepening their sense of the spiritual and enriching their lives. And remarkably, this was still the case after 25 years. In follow-up interviews by the psychologist Rick Doblin, most of the participants felt that the experience had changed them permanently, giving them a deeper appreciation of life and nature, an increased sense of joy, a reduced fear of death and greater empathy for minorities and oppressed people. As one of them told Doblin, 'It left me with a completely unquestioned certainty that there is an environment bigger than the one I'm conscious of... Somehow my life has been different, knowing that there is something out there.'[56]

For many people, drug-induced awakening experiences have been the beginning of a spiritual journey, encouraging them to investigate eastern spiritual traditions or more reliable and healthy consciousness-changing practises such as meditation. This is what happened to the Harvard professor Richard Alpert, for example, who was one of the pioneers of research into psychedelics. He conducted experiments with psilocybin at Harvard University with Timothy Leary in 1962 and continued studying the effects of psychedelics even after he was expelled from the university. However, he quickly became disillusioned with drugs, doubting that they could lead to permanent change, and travelled to India, where he learned yoga and meditation and took the name Ram Dass. He has spent the rest of his life exploring spiritual practises and teachings and spreading the wisdom he has found. And he has said himself that his experiments with psychedelics were the catalyst for his spiritual seeking.

On the other hand, using drugs as a spiritual technology may create a passive attitude and a reluctance to make the long-term disciplined effort that permanent transformation requires – as was the case with Ram Dass's colleague Timothy Leary, whose pursuit of 'chemical enlightenment' degenerated into a life of self-indulgence. As the religious scholar Huston Smith put it, 'Drugs appear to induce religious experiences: it is less evident that they can produce religious lives.'[57]

However, the second source of awakening experiences that we're going to look at has all of these advantages and none of the disadvantages.

5

LIFE-ENERGY AND AWAKENING EXPERIENCES

Of all of the different methods of transcending ordinary consciousness, the most reliable and effective is probably the practise of meditation.

Meditation seems to be natural to human beings – at least, natural in the sense that the practise arose independently in many different parts of the world. Almost every culture over the Eurasian landmass has developed a form of it. In ancient India the practise was an integral part of spiritual paths such as Vedanta, Buddhism, Jainism and Yoga, while in China the Taoist practise of *tso-wang*, 'sitting with a blank mind', became popular during the latter part of the first millennium BCE. In Islam and Judaism, the mystical traditions of Sufism and Kabbalah both developed forms of meditation, while in the Eastern Orthodox Church the 'Jesus Prayer' was clearly a meditative practise. This prayer (simply 'Lord Jesus Christ, son of God, have mercy on me, a sinner') was meant to be said aloud a specific number of times 'in silence and solitude' and then repeated silently for a longer period. After some time, the meditator moved the prayer down from their head to their heart centre, where it 'lives itself in every heartbeat'.[1]

Some modern born-again Christians are opposed to meditation, believing that quieting the mind leaves it somehow 'open' to the

Devil (the irony of this wouldn't be lost on a Christian mystic like Meister Eckhart, who would say that the mind is open to *God* when it's empty). And although it's true that meditation has never been as prominent in western Christianity, born-again Christians might be surprised to learn that centuries ago mantra meditation techniques were commonly used by Christian monks. This is highlighted by the following passage from the Christian text *The Cloud of Unknowing*, written anonymously by a man who lived in the Midlands of England in the fourteenth century:

> *The shorter the word the better, being more like the working of the spirit! A word like 'God' or 'Love'. Choose which you like, or perhaps some other, so long as it is one syllable. And fix this word fast to your heart, so that it is always there, come what may... With this word you will suppress all thought under the cloud of forgetting.*[2]

The spiritual exercises of St Ignatius, written as a guide for the training of religious novices in the 1520s, recommend the following meditative technique as a method of quieting the mind: 'At each breath or respiration, he is to pray mentally, as he says one word of the "Our Father" or any other prayer that is being recited, so that between each breath and another a single word is said.'[3]

Similarly, early Benedictine monks in the Middle East, from the sixth century onwards, would repeat mantras to themselves both when they were sitting quietly and when they were working. One of the most popular was the following phrase from the Psalms: 'O God, come to my assistance; O Lord, make haste to help me.'[4]

In addition, many Christian mystics and teachers tell us that the way to experience God is to empty and quiet the mind. According to the fourteenth-century Flemish mystic John Ruysbroeck, mystical experiences occur when 'a man is alert and undistracted in his sense by images, and free and unoccupied in his highest powers', which is a perfect description of the state we reach after a good meditation.[5] Similarly, the fourteenth-century English mystic Walter Hilton advises that 'If you want to discover your soul, withdraw your thoughts from outward and material things, forgetting if possible your own body and its five senses.'[6]

But even in conventional Christianity – and Islam too – the practise of prayer has a meditative purpose for many people. Prayer isn't just a matter of talking to God and asking him for guidance or favours; it may also have an awakening effect by quieting the mind and generating a sense of inner peace. A student of mine described to me her experience of prayer:

When I pray I feel as though I find inner peace. I forget about all my daily concerns and go deep into myself. I feel a powerful, rich energy flowing into my being. It feels like a sanctuary from all the rushing to and fro of everyday life.

THE EFFECTS OF MEDITATION

There are hundreds of different techniques of meditation, but they all follow the same basic principle. The aim is to quiet the mind, to slow down the chattering thoughts that continually whizz through it, until eventually they fade away and we experience a state of mental stillness or pure consciousness. In meditation we do this by *focusing the mind,* trying to keep our attention fixed on a certain point, object or image. Different techniques recommend different objects of concentration: a mantra, the breath, a point inside our own consciousness, an imagined image or a real object such as a candle flame or a sacred symbol such as a mandala. Focusing our attention leads to mental quietness because our normal thought-chatter is fuelled by the attention we give to it. If we're immersed in it, it keeps whirling away, spinning from one association to the next. But if we focus our attention on another object, it naturally fades away, like a fire which has run out of fuel. Some practises recommend letting go of the focusing device when the mind has become quiet, so that we can experience the stillness and peace at the heart of our being without any obstruction.

I should also mention that there's another type of meditation which doesn't use objects of concentration as such: *vipassana,* or insight meditation. As taught by the Buddha, the aim of *vipassana* is to stand apart from the flow of your thoughts and sensations and just observe them as they arise and pass away. The important thing is to not let yourself be carried away by the flow, to be a detached witness of it. In this way, you gain insight into the workings of the mind and become aware of how impermanent mental and emotional states are. You begin to 'dis-identify' with the flow, to realize that your true self is distinct from thoughts and feelings. The Buddha recommended that *vipassana* should be practised alongside 'object meditation' (*samatha,* as it is called in Buddhism).

For such a simple practise, meditation is incredibly effective on a variety of levels. Studies have shown that it can bring an almost dizzying array of physical benefits: it can reduce heart rate and blood pressure, and has been successfully used to treat hypertension and cardiovascular disease; it can stimulate the immune system, reduce chronic pain, help alleviate asthma and even aid recovery from cancer. If any drug had these effects it would quickly become known as a 'wonder drug' and find its way into every bathroom cabinet in the world. But even more than this, meditation has powerful psychological benefits. Many studies have shown that regular meditation leads to reduced anxiety and stress and can help people overcome insomnia, depression, alcoholism and drug addiction.[7]

More generally, the practise has been found to increase well-being. For example, in a 2007 study at the University of Oregon in Eugene, 40 people were given a five-day training course in mindfulness meditation and relaxation. Compared to a control group, the meditation group had more positive moods and lower levels of cortisol, a hormone linked to stress.[8] Also, in 2003, a study at the University of California found that long-term Buddhist meditators had less activity in the amygdala, the part of the brain linked to fear and anxiety; and that they experienced less confusion, shock and anger than other people.[9] Again, these benefits appear to be greater than Prozac or Valium or any other mood-altering drug, and it's not surprising that a great many physicians now recommend meditation to their patients.

Meditation has just as powerful effects on the spiritual level too. One important difference between it and the 'homoeostasis-disrupting' practises we looked at in the last chapter is that its main focus is *long term*. It isn't so much about inducing a temporary change in consciousness as a gradual but permanent change of being. Its ultimate aim is to 'tame' the ego-mind, to permanently quiet its thought-chatter and transcend our normal separateness and 'ego isolation'. And this change – even if it only happens to a degree – is accompanied by an 'identity shift'. Your centre of gravity will shift from your chattering ego-mind to a deeper self. You will feel that your normal sense of 'I' was only really the product of the constant thoughts and desires that ran through your mind and that beneath that thought-chatter there is another self which seems more essentially you, and stronger, more complete. As I mentioned above, this 'dis-identification' from the flow of thought is one of the direct aims of *vipassana,* but it occurs through 'object meditation' too. (We will look into these long-term effects in more detail later.)

However, meditation can certainly have very powerful short-term effects too. In fact, a good meditation practise, in which you keep your mind fairly well focused on the mantra or your breath, almost always induces a low-level awakening experience. I described my own experience of this in Chapter 1: after a good meditation, colours seem brighter, objects seem more real and beautiful, and I notice details which I don't normally perceive.

In her study of mysticism first published in 1911, Evelyn Underhill suggests that anyone can have a rudimentary spiritual experience by looking at a particular object 'in a special and undivided manner'. She advises us to 'wilfully yet tranquilly refuse the messages which countless other aspects of the world are sending' and tells us to try not to think. The result of this will be:

*You will perceive about you a strange and deepening
quietness ... you will become aware of a heightened
significance, an intensified existence in the thing at which
you look... It seems as though the barrier between its life
and your own, between subject and object, has melted
away. You are merged with it, in an act of communion:
and you know the secret of its being.[10]*

Underhill is clearly advising us to practise a form of meditation here
and the effects she describes are exactly those of a low-intensity
awakening experience.

More than half a century later, the American psychologist
Arthur Deikman followed a very similar procedure in a series of
'experimental meditation' sessions. He asked the participants to
focus their attention on a vase for periods up to half an hour and they
reported that the vase became richer and more vivid as an object, that
it 'seemed to acquire a life of its own, to be animated', and also that
there was a 'decrease in [their] sense of being separate' from it. After
the sessions, the participants found that this heightened perception
of the vase was extended to their whole environment. One of them
reported that he was amazed at the beauty he could see everywhere,
which he described as 'perception filled with light and movement,
both of which are very pleasurable'. Another participant stated that
everything he saw was 'clamoring for [his] attention'.[11]

High-intensity awakening experiences are less common in
meditation, but they certainly occur too. Below, for example, an
acquaintance of mine describes a powerful 'ingoing' experience she
had while doing a group meditation on a spiritual retreat. As well as
showing the power of meditation, this experience illustrates that, as
I mentioned at the beginning of Chapter 2, awakening experiences
are often communal:

*We were doing some mantra meditation and the energy in
the group was incredible. But I was quite uncomfortable
for the first 20 minutes or so. I kept having to change my*

*position and my mind was chattering away. But as I
repeated the mantra I became less aware of the pain in
my back and I felt myself slipping into this other place. I
became separate from the chattering of my mind and lost
all bodily awareness. I was pulled to this place of pure love
and joy. It was just pure consciousness. It was as if I was in
this huge cave that was filled with a golden brightness, and
I was the colour and the mantra. Everything melded into
one. I felt ecstatic and massively serene at the same time. It
was a connection to something huge.*

*I was on a massive high for a couple of hours afterwards.
And even the next day I still felt very connected to
everything, and everything seemed illuminated.*

The Victorian poet Alfred Lord Tennyson practised a form of mantra
meditation – even though he might not have recognized it as such
– in which he silently repeated his name to himself. This frequently
induced high-intensity awakening experiences in which he lost all
sense of separateness and became part of the formless spiritual
'ground' of the universe. As he describes it:

*[I]ndividuality itself seemed to dissolve and fade away
into boundless being, and this was not a confused state but
the clearest, the surest of the surest, utterly beyond words
– where death was an almost laughable impossibility – the
loss of personality (if so it were) seeming no extinction but
the only true life.*[12]

AWAKENING EXPERIENCES
AND LIFE-ENERGY

But why does meditation have this awakening effect?

In my view, it's because meditation has the effect of intensifying
(and stilling) our inner energy, our 'life-energy'. By this term, I mean

the essential non-physical energy of our being. Scientifically speaking, when we use the term 'energy' we think in terms of the light and heat of the sun, which plants and animals (including human beings) absorb. When we eat plants and animals, we take energy from them (in the form of calories) and use this energy to fuel our body. But there seems to be another kind of energy inside us besides this physical one.

This is the energy used by our mind when we think, concentrate, perceive the world around us and process information. This energy is also used by – and flows through – our body. If you close your eyes now and relax, you should be able to feel it: a soft and subtle vibrating (perhaps even tingling) energy that flows through your feet, your legs, your upper body, your hands and arms and up into your head. This is what traditional Chinese philosophy calls *chi* and ancient Hindu philosophy calls *prana*. (As we'll see in a moment, many other cultures had concepts of 'life-energy' too.) As Chinese and Indian medicine tell us, this energy also flows through to the different organs and structures of the body and has the job of keeping them – and the overall organism – healthy. Life-energy can also manifest itself as sexual energy, just as, when it is used for mental functions, it expresses itself as mental or psychic energy. When you become sexually aroused, you can feel it tingling through your lower body, intensifying and exploding when you have an orgasm.

In normal life, there is a continual outflow of our life-energy. It's drained away by the thought-chatter that continually fills our mind, by the tasks and chores that continually occupy our attention and by the constant processing of sights, sounds and smells around us, as well as the information that comes to us from the media or from conversations with others. More intermittently, we also expend life-energy through emotions, when circumstances, or our own thoughts, trigger feelings of anger, guilt, resentment, bitterness, jealousy, etc.

But meditation halts this outflow. When we sit down to meditate, we no longer give our attention to tasks, and the information that we process from our surroundings is reduced to a trickle. Our thought-chatter slows down too, and we normally become free of emotional activity and sexual desire. As a result, after meditation there is an *inner concentration* of our life-energy. It's concentrated and intensified rather than dispersed and dissipated – and this generates an 'awakened' state of consciousness.

It's true that meditation causes physiological changes too – for example, reduced oxygen consumption and blood lactate levels, and (as we saw above) a slower heart rate and lower blood pressure – and could therefore be seen as another method of disrupting homoeostasis. But with meditation this disruption is only a secondary effect. The really significant change isn't to our physiology or brain chemistry, but to our inner being, or life-energy.

The philosopher Phillip Novak explains the awakening effects of meditation in a similar way. He notes that we normally see the world around us as a half-real one-dimensional place because the 'endless associational chatter' – that is, thought-chatter – of our mind monopolizes our psychic energy, leaving none available for us to devote to what he calls 'open, receptive and present-centred awareness'. But when we meditate we don't give any attention to what Novak calls the 'automatized structures of consciousness' which produce thought-chatter. As a result these structures start to weaken and eventually fade away, which frees up the energy which they normally monopolize. And this energy transfers to perception. We use the surplus energy to *attend* to our surroundings and experiences, to really *see* the objects and phenomena around us rather than just glossing over them. In Novak's own words, 'Energy formerly bound in emotive spasms, ego defence, fantasy and fear can appear as the delight of present-centredness.'[13]

Similarly, Arthur Deikman explains mystical experiences in terms of a 'de-automatization of perception'. From a survival point of view, he suggests, we need to conserve as much energy as possible, so that we can devote all our energy to the practical business of keeping ourselves alive – finding food, dealing with problems and dangers, protecting ourselves against the elements and so on. This is why our normal perception of the world is automatic – we conserve energy by not putting it into the act of perception. But in spiritual or mystical experiences, Deikman argues, these structures which 'ordinarily conserve attentional energy for maximum efficiency in achieving the basic goods of survival' are 'set aside or break down, in favour of alternate modes of consciousness'.[14] This is what he refers to as a 'de-automatization of perception'.

In other words, this is the reverse of the process of losing the naturally awakened state of indigenous peoples. In meditation, we take back the psychic energy that is normally used up by the ego. In my own terminology, this means that the desensitizing mechanism which normally edits out the reality of our experiences no longer needs to function. Since the ego is quiet, there's a surplus of energy, and so this mechanism doesn't need to perform its energy-saving role. It no longer acts on our perceptions, and so we see the is-ness and beauty that are normally hidden from us.

This concept of an intensification of life-energy doesn't only help to explain meditation experiences, but awakening experiences in general. It is, I believe, the second major source of awakening experiences, with states of homoeostasis disruption (HD states) being the other. This can be summarized as follows:

Awakening experiences occur when there is a more intense than usual concentration – and a greater than usual stillness – of 'life-energy' inside us.

While HD states give rise to wild and ecstatic experiences (that is, 'high-arousal' experiences), awakening experiences caused by an intensification and stilling of life-energy tend to be sedate and serene ('low-arousal experiences').

THE EXISTENCE OF LIFE-ENERGY

However, since the concept of life-energy is quite controversial, perhaps we should examine it a little more before we go any further.

The existence of 'life-energy' – or vitality – used to be taken for granted, even by psychologists and philosophers, but was a casualty of the rise of materialistic science during the twentieth century, with its belief that matter was the only reality. Since life-energy is non-material, it has no place in the scientific worldview.

However, in terms of our own experience as human beings, its existence makes a great deal of sense. For example, why is it that we sometimes feel more alive than at other times? Why do we sometimes feel a kind of glow of health and vitality inside us which makes us feel cheerful, while at other times – say, after a hard day at the office or a few hours' travelling – we feel so drained of energy that we have to lie down for an hour or two to recuperate? When we rest we can sometimes *feel* life-energy recharging itself inside us, flowing through our body and making us feel stronger and mentally more alert. To a large extent, our 'energy levels' seem to determine our moods: a buoyant, optimistic mood usually equates with a high energy level, while a miserable and pessimistic mood usually equates with being drained of energy.

You might argue that this can just be explained in terms of muscular energy – we feel energetic and cheerful when we've absorbed a lot of energy from food but haven't expended any yet, and we feel 'drained' when we've been physically active because we have expended a lot of muscular energy. But one argument against this is that we often become tired in situations where we expend hardly any physical or muscular energy. For example, an office worker who spends all day filling in forms and typing information into a computer doesn't expend very much physical energy at all. Neither does a student who spends the day reading textbooks or a writer who feels exhausted after a four-hour stint in front of the computer screen. The energy that we use in these situations is not muscular – if anything, it's *mental* rather than physical energy.

Conversely, we can often feel very energetic and alive at times when we *have* expended a lot of physical energy. Every morning I do yoga *asanas* for about 15 minutes and afterwards I always feel new waves of energy flowing through my body. I always feel somehow purer and more alive. Almost everybody who does yoga *asanas* or related practises such as *chi gung* or *tai chi* experiences this – in fact, this is the main purpose of the practises. People who play sports and go for vigorous walks or climbs know this feeling too: at the end of the activity they might feel physically tired but at the same time experience a strange kind of mental glow and feeling of being more alive. This sometimes happens after sex too – despite all the muscular energy we've expended, we often feel gloriously alive. In terms of physical energy this doesn't make sense. Of course, the release of endorphins may cause feelings of well-being, but there's no reason why they should fill us with energy too. Expending physical energy should make us feel *less* alive and energetic. But it seems that there is a non-physical energy inside us which can, paradoxically, be *intensified* by certain forms of exercise.

On an everyday level, most of us take the existence of life-energy for granted, even if we're not aware of it. We talk about feeling 'run down' or 'drained', or say that we need to 'recharge our batteries'. Our experience tells us that there is a kind of 'energy battery' inside us which can be recharged by rest and sleep. We also talk about people who are 'full of life' or 'full of vitality', implying that these people have a higher than usual level of 'life-energy' inside them.

THE PROBLEM
OF SLEEP

In fact, the concept of life-energy may provide a common-sense solution to a problem that still vexes scientists: that of why human beings need to sleep for several hours every night. Some popular theories suggest that the purpose of sleep is to replenish the body's energy and repair the physical 'wear and tear' that the day has brought to our organs and tissues and other bodily structures. However, as the sleep scientist Jim Horne, director of the Sleep Research Centre at Loughborough University, points out, in terms of physical energy, sleep doesn't have a particularly strong restorative effect. When mammals such as rodents sleep, their metabolic rate falls very significantly and they do restore a great deal of energy. But our metabolism only slows down by 5–10 per cent during sleep (compared to when we rest), and sleep has no more of an energy-conserving effect than resting and relaxing while being awake. As Horne puts it, 'There is only a modest further energy saving to be gained by sleeping.'[15]

Sleep is no more effective than rest in terms of restoring the functioning of our body either. Most of the body's restorative functions are carried out while we're awake, and in some cases sleep actually reduces these functions – for example, tissue repair slows down during sleep, due to lower levels of amino acid in the blood. As Horne writes, 'There is little or no evidence that outside the brain any other organ undergoes any heightened degree of repair during sleep. Relaxed wakefulness has an equally restorative effect.'[16]

If the purpose of sleep were to repair the body, we would expect severe sleep deprivation to cause serious physical problems, but this isn't the case. In fact, studies have shown that people can go without sleep for up to eight days without any signs of physical illness or unusual hormonal levels, or any significant physical changes of any kind. This is not what you'd expect if the purpose of sleep were to restore energy and repair the 'wear and tear' of wakefulness.

But if this is the case, why do we *feel* that sleep has such a powerful energy-restoring effect? Why do we often wake up after a short nap and feel full of energy again? And why do we sometimes feel so drained of energy that we *have* to sleep? Since sleep only has a limited energy-restoring effect (in terms of physical energy), this doesn't seem to make sense.

The important point here may be that the energy that is restored in sleep is not *physical* energy. Perhaps the real purpose of sleep is to regenerate our *life*-energy. Our life energy becomes so depleted after 16 hours full of concentration and information processing that we need to completely 'switch off' – to become inactive and unconscious – for it to regenerate. Our metaphor of 'recharging batteries' may be exactly what happens. When we withdraw our senses from external stimuli and our mind ceases being active, our life-energy naturally recharges itself. On the other hand, if we don't get enough rest and sleep, we become 'drained' or 'run down' – and often ill, too, perhaps because there's not enough life-energy inside us to maintain the health of the body. (This is the view of ancient Chinese medicine, which suggests that we become vulnerable to disease when our *chi*, or life-energy, is generally diminished, or isn't flowing to different parts of the body.)

OTHER CONCEPTS OF LIFE-ENERGY

Some psychologists take the existence of a non-physical energy for granted too, even if they don't say so directly. They use terms like 'psychic', 'mental' or 'attentional' energy to describe the energy we use when we concentrate on activities, focus our attention or think. As the Italian psychologist Marchetti puts it, for example, 'Every time we direct our attention towards an object, we spend our [attentional] energy on it.'[17] In a similar way, the psychologist Mihaly Csikszentmihalyi speaks of the 'allocation of psychic energy' which takes place when we focus our attention, or the psychic energy which we 'invest in experiences'. He suggests that one of the benefits of the state of 'flow' – being absorbed in a challenging and stimulating activity – is that it gives us control over our 'psychic energy'. As he sees it, in ordinary life a lot of our psychic energy is taken up with 'preoccupation with the self', but in a state of 'flow' we forget ourselves, and so the psychic energy we normally waste is retained.[18]

In a similar concept to mine, the American psychologist and philosopher Michael Washburn suggests that our essential life-energy expresses itself in three different ways: as psychic energy, as libido (or sexual energy) and as spiritual power. He notes that psychic energy is used continually, fuelling our ongoing conscious experience, while libido and spiritual power are both 'potential' energies which are usually latent but become 'activated' by certain stimuli.[19] (Washburn's theory of spiritual awakening is similar to mine and I will refer to him again later.)

Earlier psychologists also used the concept of life-energy very freely. Both Freud and Jung, for example, used the term *libido* for psychic energy. Although they had different views on the nature of this energy – typically, Freud saw it as sexual in origin – they both saw the psyche as a 'closed system' with a finite amount of energy, which could be 'portioned out' in different amounts to the different structures and functions of the mind. In Freud's model, the id, the ego and the superego competed against one another to monopolize psychic energy. If you spend most of your time chasing after hedonistic pleasures like sex and food, your id is monopolizing your psychic energy, leaving little over for the ego and the superego, whereas if you have a very powerful conscience and are constantly assailed by feelings of guilt, your superego is monopolizing most of your psychic energy. Freud also believed that one of the problems caused by repression was that the act of repressing instincts or old experiences could take up a large portion of the *libido,* leaving less energy for other functions.[20]

For Jung, psychic energy was the power behind all of our experience – such as thinking, concentrating, instincts and sexual desire – but was of a different nature from that experience. As he saw it, psychic energy could be *actual,* manifesting itself as the 'dynamic phenomena of the psyche, such as instinct, wishing, willing, effect, attention, capacity for work, etc.', or it could be *potential,* showing itself as 'possibilities, aptitudes [and] attitudes'.[21] As in Freud's view, he believed that if a lot of energy was used up by one of these functions, then there would be less available in other areas.

The great American psychologist William James also took the existence of psychic energy for granted. He often referred to it as 'vitality' and in his essay *The Energies of Man* he puzzled over the question of why we all feel more or less alive on different days and how most of us feel as if we should be more alive than we are, as if there are reserves of vitality inside us which 'the incitements of the day do not call forth'. James notes that it's only when we make an effort to *act* that we are able to 'raise the sense of vitality'. As he puts it, '*Excitements, ideas* and *efforts* … are what carry us over the dam.'[22]

From an anthropological perspective, our modern scientific culture seems to be the first in history not to accept that there is such a thing as life-energy. Concepts of life-energy or psychic energy are common throughout the world. The ancient Indian and Chinese philosophers developed very detailed and complex concepts of *prana* and *chi* respectively. According to Indian Tantric philosophy, *prana* – which can be translated as both 'breath' and 'life' – flows through thousands of tiny channels throughout our body, called *nadi*. The body has seven main energy centres, the *chakras*, which can be active to different degrees and utilize different amounts of *prana*. One of the purposes of the *asanas* of hatha yoga is to affect the flow of *prana* through our body.

Similarly, in China, *chi* is believed to travel through 12 major meridians through the body, as well as thousands of smaller ones. Like hatha yoga, the exercises of *chi gung* and *tai chi* are designed to stimulate its flow. Acupuncture is believed to do the same, raising the general level of *chi* and removing blockages in its flow which can lead to illness. Acupuncture has now received widespread scientific validation from numerous studies but, tellingly, western scientists are still puzzled by the question of *how* it works.[23]

In Tibetan Buddhism, the essential energy of our being is known as *thigle,* which has been translated as 'bioenergetic volume'. This energy flows through our body as *lung,* through tiny channels called *tsa*. The ancient Egyptians believed that the whole of nature was pervaded with an animating spirit called *ba,* which was an expression of the universal energy of *akh,* or 'spirit-force'. The energy of *ba* was 'channelled' into human beings by the body's 'shadow' or 'double', *ka,* so that it became a person's life-energy. In a similar way, the Stoics of ancient Greece believed that the whole of the universe was pervaded with *pneuma,* which they called 'the soul of the universe' – in other words, this was their concept of spirit-force. And *pneuma* was also the force which animated living beings.

Living beings could have different concentrations of *pneuma* inside them, so that some creatures were more alive – and therefore more intelligent and conscious – than others.

Most, if not all, of the world's tribal indigenous peoples also have concepts of this energy. The Maoris of New Zealand refer to it as *tapu*, in parts of New Guinea it's called *rokao* and the Algonquian Native Americans called it *orenda*. Like the Egyptians and the Stoics, many of these peoples see life-energy as an expression of an all-pervading spirit-force and as essentially the same in nature. One of the tribal peoples of Japan, the Ainu, use the word *ramut* for both an individual's life-energy and the spiritual energy that fills the world. The anthropologist Neil Gordon Munro writes of their beliefs, 'When living things – men, animals, trees or plants – die, *ramat* leaves them and goes elsewhere, but does not perish.'[24] Similarly, the Ufaina tribe of the Amazon believe that when a person is born, a small amount of *fufuka* (their term for universal spirit) enters them. They, and their tribal group, 'borrow' it from the total 'stock' of spirit. While they live, this spirit-force is always the essence of their being and at death it is released and returns to its source.[25]

Therefore, it seems justifiable to believe that there is such a thing as life-energy and that it is the key to understanding awakening experiences of the 'low-arousal' type, as opposed to the 'high-arousal' experiences induced by disrupting homoeostasis – that is, serene and sedate experiences rather than wild, ecstatic ones. In any situation where our normal outflow of life-energy is halted and a higher-than-usual intensification of energy builds up inside us, an awakening experience occurs.

Incidentally, I should perhaps explain why I've used the term 'life-energy' rather than 'psychic energy'. Despite Freud and Jung's general use of the term, I feel that 'psychic energy' is a little misleading, since it suggests that this energy is used purely by the psyche, or the mind, and is situated there, when in fact it flows through the body too. As I've said already, this energy is *used* as psychic energy but it also manifests as sexual and emotional energy. There is one essential life-energy which is channelled into different functions.[26]

As we'll see in the next chapters, awakening experiences are often related to changes to the psyche, but they can be related to the body too. After doing yoga *asanas* or *tai chi,* it's quite common to experience a sense of inner well-being, a sense of connection to the world and a heightened awareness of your surroundings. And this is because the exercises have the effect of intensifying life-energy *in the body,* just as meditation does in the *psyche*. Since the energy is essentially the same, the effect is the same.

I believe that Freud and Jung were right in that there is a finite amount of life-energy inside us which can be 'portioned out' in different ways. (Both Deikman and Novak obviously take this for granted too, since they talk about 'conserving' and 'freeing up' psychic energy.) The energy level inside us continually fluctuates, rising and falling according to how much we have expended through the different functions of the mind and body and how much we have rested or slept. By far the largest portion of it is used as psychic energy, through thinking, concentrating and information processing. But at certain times it might be mainly used as emotional energy (for example, when you're having an argument or feel very upset) or as sexual energy. And there are also certain times when the energy isn't expended in these ways, when it is in a state of quiescence and becomes intensified, which is when awakening experiences occur.

In a sense, this connection I'm making between awakening experiences and life-energy is nothing new. Many mystics and spiritual teachers have interpreted mystical experiences in similar terms. The ancient Hindu text the *Moksha-Dharma,* for example, compares the transcendental Self to a sun and notes that when the *yogin* concentrates his attention, he gathers up the 'rays' of the sun – or the 'whirls' of consciousness – and focuses them inwardly. In other words, he gathers up the life-energy which the whirls of consciousness usually dissipate, which becomes concentrated – or intensified – within his being. As a result he experiences the intense radiance of the Self and attains a state of *samadhi*.[27]

In the Christian mystical tradition, Meister Eckhart describes how mystical experience occurs when '*you are able to draw in your [intellectual and sensory] powers to a unity* and forget all those things and their images which you have absorbed'.[28] He says that in order to become one with God, 'a man must collect all his powers as if into a corner of his soul'.[29] In our terms, he has to stop his life-energy being dissipated, to stop its normal outflow and *retain* it, so that it becomes concentrated and intensified in his inner being. In a similar way, St Gregory of Sinai describes an awakening experience as 'the total lifting of the powers of the soul to what may be discerned of the entire majesty of glory'.[30]

Back in India, the Tantric sects of Hinduism and Buddhism, which developed in medieval times, were clearly aware of the connection between intensifying life-energy and awakening experiences. They used meditation, breath control and yoga *asanas* to intensify the flow of *prana* through the body, attempting to raise it to the higher *chakras* and to release *kundalini,* the serpent energy at the bottom of the spine. In Chapter 9, we'll see that many mystics and spiritual teachers have seen long-term spiritual development in these terms too, as a process of taming their physical desires and reducing their attachments so that they could build up a *permanently* high concentration of life-energy inside them.

THE STILLING OF LIFE-ENERGY

However, it's important to note that it isn't quite enough for life-energy *just* to be intensified. For awakening experiences to occur, it usually has to be *stilled* – or purified – as well.

The biggest single outflow of our life-energy is the constant thought-chatter that fills our mind, which is why awakening experiences can occur simply through quieting that chatter. However, thought-chatter causes another major problem: a constant disturbance inside us. In Meister Eckhart's phrase, we're afflicted by a 'storm of inward thoughts',[31] a chaos of swirling images and impressions which we have absolutely no control over. In fact, the 'storm of inward thoughts' largely controls *us*, changing our moods and triggering emotions which can become powerful disturbances in their own right. In addition, our *desires* create disturbance, whether they are physical desires for sex or food, or – more frequently – psychological desires for affection, excitement or self-validation.

Many spiritual traditions and teachers have told us that in order to gain spiritual insight or to 'find God inside' we must attain a state of complete inner stillness, where the mind is completely free of the movement of thoughts, desires and emotions. The *Bhagavad-Gita* describes how the 'storm of the sense-desires' (the similarity to Meister Eckhart's phrase is striking) makes us ignorant and confused, and states that in order to reach *brahman* we should 'dwell in the solitude of silence' with 'thoughts and words and body in peace'.[32] Similarly, Meister Eckhart says that 'If God is to speak His word in the soul, she must be at rest and at peace.'[33]

To illustrate this, let's freeze a person at one particular moment in their day – say, an 18-year-old girl who's in the middle of her shift at a pizza restaurant and about to walk over to a table to take another order. Since it's not a job which engages her attention, her mind is filled with the disturbance of thought-chatter. She might be thinking about what she's going to do when she leaves work tonight or daydreaming about meeting a new boyfriend. Emotions like frustration and bitterness may occasionally arise inside her because she doesn't like her job and wants to do something more fulfilling. She might also feel a tinge of jealousy and hatred towards some of the customers, the ones that look as though they have good jobs and lots of money. If this is the case, there will also be desires inside her – to get a different job, to eat some chocolate or to go and get drunk to forget about her unhappiness. And all of this creates disturbance within her being.

But if she goes home and sits down quietly to meditate, she might find that most of this disturbance fades away. As the chattering of her mind slows down and dies away, so will her desires and emotions (which are largely triggered by thought-chatter, after all), so that her being becomes still and peaceful, like the still surface of a lake, rather than a stormy sea. And this will contribute to the spiritual feelings she has after the meditation, particularly the inner feelings of well-being and peacefulness, and of connecting to a deeper and truer self.

In almost all cases, this stilling of life-energy goes together with its intensification. The two usually don't happen separately, since in order for it to be intensified, life-energy *has* to be stilled. Awakening experiences 'need' the energy which our thought-chatter, desires and emotions normally dissipate. However, when there is a large input of energy from another source, this doesn't necessarily have to be the case. In *kundalini* awakening, for example, which we'll look at in more detail in Chapter 7, a massive reserve of energy at the bottom of the spine is released and there is a sudden intensification of life-energy without its stilling.

Before then, in Chapter 6, we're going to look at other, more spontaneous, situations where our life-energy becomes intensified and stilled.

6

SPONTANEOUS AWAKENING EXPERIENCES

Meditation is a direct attempt to close down our normal energy leaks and intensify and still our life-energy, but there are also many situations in which this can occur accidentally.

This is why nature is such a powerful trigger of awakening experiences. In 1961 the English author Marghanita Laski made a survey of the triggers of higher states of consciousness for her book *Ecstasy* and found that nature was the most common one. Over 20 per cent of the awakening experiences she examined were in some way related to natural surroundings.[1]

For me personally, nature has always had a powerful awakening effect. The third experience I described in the introduction was definitely the result of contemplating the hills and fields around me, and the first was at least partly, if not mainly, the result of staring intently at the sky. I have low-intensity awakening experiences very frequently when I'm amongst nature. If I go walking in the countryside on my own (it doesn't happen so often with other people), there usually comes a point when a feeling of well-being begins to well up inside me and when the trees and the fields and the sky around me seem to be more alive and beautiful and to be shining with a new radiance. The clouds above me seem to be moving with a dramatic beauty and a strange sentience, and the spaces of sky seem to be tinged with the presence of spirit-force. In fact, I had a series of these experiences shortly before writing this, while on holiday in Anglesey – the same place where I had the experience described in the introduction.

It doesn't have to be the countryside, though. I have spent most of my life in cities and had most of my awakening experiences there. They usually occur if there's a small space of nature, such as a field surrounded by trees or a park, where there is a large expanse of sky. When I walk through the field I usually find myself staring at the sky, captivated by the beauty of the clouds and/or the sunlight, and quickly begin to have 'spiritual' feelings and perceptions. Here, for example, is an experience I had 12 years ago, which I described in my 'spiritual experience journal' as follows:

> *For some reason I felt a bit exhilarated and decided to go for a walk around the big field behind the sports centre. It was a beautiful evening – clear blue sky beginning to get dark, orange where the sun was going down, a few stars beginning to shine through. I walked around the field several times, looking at the sky, amazed at how beautiful it was. I wasn't thinking – my mind was quiet and I felt full of vitality… I felt as though I was being engulfed in the sky and my normal sense of space was changing. The sky didn't seem 'up there', it seemed to be around me, a part of me…*
>
> *I felt that the universe was alive – that the blue-black space around me was alive. It almost seemed to have a personality. The whole universe was living and breathing. Every time I stared at it and kept my mind quiet, the feeling grew stronger. It only stopped when my mind started thinking again.*

We've already looked at some awakening experiences which seem to have been induced by contact with nature, for example the person on page 12 who was sitting at the top of a mountain waiting for friends when he became aware of an 'immensely powerful benign force' pervading his surroundings, or the woman on page 8 who, as an eight-year-old girl, had a low-intensity awakening experience while looking at the meadows and the sunrise beyond her garden. Most of these experiences, including my own, can probably be classified as low- to medium-intensity awakening experiences, but nature can certainly give rise to high-intensity experiences too. Here, for example, a person becomes one with the blazing 'ground' reality of the universe:

> *One day, when I was four, I found myself standing at the back, alone. The sea touched the sky. Breathing with the waves, I entered their rhythm. Suddenly there was a channelling of energy: the sun, the wind, the sea were going right through me*
>
> *A door opened and I became the sun, the wind, and the sea. There was no 'I' any more. 'I' had merged with everything else. All sensory perceptions had become one. Sound, smell, taste, touch, shape – all melted into a brilliant light. The pulsating energy went right through me, and I was part of this energy.[2]*

Of course, countless poets have written of the states of awe and ecstasy they've experienced whilst alone in nature. This is what Wordsworth's poetry is most famous for – his sense that nature is pervaded with a benign unifying presence and the joy and serenity he describes while contemplating it. His near-contemporary Percy Bysshe Shelley was also a 'nature mystic' who saw a 'Spirit of Beauty' pervading the whole of nature and an 'awful shadow of some unseen power / [which] Floats though unseen among us'.[3] Similarly, the nineteenth-century English poet and priest Gerard Manley Hopkins described how 'The world is charged with the grandeur of God. / ... like shining from shook foil.'[4] Other poets like Walt Whitman, D. H. Lawrence, Emerson, William Blake and W. B. Yeats have also left us many descriptions of the sense of meaning and harmony and inner joy they experienced while contemplating natural scenes.

It's perhaps tempting to believe that these experiences are directly *caused* by nature, as if it has some special awakening power which man-made environments don't have. This is what some Romantic poets believed. Shelley, for example, saw the 'unseen power' he perceived as a kind of spirit which came and went of its own volition. This may be true to a degree. *Brahman,* or spirit-force, does seem to be easier to perceive in nature, perhaps because it manifests itself more purely there. Of course, the whole world is pervaded with spirit-force – even a city street in which there's nothing except concrete, metal, glass and plastic is full of *brahman.* But it's possible that when natural forms like stone and sand are manipulated and turned into buildings, or when we create synthetic materials like plastic, spirit-force may somehow get diluted and become less apparent. As Eckhart Tolle puts it, in contrast to man-made objects, natural forms like stones and crystals have an 'ethereal nature' which means that their 'form obscures the indwelling spirit to a lesser degree'.[5]

But the main root of all of the above experiences is, I believe, that contemplating nature can intensify, still and purify our life-energy in the same way as meditation. The natural world has powerful qualities – stillness, open space, beauty and majesty – which can readily induce a 'spontaneous meditative state' and therefore an awakening experience.

The stillness of nature means that we process much less sensory information there than in an urban environment. Instead of the barrage of sensory information we have to deal with on city streets, or even in our own houses (where the TV might be on and the phone might be ringing), there is no activity except, say, the blowing of the wind, the rustling of leaves and birds flying. We also lose very little energy through mental (or concentrative) effort. When you're walking through the countryside you usually aren't actively doing anything; your mind isn't engaged in any tasks. As a result, you have effectively closed – or at least reduced – the doing and information-processing channels of your energy outflow. And contemplating nature can close the 'thinking' channel too. Nature can make your mind quiet simply because it's so impressive and attractive that it holds your attention in much the same way as a mantra in meditation, allowing your normal thought-chatter to fade away. As a result your life-energy becomes intensified, stilled and purified and you begin to feel a sense of inner well-being and gain a heightened perception of your surroundings, making the scene around you seem even *more* beautiful and dramatic and real.

ON THE POINT OF WAKING UP

In his autobiography *In My Own Way* the author and spiritual teacher Alan Watts described how he always experienced an awakened state at the moment of – appropriately enough – waking up in the morning. As he wrote:

> *Every morning, when I first awaken, I have a feeling of total clarity as to the sense of life, a feeling of myself and the universe as a matter of the utmost simplicity. 'I' and 'That which is' are the same. Always have been and always will be.*[6]

Another famous spiritual teacher, Jiddu Krishnamurti, described a similar experience. As a young man in India, he woke up in the middle of the night and felt that he was one with a source of pure energy. As he described it in one of his dialogues with the physicist David Bohm:

> *I hesitate to say this because it sounds extravagant [but] the source of all energy had been reached. And that had an extraordinary effect on [my] brain. And also physically. I'm sorry to talk about myself but, you understand, literally, there was no division at all; no sense of the world, of 'me'. You follow? Only this sense of a tremendous source of energy.*[7]

My wife sometimes has a similar (though perhaps not as intense) experience. Occasionally she wakes up in the morning with a feeling of what she describes as 'pure happiness' inside her, a sense of harmony and peace, a feeling that 'everything is well' and that there are no problems. The feeling usually only lasts for a second or two, until, in her words, 'I remember the day ahead of me and the day before, and memories and thoughts start running through my mind.' In other words, the feeling lasts until her ego starts chattering away. It's as if for a moment her ego is caught off guard, is a little slow off the mark and doesn't wake up with the rest of her mind, so that she has a brief taste of pure egoless consciousness.

You may remember that the second experience I described in the introduction, the most powerful awakening experience I've ever had, happened when I woke up in the middle of the night. In some respects, this experience was similar to Krishnamurti's: I also felt as if I had become part of a tremendously powerful energy source, one which was the essential reality of the universe. In fact, I often experience a kind of heightened awareness when I wake up in the middle of the night (for me this never happens in the morning after a whole night's sleep, for some reason). The experience is almost always the same: I'm lying in bed or sitting on the toilet – my weak bladder is usually the reason why I wake up – and I have a strong sense of a power or presence that seems to fill the sky, although I don't have to be looking at it. It seems to somehow *press down* from the sky and I can sense that it's limitless. I sense that what we think of as 'the sky' doesn't really exist, since there's only space that fills the Earth's atmosphere and stretches through the solar system and onwards towards infinity. And the whole of this space is full of this powerful force.

These experiences don't appear to be very common, but they do make some sense in terms of an intensification and a stilling of life-energy. After all, sleep is a state of withdrawal from the world. We're inactive, our mind is largely empty, processing very little information, and our life-energy is regenerating itself. Our mind is active when we dream, of course, but it's likely that these experiences of heightened awareness occur during deep sleep, when we don't dream and the mind is empty. As a result, there is a state of energy concentration and stillness which is equivalent to a state of awakening. It's significant that one of the beliefs of Indian philosophy – as the great mystic Ramana Maharashi often remarked, for instance – is that we're always in a state of *samadhi* during deep sleep, only we aren't aware of it because we're unconscious. But sometimes, it seems, when we wake up, *samadhi* can linger for a short while.

QUIETNESS AND STILLNESS

A state of intensification and stilling of life energy, or 'ISLE state', can also just occur when we're relaxing and resting in quiet and still surroundings. When we rest, we purposely reduce the normal outflow of our life-energy – we stop being active, remove ourselves from external stimuli and allow our chattering mind to slow down. This is what resting is: closing down the channels through which our energy leaks away so that we can 'recharge our batteries'. Our life-energy regenerates, becomes more concentrated again, and as a result we might experience an awakened state.

This might happen when we're sitting in darkness in a room or going for a walk at night through quiet and empty streets. Here, for example, a friend of mine describes how he sometimes used to experience a low-intensity awakening experience when he stayed up late at night on his own:

I used to love staying up until two or three o'clock in the morning because everything was so peaceful. I used to love sitting by my window and looking out on to the streets. The trees seemed alive. I could sense a kind of atmosphere in the air, like a vibration, a kind of peacefulness. Not something that was just the absence of noise, though – a kind of peaceful force. It's always there, I think, but we're usually too busy to pay attention to it.

It's significant that Richard M. Bucke says that his experience of 'cosmic consciousness' which I quoted on page 30 happened when he was in a deeply relaxed state. His mind was 'calm and peaceful' and he was in a state of 'quiet, almost passive enjoyment, not actually thinking, but letting ideas, images, and emotions flow of themselves, as it were, through my mind'.[8]

However, it's quite rare for relaxation to be the sole cause of awakening experiences. Our mind may quiet down and empty to a degree when we relax, but for it to quiet down enough for awakening to take place there also has to be an activity or object which focuses our attention, for example nature or music. Often relaxation works together with these focusing 'objects'. For example, in her book *The Experience of No-Self,* the modern mystic Bernadette Roberts describes an experience of oneness which was probably the combined effect of nature and relaxation. During a retreat at a monk's hermitage in Big Sur, California, she went for a walk along a hill overlooking the ocean:

> *A seagull came into view, gliding. Dipping, playing with the wind. I watched it as I'd never watched anything before in my life. I almost seemed mesmerized; it was as if I was watching myself flying, for there was not the usual division between us. Yet, something more was there than just a lack of separateness, 'something' truly beautiful and unknowable. Finally I turned my eyes to the pine-covered hills behind the monastery and still there was no division, only something there that was flowing through every vista and particular object of vision. To see the Oneness of everything is like having special 3D glasses put before your eyes…[9]*

Here the quietness and inactivity of the retreat must have gone some way to creating an ISLE state to begin with, making Roberts more sensitive to the effect of nature. (Of course, the retreat presumably involved spiritual exercises such as prayer and meditation, which would have also helped to create an ISLE state.)

This is the whole purpose of spiritual retreats, of course – to go into a quiet, stress-free environment in which we can rest and recharge our life-energy, away from the barrage of information and the endless busy-ness which normally fill our life and drain our energy away. Most spiritual retreats involve practising some form of mind-quieting techniques as well, usually meditation. It's possible that on a retreat a kind of spiritual atmosphere will build up too, emanating from the group as a whole, which will also affect us. The end effect will – hopefully – be an intensification and stilling of our life-energy which brings a heightened awareness of our surroundings and/or an inner feeling of well-being, love or joy. Here, for example, the author Elizabeth Debold describes a high-level awakening experience she had at the end of a week-long silent retreat with the American spiritual teacher Andrew Cohen:

> *My perception is heightened – colors vibrate, the rushing river voices a soundless roar, and this extraordinary light suffuses everything. It's alive, I realize: the light is alive. Everything around me, the entire world, is transparent, lit from within. I have the sense that I could simply reach out and tear the surface of reality to reveal this underlying blaze. But the ordinary sense of I-am-here-and-the-world-is-out-there is gone. All of the space between is filled – it's all One – and I am not separate from that, I am completely empty and this fullness is everywhere.*[10]

This is part of the purpose of the monastic way of life too. Monks live in a quiet and still environment and have designated periods of silence and solitude, as well as periods of prayer and meditation. As a result, it's possible that they may experience an almost constant ISLE state, at least at a mild level, and therefore an almost constant state of mild wakefulness.

In 2005, the BBC broadcast a TV series called *The Monastery*, which documented the experiences of a group of five men who lived as Benedictine monks for several weeks. Most of them were powerfully affected by the silence, stillness, prayer and meditation and experienced strong 'spiritual' feelings. In other words, the monastic life had the effect of intensifying and stilling their life-energy. As one of them, Tony, described it, 'I was put in touch with a spirituality deep inside me which has given me the energy and inclination to strive for so much more in my life and appreciate what's important and be a better person and lead a better life.'[11]

In a similar way, and around the same time, the German film-maker Philip Groening spent six months living in a Carthusian monastery in the French Alps, spending most of his days in silence and solitude like the monks. After a few weeks he realized that he was changing inside and starting to see his surroundings differently. He began to feel an altered sense of time and a sense of presentness and alertness. Seemingly mundane objects became intensely real and beautiful to him. 'There was a change as my perception of the present moment helped me to see more,' he says. 'My level of awareness became different.'[12] As a result, his film of the time he spent in the monastery, *Into Great Silence,* is full of strikingly beautiful images. Again, the quietness and inactivity of the monastic way of life had an awakening effect on him.

In other words, rest, relaxation, stillness and quietness make awakening experiences much more likely to occur. They stop us using up our life-energy in activity and perceiving and processing information and lead to a quieting of our mind. Philip Groening started to see his surroundings in a different way because the higher level of life-energy generated by the silence and stillness of the monastery meant that his desensitizing mechanism no longer needed to function and no longer edited out the is-ness of reality.

This is probably why some of my own most powerful awakening experiences have happened on holiday, at times when I was very relaxed and rested.

MUSIC AND OTHER ART FORMS

A friend of mine had a powerful awakening experience while listening to a concert performance of Brahms's fourth symphony:

> *The first movement just seemed to warm me up in some way. I was listening more keenly, going with the flow of the music. I seemed to be able to shut out any distracting thoughts. The slow movement began and I recognized it as a particularly beautiful one. The magical moment came and suddenly it was like glittering petals of sounds exploded. It was as though the orchestra, the composer, and my spirit, our spirit – the audience's – were just opening there and then. We were just opening to generous sunshine. It felt as though some flower inside me had been tight shut, [and] was suddenly just able to open wide.*
>
> *I could immediately feel the stream of life flowing around me. It was a movement of feeling as though I was experiencing heaven on earth. I felt as though I was a reed in a stream, bending to the rhythm of a stream… [I felt] a huge sense of euphoria, an intense sense of well-being. Life became idyllic, and it carried on for days. For five days I felt completely energised.*

We've already heard (on page 25) from another person who had a powerful ingoing awakening experience while listening to Brahms, stating – significantly – that he was 'completely relaxed' and 'seemed to be beyond the boundary of my physical self. Then an intense feeling of "light" and "love" uplifted and enfolded me.'[13] Marghanita Laski reports the similar awakening experience of a person who, while listening to Mahler's tenth symphony, experienced a sense of weightlessness, a 'complete sense of liberation … a tremendous expansion, a different dimension altogether'.[14]

Music is a powerful trigger of awakening experiences, partly because it puts us into a relaxed state, so that our life-energy recharges and becomes more concentrated. Perhaps more significantly, though, it can be a focus for our attention. Some pieces of music are so powerful and beautiful that we become completely immersed in them. All our normal thought-chatter fades away as our mind becomes quiet and still. My friend, for example, wrote that he 'seemed to be able to shut out any distracting thoughts'.

But in addition to the relaxing and mind-quieting effect of music, it's also important that pieces of music are often *inspired* by and created in higher states of consciousness. The composer or songwriter may feel a sense of exaltation or a vision of beauty and is-ness which they try to express through the music and which comes through to the listener (as long as they are in a receptive state). This is certainly true of composers like Mahler and Beethoven, and also of more modern composers like Henryk Gorecki (my own personal favourite) and John Tavener. It's certainly true of Indian music too, which has a very close relationship to spirituality. With its repetitious, circular, modal nature, it seems almost designed to induce a state of intense absorption in the listener and in the musicians. In this way, music can be a *transmitter* of spiritual feelings.

A few years ago I went to a performance of Mahler's eighth symphony, the so-called 'Symphony of a Thousand'. In the last movement, Mahler sets the closing scene of Goethe's play *Faust* to music. The closing lines – describing how Faust's soul ascends to the highest spheres of heaven – seem to describe a mystical state of being in which 'The unattainable is here attained / The indescribable is here accomplished.' I was reading those lines from the programme as the choir was singing them. I felt that Mahler's hauntingly ethereal and other-worldly music was the perfect expression of the serenity and exaltation of mystical experiences, and a rush of euphoria built up inside me. My inner being seemed to be glowing and pulsating, as if a higher state of consciousness was being transmitted to me through the music.

Higher states of consciousness induced by music are always

ingoing. They usually occur when the listener's eyes are closed, when they have withdrawn from external stimuli (apart from the music itself) and their attention is resting within their own being. And although the musical experiences we've looked at are low-intensity ones, occasionally music can induce ingoing experiences of the highest intensity, when we become one with the formless 'ground' of all reality.

One evening the author Warner Allen was listening to a performance of Beethoven's seventh symphony and became enraptured by the music. He closed his eyes and had an intense experience of 'illumination':

> *A silver glow ... shaped itself into a circle with a central focus brighter than the rest. The circle became a tunnel of light proceeding from some distant sun in the heart of the Self. Swiftly and smoothly I was borne through the tunnel and as I went the light turned from silver to gold. There was an impression of drawing strength from a limitless sea of power and a sense of deepened peace...*
>
> *I am absorbed in the Light of the Universe, in Reality glowing like fire with the knowledge of itself, without ceasing to be one and myself, merged like a drop of quicksilver in the Whole...* [15]

Other art forms can trigger awakening experiences too. Although music is an especially powerful trigger because of the 'transmitting' effect I've mentioned, in theory any kind of performance which intensely focuses the attention for a long period can induce awakening experiences. Here are two examples (one of which I mentioned previously) of awakening experiences from my students which occurred during dance performances:

> *Twenty years ago at the Alhambra Theatre in Bradford, the first time the Alvin Ailey dance group had ever visited the UK, they danced a piece called* Revelations, *based on gospel*

*stories, using gospel music. I became totally immersed in
the performance. I felt in awe of these beautiful bodies
moving in such expressively beautiful ways. I almost
felt I was up there with them. I was on a real 'high' and
remember a feeling of such happiness and serenity and an
appreciation of the human body and the wonderful way it
can move.*

*Attending the swirling Turkish Dervishes' performance at
the Royal Northern College of Music ... was a very spiritual
experience. The theatre fell silent – no babies crying, no
movement or sounds from the audience, only the gentle
swishing sounds of white skirts twirling and the soft sounds
of felt gliding on the stage. [There was] a feeling of intense
peace and calm, happiness and tranquillity. Nothing else
mattered in the world and outside the theatre. We all felt as
one – it was a mesmerizing experience and unforgettable.*

This is true of literature and art too. Poetry and paintings can
sometimes have an awakening effect when we're so struck by their
beauty that our mind becomes quiet and still. In this case, the
'transmission' effect is very important. Poets like Wordsworth and
D. H. Lawrence (who wrote over 1,000 poems as well as his famous
novels) transmit their spiritual vision to us through their poetry. And
the same is true of artists like Turner, Monet or van Gogh. We only
need to look at their paintings to recognize that they were intensely
'awake' to the is-ness of their surroundings and had a sense of the
underlying radiance and harmony of the world, and something of
their fresh and intense vision is transmitted to us.

Of course, we shouldn't forget that performers and artists
– especially of music and dance – can have powerful awakening
experiences too. In Chapter 1, for example, we looked at the
experiences of a morris dancer and a folk musician.

SPORTS

Sports can give rise to awakening experiences too, especially solitary sports which involve long periods of monotonous rhythmic activity, such as long-distance running or swimming.

When the psychiatrist Thaddeus Kostrulaba took up jogging he was surprised by how energetic and cheerful he felt after every run. He wrote that he felt 'an odd shift in feeling … a sense of well-being, a sense of energy'.[16] He realized that the jogging was functioning as a kind of meditation and that the repetitive rhythm of running was serving the same function as a mantra, quieting his mind. As he wrote, 'Eventually, at somewhere between 30 and 40 minutes, the conscious mind gets exhausted and other areas of consciousness are activated.'[17]

This is an example of the paradox we looked at in the last chapter: that you can feel more alive and energetic after expending a lot of muscular energy. You can conserve and regenerate life-energy at the same time as expending muscular energy, particularly when your mind becomes focused and your normal thought-chatter fades away. This was probably the main source of the well-being that Kostrulaba felt inside him: a higher concentration (and a greater stillness) of his life-energy.

This is probably a major reason why running and jogging – and perhaps swimming too – are such popular sports. As well as keeping us fit physically, they give us a sense of being mentally alive and full of well-being. One acquaintance told me that he loves running because 'It's the only situation in my life where my mind quiets down, when I'm free of worries and thoughts buzzing round in my head. At the end of a run I feel refreshed, all clean and alert inside.' Similarly, the American marathon runner Kathy Switzer describes how she becomes much more 'awake' when she's in training: 'I'm more physically sensitive to food, to weather, to touch … I also become more mentally sensitive to social problems, the ills of the world and so on… Everything I see and feel is more extreme.'[18]

This is what inevitably happens when the ego-mind quiets down and fades away. As Novak noted, the psychic energy that is usually monopolized by the ego is 'freed up' and transferred to perception, so that we become more alert to our surroundings and experience.

Here is an example of the awakening effect of running from one of the most famous runners of all time, Roger Bannister, the first person ever to run a four-minute mile. Here he describes an ecstatic experience which made him aware of the joy of running. As a child, he was running along a beach and stopped for a moment, gazing at the sea:

> *The air had a special quality to it, as if it had a life of its own... I looked down at the regular ripples on the sand, and could not absorb so much beauty. I was taken back – each of the myriad particles of sand was perfect in its way...*
>
> *In this supreme moment I leapt in sheer joy. I was startled, and frightened by the joy that so few steps could create... I was running now, and a fresh rhythm entered my body. No longer conscious of my movement, I discovered a new unity with nature. I had found a new source of power and beauty, a source I had never dreamt existed.*[19]

I've recently taken up running myself and had similar experiences. I usually run for 20–25 minutes around the fields close to my home. I'm not particularly fit or athletic (at least not at the moment), so I find it a little awkward to begin with and feel that I'm not going to be able to run for very long. But after a few minutes I fall into a rhythm. The running becomes more effortless and my state of mind begins to change. If my mind is busy with chattering thoughts, I begin to 'dis-identify' with them, to detach myself from them and allow them to fade away. After 15 minutes or so I stop – partly for a short rest but mainly so that I can look at my surroundings. Everything around me looks more beautiful and striking – the trees seem more real and distinct and the dark of the sky seems more rich and powerful. When I look at the sky I sometimes have a sense that I'm really *here,* on the surface of this planet, with the universe stretching everywhere around me. It feels amazing to be alive in the midst of it all. Sometimes my individuality seems to fade away and I become aware of myself as a part of the whole universe. I sense that the universe is alive and its 'aliveness' flows through me and is a part of me.

I run for another 5 or 10 minutes after my break and by the time I get home I'm filled with a glow of well-being which lasts for the rest of the evening. I feel content and complete and my mind seems impervious to worries, resentments or aversions. As a result, running has become a form of spiritual practise for me.

Admittedly, it's difficult to separate the meditative effect of running from other factors. For me personally, I'm sure that the contact with nature I have when I run contributes to awakening. It's also likely that part of the awakening effect of any physical exercise comes from disrupting homoeostasis. After all, strenuous exercise certainly produces major physiological changes, such as increased oxygen intake, increased heart rate and a higher body temperature. Another possibility is that the feeling of well-being is partly caused by the endorphins that our body produces when we exercise. But in my view the meditative effect is probably the most important, since the type of awakening I have after running is more similar to an ISLE than an HD state. It's a calm and serene state which lasts for a few hours, similar to a meditation experience, rather than the wild, ecstatic and unstable (and unusually quite temporary) states induced by sleep deprivation, fasting or drugs.

Other, more sedate, sports can give rise to awakening experiences too. The English poet Ted Hughes often experienced a meditative state while fishing. In an essay on writing poetry, he notes that in order to write poetry you have to have the ability to intensely focus your mind and believes that he acquired this ability through fishing. He describes the effect of staring at a float for long periods: 'All the nagging impulses that are normally distracting your mind dissolve … once they have dissolved, you enter one of the orders of bliss. Your whole being rests lightly on your float, but not drowsily, very alert.'[20] This could easily be a description of a meditation experience – and in fact, it *is* a meditation experience in all but name, with the float serving as an object of concentration.

There are other aspects of sport, besides this rhythmic or mantra-like effect, which can help give rise to awakening experiences. In some sports, such as fell-running or climbing, solitude and nature may act as triggers too. Here, for example, the adventurer Richard Byrd describes a mystical experience he had while exploring the Arctic Circle:

> *The day was dying, the night being born – but with great peace. Here were the imponderable processes and forces of the cosmos, harmonious and soundless. Harmony, that was it! That was what came out of the silence; the strain of a perfect chord, the music of the spheres, perhaps. It was enough to catch that rhythm, momentarily be a part of it.*
>
> *In that instant I could feel no doubt of man's oneness with the universe.*[21]

The physical movement of sport may be another factor too. As Kostrulaba found, physical exercise can affect the flow of energy in our body. Sometimes when we've been sitting down for too long, our energy feels stagnant, as if it isn't flowing to all parts of the body. But when we exercise, blockages seem to be removed and the flow seems to intensify again, making us feel alive and energetic – and possibly contributing to a state of awakening.

And this, of course, leads us on to eastern forms of exercise such as hatha yoga, *chi gung*, *tai chi*, judo and karate. These practises combine the usual breath control and attention focusing of meditation with physical exercises designed to generate or awaken new energy inside us and remove blockages which may be preventing energy flowing to certain parts of our being. Anyone who has seriously practised any form of yoga or *chi gung* will certainly have noticed this vitalizing effect.

It's always been accepted that these exercises have a spiritual dimension to them – and we should recognize that sports like swimming and running have this aspect too. We should really see them as western forms of yoga. One of the reasons why we play sports and do athletic activities is because of their awakening effect. And as I mentioned at the beginning of Chapter 2, it's significant that when sportspeople have these awakening experiences, their performances improve: everything they do seems spontaneously perfect and time seems to slow down.

SEX AND LOVE

Another physical activity which can give rise to higher states of consciousness – and for very similar reasons – is sex.

The liberating power of sex was one of the major themes of D. H. Lawrence's novels and the main reason why they often fell foul of the censors. (His last novel, *Lady Chatterley's Lover,* was not published in the UK until more than 30 years after his death.) For Lawrence, sex was a consciousness-changing practise which had the power to free us from our usual sense of ego isolation and put us in touch with what he called the 'marvellous rich world of contact and sheer fluid beauty'.[22] He talks of 'the strange, soothing flood of peace, the sense that all is well, which goes with true sex'.[23] And here he describes how Lady Chatterley's vision of the world is completely transformed when she's walking home after making love to her gamekeeper:

The trees seemed to be bulging and surging, at anchor on a tide, and the heave of the slope of the park was alive... The universe ceased to be the vast clock-work of circling planets and pivotal suns which she had known. The stars opened like eyes, with a consciousness in them, and the sky was filled with a soft, yearning stress of consolation. It was not mere atmosphere. It had its own feeling, its own anima. Everything had its own anima.[24]

This is a beautiful description of a lower-intensity awakening experience in which we become aware that the so-called 'inanimate' objects around us are alive and have their own inner being. There is also a hint of spirit-force pervading the sky, creating that 'soft, yearning stress of consolation'.

Probably most of you have experienced something like this during or after sex: a feeling of well-being which goes beyond sensual pleasure and is caused by a change of consciousness. Perhaps earlier you felt stressed and worried, as if your life was full of problems, but now everything seems miraculously different. Your problems have disappeared (proving that to a large extent we create our own problems *by* worrying) and you seem to be glowing inwardly, as if a kind of dynamo has been switched on inside you, filling you with a feeling of completeness and serenity. As with long-distance running, you might feel tired physically, in terms of muscular energy, but in terms of life-energy you feel fantastically alive. And if you look outside you might sense the harmony and animacy that Lady Chatterley saw. Here, for example, an acquaintance of mine describes how she feels after she has orgasms:

> *I feel as if I haven't got any weight. There's a warm feeling running all through my body… Nothing else seems to matter, problems cease to exist, as if the feeling takes you over so much that there's no room for anything else. I feel capable of doing anything…*
>
> *I also look at things more clearly, look beyond what I usually look at. The colours seem more distinct; if you look at, say, a tree, you see it for what it really is, not just as a tree. You see it as nature, not just as an object.*

The transpersonal psychologist Jennifer Wade spent several years collecting examples of altered and higher states of consciousness occurring during sex. She found that many people talked about 'seeing' a blindingly brilliant light, having feelings of intense well-being and euphoria, expanding and becoming one with the universe or feeling the presence of the divine. One person told her that when she had sex with her lover she always felt 'a sense of great peace ... like it's the Universe's way of reassuring me that everything is right, as if I were a dog in front of a fireplace, and this giant, gentle hand is patting me, it just feels so good and comfortable',[25] while another person told her that: 'It was more like we were just steeped in Divinity, and it was all One. And the feeling of love was just tremendous ... just being imbued with something Other, something Divine.'[26] And here Wade describes a high-intensity awakening experience that she personally had during sex, when she transcended the world of form and became one with the ground of reality. This experience is very similar to the experience of Ramakrishna that I quoted in Chapter 1:

> *I had a [transcendent] episode that was too big to contain.*
> *The whole world disappeared in a wash of white light*
> *that became clear, and then nothingness, non-duality, the*
> *Void... When I came back to normal consciousness, I was*
> *awestruck, jubilant. Suddenly I got it* – this *is what the*
> *saints and sages were talking about, this is what is true.*[27]

Perhaps disrupting homoeostasis is a factor here, and there's no doubt that the ecstatic feelings that sex can induce are partly connected to chemical changes such as the release of endorphins. But I believe these awakening effects are partly due to the fact that sex can intensify and still our life-energy in a similar – but often stronger – way to contemplating nature or listening to music. The sheer pleasure of sex creates a state of intense absorption. Our attention is taken away from the chattering of our mind, which quickly begins to subside. This is why we may feel that we don't have any problems – because the worrying thoughts that created the 'problems' are no longer there. When we have sex there's usually silence, stillness and darkness around us as well, so that our energies are no longer leaking away through absorbing stimuli. And sex overwhelms us to such an extent that our attention is effectively closed to everything beyond the desire and pleasure we feel.

Like physical exercise and yoga – although again in a more powerful way – sex also appears to generate new energy inside our body, or at least to unblock and ease the flow of energy. People who have transcendent sexual experiences often report feeling that they have awakened new energies inside them. As Wade describes it, 'Some people report strange energies coursing through the body. Sometimes it starts with a sense that the sexual charge normally rooted in the genitals is spreading throughout the entire body, lighting it up with crackling power and fireworks.'[28] One person told her that 'The movement of energy was very clear, spreading through the body, through the arms and legs, reaching the areas of the hand and mouth that were extremely charged.'[29] It's because this release of new energy is often so strong during sex that sexual awakening experiences can be so powerful.

Religions tend to see sex as something to be slightly ashamed of, a 'weakness of the flesh', a part of the lower, instinctive being which we shouldn't pay much attention to, or should even try to overcome. But, perhaps not surprisingly, some esoteric religious groups had a more spiritual view of sex. The Tantric sects of Hinduism and Buddhism see sex as a symbolic expression of the unity of the universe and believe that sexual partners can directly experience the bliss that is the nature of the absolute reality of the universe. According to Tantra, the whole of the body is filled with divine energy which becomes aroused during sex and which we can learn to control – and on the basis of the experiences we've looked at, this does seem to be the case. Even within Christianity, the heretical medieval sect, the Brethren of the Free Spirit, had a similar attitude: to them a controlled form of sex was as acceptable as a spiritual practise as prayer or meditation.

In Chapter 4 we saw that any activity or experience which disrupts homoeostasis can potentially give rise to a 'high-arousal' awakening experience. Similarly, in theory almost any activity which focuses the attention strongly and takes place in a quiet and still setting (and/or helps to ease or unblock the flow of life-energy through the body) can bring about an ISLE state and so induce a 'low-arousal' awakening experience.

In the next chapter we're going to look at some more unusual phenomena which can give rise to ISLE states.

7

OTHER TYPES OF ENERGETIC AWAKENING

The connection between life-energy and awakening experiences manifests itself in an extreme way in the experience of *kundalini* awakening. According to Tantra, *kundalini* – literally 'serpent' or 'snake lady' – is a highly concentrated and powerful source of life-energy 'coiled' at the base of the spine. The energy is normally dormant, but may be awakened after intense and prolonged periods of yoga and meditation, or even after intense periods of normal concentration.

A friend of mine had such an experience shortly after she started practising Buddhist meditation. She had been meditating regularly for several weeks and felt that she was gaining a great deal of benefit from the practise. One afternoon she was meditating at her Buddhist centre, following her teacher's instructions, when she felt what she described as a 'forceful, pushing sensation near the base of my spine'. She felt that she was making a deep connection with a divine force, which her breath was both coming from and entering into. As she continued breathing,

This sensation continued to rise in my spine, getting higher and higher with each in-breath. It was a magnificent but intensely intimate and sexual experience. It was at the

point where the sensation was arriving at my neck that
I panicked. I knew that if I did not resume control, this
force would pass through my head and out through the
crown and as a result I would scream and be forced to run
around the room like some crazy person.

She felt that a massive previously unknown source of energy had been released inside her. She felt like a different person for weeks afterwards; everything around her 'had changed suddenly and dramatically'. She felt exhilarated, with a fresh vision of the world, although at the same time slightly bewildered by some of the intense emotions flooding through her. People around her noticed the change too:

My face shone with a new happiness and many people
commented on the 'new image' – lively, awake and
laughing. I had boundless energy and required little or no
sleep. I was surrounded by people wanting to talk to me ...
problems disappeared as soon as I went to investigate them,
patients recovered from their illnesses and all around me I
saw beauty.

Similarly, but even more powerfully, an American student named Yvonne Kason had been studying hard for several hours without a break when she became aware of an intense pressure headache. A friend started to give her a head massage, which seemed to suddenly unleash powerful waves of energy inside her. Her whole body started shaking and jerking with the pulses of energy, and this continued for six hours. When the energy rushes and the shaking finally stopped, she felt incredibly tired but at the same time 'as if I had experienced a release of some sort'. She fell asleep for a few hours and when she woke up she 'felt as if [she] had been reborn':

When I opened my eyes, the world seemed to have become
a magical place. I felt as if I were in love with the world,
and that the universe and I were making love to each

*other. It seemed as if the world was filled with light; all the
colours and dimensions of objects seemed clearer and
more beautiful. Every sensation was enhanced. It was as
if I was breathing in the life energy of the universe with
each breath. I felt as if my consciousness had expanded
to immense proportions, and I felt totally at one with the
entire universe. I felt the oneness of all things, and I felt that
all was well in the Divine plan of the universe.[1]*

As Yvonne Kason found, this energy can be extremely volatile, like a
bolt of electricity shooting through the body. Unless you're prepared
for it, *kundalini* awakening is too powerful for the mind or body
to contain and can cause massive disruption, both mentally and
physically.

This was also the experience of the Indian yogi Gopi Krishna.
He had been meditating in the lotus position for hours when he felt
a strange sensation at the bottom of his spine. He focused on the
sensation and it grew stronger, until suddenly he felt 'a stream of
liquid light entering my brain through the spinal cord'. This led to a
high-intensity awakening experience of the formless void, which he
describes as follows:

*I felt the point of consciousness that was myself growing
wider, surrounded by waves of light... I was now all
consciousness, without any outline, immersed in a sea of
light simultaneously conscious and aware of every point,
spread out, as it were, in all directions without any barrier
or material obstruction. I was no longer myself, or, to be
more accurate no longer as I knew myself to be, but instead
was a vast circle of consciousness in which my body was
but a point, bathed in light and in a state of exultation and
happiness impossible to describe.[2]*

Unfortunately this didn't lead to an instant state of enlightenment,
though. Once the energy had been awakened, Gopi Krishna couldn't

control it. For months he was in a state of agony, feeling exhausted but unable to sit still, rest or even eat. He suffered from hallucinations and sharp pains all over his body. It was only after years of effort that he managed to 'tame' the wild energy and finally attain a state of permanent *samadhi*.

Kundalini may seem like an esoteric concept, but if, as Indian and Chinese philosophies tell us, there are a number of main centres of life-energy throughout our body (the *chakras* or meridians) there's no reason why we shouldn't also accept that there is an especially intense concentration of this energy at the bottom of our spines.

In fact, *kundalini* awakening is a good illustration of the connection I'm making between the intensification of life-energy and awakening experiences. During a *kundalini* awakening, life-energy *explodes* through us, like a river bursting its banks, causing a very sudden and dramatic intensification of energy. And since the intensification is so powerful, the awakening experiences that go with *kundalini* awakening are usually high-intensity ones, often an experience of union with the whole cosmos.

The difference between *kundalini* experiences and more sedate types of awakening experiences is that during a *kundalini* awakening our life-energy isn't *stilled* at the same time as intensified. As I've said, normally our life-energy has to become stilled for an intensification to occur: our thoughts and emotions have to become quiescent so that the energy they normally use up can be conserved. But since *kundalini* awakening is a massive release of energy which isn't normally available, this doesn't have to happen. And of course, it's because the energy is so restless and wild that it can cause such havoc.

It's tempting to suggest that some of the sexual experiences we looked at in the last chapter, where people were aware of strange energies flowing through their bodies, were forms of *kundalini* awakening too. One person spoke of an 'electric charge', while another described an 'electrical feeling that moves up my body and just goes out my eyes. When it's intense, it's almost blinding.' These experiences aren't as intense as Yvonne Kasen's or Gopi Krishna's, though, and don't involve the same extreme physical effects. So perhaps they were only a partial kind of *kundalini* awakening, or the release of a different, less powerful form of energy. Or perhaps they were simply the result of the unblocking of our *normal* flow of life-energy.

NEAR-DEATH EXPERIENCES

Another phenomenon which makes sense in terms of the view of awakening experiences I'm putting forward is the near-death experience (NDE).

The basics of the near-death experience are probably familiar to all of you already. Many people who clinically die for a short time – when their breathing and their hearts stop and their brains show no electrical activity – find that their consciousness continues and they undergo an incredibly blissful and exhilarating experience which is so powerful that they may not actually want to return to life and may even be angry with the doctors who have resuscitated them.

Near-death experiences first came to wide public attention during the 1970s with the research of psychologists such as Raymond Moody. However, examples have been recorded throughout human history, beginning with Plato's account in *The Republic* of a soldier who was apparently killed in battle and taken home to be buried. Fortunately for him, he revived on the funeral pyre and stated that while unconscious he had left his body and travelled to a strange country where he had seen other dead soldiers choosing their next life.

Due to the advances in modern medicine, particularly in resuscitation techniques, reports of the experiences have become very widespread over recent decades. Different studies have found that between 12 per cent and 43 per cent of people who have been clinically dead and then revived have had the experience.[3] In a typical case, it begins with a feeling of separation from the body (in many cases an out-of-body experience in which you look down on 'yourself' from above), followed by a journey through a dark passage towards a place of light. There is a feeling of great peace and euphoria and sometimes an awareness of the one-ness of everything. In some cases there is a 'life review' in which all the events and experiences of your life flash before you. Often people meet deceased relatives or beings of light, who sometimes tell them that 'it's not your time yet' (as a friend of mine who 'died' during a heart operation was told by his father) and persuade them to return to their body.

What's most significant about near-death experiences for us, though, is that there is always a profound spiritual aspect to them. In the great majority of cases, the near-death experience is also a powerful awakening experience. For example, when a person leaves their body or travels through the tunnel towards the light, they almost always have an intense feeling of well-being. According to a survey of 300 NDEs by one of Britain's leading NDE researchers, the psychologist Peter Fenwick, 88 per cent of people undergoing them experienced feelings of serenity and joy.[4] One heart-attack victim who watched from above while paramedics tried to restart his heart, and then passed through a tunnel towards a light, commented that 'there is no comparable place in physical reality to experience such total awareness. The love, protection, joy, giving, sharing and being that I experienced in the Light at that moment were absolutely overwhelming and pure in essence.'[5] A woman who had a near-death experience during childbirth said that the most striking aspect of the experience was 'the absolute peace, the oneness, the completeness'.[6] This is without doubt the same profound peace, harmony and sense of being one with the universe that high-intensity awakening experiences bring.

The incandescent light that people often see during NDEs is also surely the same (or at least of the same nature) as the light that is frequently a part of awakening experiences, such as Ramakrishna's or Gopi Krishna's – that is, the brilliant light of spirit-force itself. As one person reported:

It was just pure consciousness. And this enormously bright light seemed to cradle me. I just seemed to exist in it and be part of it and be nurtured by it and the feeling just became more and more ecstatic and glorious and perfect.[7]

This is clearly an experience of the formless void, the ground of reality, and indistinguishable from any other high-level mystical experience.

Other descriptions of near-death experiences contain phrases such as 'a sense of exultation was accompanied by a feeling of being very close to the "source" of light and love', 'Time no longer mattered and space was filled with bliss – I was bathed in radiant light and immersed in the aura of the rainbow' and 'There was no separateness at all. The peace I felt was indescribable.'[8] Any of these could have come from a collection of mystical experiences such as Hardy's or Hoffman's.

But why should the near-death experience also be an awakening experience? It could be interpreted as being caused by homoeostasis disruption. Obviously, when a person is close to death, their physiological functioning is vastly different from normal. But the essence of the experience takes place when the body is biologically dead, without any physiological functioning whatever. And because of this, in my view, it makes more sense to see NDEs as another example of the connection between life-energy and awakening experience. At the moment of death, it seems, our life-energy (or spirit, if you like) departs from the material body. And at this moment of departure, our energy is probably more intensely concentrated than normal, partly because it no longer has to fuel the material body's physiological functioning. Most people who have near-death experiences feel that during them they still have a body of some form, but a lighter and less crude one (this may be what esoteric traditions have called the energy body or the astral body), which probably uses less life-energy. It's likely that at the point of death there will be a smaller outflow of life-energy from the ego too. After the experience of dying – perhaps involving periods of unconsciousness, or of pain and trauma – the ego-mind is likely to be much stiller and more subdued than normal.

The process of dying is often a process of detachment as well. In ordinary life, our identity is bound up with a whole host of extraneous things: possessions, status, knowledge we've accumulated, hopes, beliefs, etc. In the process of dying – particularly if it's a drawn-out process – we may let go of these attachments, realizing that we can't take them with us and that our true identity lies apart from them. These attachments can be seen as 'psychic structures' which also use up life-energy and create disturbance inside our being, and so being released them from them would also create a higher intensity and stillness of life-energy. (We'll look at this process of detachment in more detail in the next chapter.) Because of these factors, it's possible that just after the moment of death we will be in an ISLE state.

The good news is that this intense awakening experience – of the formless void which is the essence of all reality – may be awaiting all of us. Many mystics have told us that there's no reason to be afraid of death, not just because life continues but because the process of 'dropping off' the material body is a euphoric, liberating experience. D. H. Lawrence saw death as the beginning of a 'great adventure' in which – as he writes in his poem 'Gladness of Death' – 'the winds of the afterwards kiss us into the blossom of manhood'.[9] After the painful experience of dying there is, he writes, 'an after-gladness, a strange joy'. In a similar way, Walt Whitman heard 'whispers of heavenly death' around him, and wrote that 'To die is different from what any one supposed, and luckier.'[10] Or, as the *Tibetan Book of the Dead* describes our initial experience of death:

> *Your respiration ceases, all phenomena will become*
> *empty and utterly naked like space. [At the same time] a*
> *naked awareness will arise, not extraneous [to yourself],*
> *but radiant, empty and without horizon or centre. This*
> *intrinsic awareness, manifest in a great mass of light, in*
> *which radiance and emptiness are indivisible, is the Buddha*
> *[nature] of unchanging light, beyond birth or death.*[11]

This spiritual state may not last indefinitely – after a certain amount of time it seems we reach a 'cruder' state of existence, which is in some ways similar to our life on Earth, although subtler and more ethereal. (For a summary of the evidence for an afterlife and an overview what the 'next world' might actually be like, see David Fontana's excellent book *Is There an Afterlife?*) However, it appears that the horror and trepidation many people feel when they think about death are misplaced.

ENLIGHTENMENT AND *SATSANG*

In awakening experiences caused by an ISLE state, the structure and organization of our psyche changes. The ego becomes quieter and less dominant and the desensitizing mechanism stops functioning. As a result, there is a surplus of energy, which is used perceptually.

However, usually it's not long before our normal psychic structure re-establishes itself. When you wake up the morning after an awakening experience you might still feel a sense of ease and inner well-being, but at the same time you can feel that you're back to your old self, with the same sense of separateness, the same thought-chatter running through your head and the same self-concept and the same attachments. The ego is just as powerful as before, monopolizing your psychic energy in the same way, with the desensitizing mechanism functioning to conserve energy on its behalf. That's why most awakening experiences are only temporary – because the mould of our normal psychic structure quickly reforms.

However, this doesn't have to be the case. There are some people who have permanently changed the structure of their psyche, for whom the ego is permanently tamed and quieted, and the desensitizing mechanism no longer functions. This is what is meant by the term 'enlightenment' – a permanent higher state of consciousness, a state of permanent 'wakefulness' in which you can continually sense the is-ness, wonder, harmony and oneness of the world, and in which you continually feel a sense of relatedness to the world and a permanent inner bliss and serenity. (We'll look at how to move towards this permanent state of wakefulness in more detail in Chapters 9 and 10, and I plan to look at the phenomenon of enlightenment in its own right in a later book.)

In a sense, the wakefulness of these people isn't just *theirs*. It radiates from them and spreads to everyone they come into contact with. And this can, in fact, be another significant source of awakening experiences: close contact with an enlightened person.

Enlightened people are like spiritual dynamos. Their presence is so strong that even people who aren't at all 'spiritual' feel a sense of well-being in their company and so are attracted to them without knowing why. And for people who have made some spiritual progress already, the effect can be extremely powerful. Contact with an enlightened person may enable them to make the final jump to permanent enlightenment themselves.

This type of awakening experience isn't common, simply because there are so few enlightened people around. But when it does happen, it can be as dramatic as a *kundalini* experience, although usually without the volatile and unpredictable side effects. This is one of the reasons why many spiritual traditions place so much emphasis on the role of a guru. The guru is important not just because of the advice and guidance they can give you, but because they can transmit their spiritual power to you, giving you a taste of enlightenment and speeding up your spiritual development. (In Sanskrit, this is called *satsang,* literally 'good company'.)

RICHARD M. BUCKE AND WALT WHITMAN

One of the western world's most highly developed mystics of recent times was the great American poet Walt Whitman, whose 'whispers of heavenly death' I've just referred to. In his book *Cosmic Consciousness,* Richard M. Bucke places Whitman alongside the Buddha, Jesus, Moses and others as one of the small number of human beings throughout history who have developed a permanent mystical consciousness. In fact, Bucke goes so far as to see Whitman as the 'highest instance of cosmic consciousness' because he was able to integrate his mystical consciousness into his ordinary personality without allowing it to completely take over and 'tyrannize over the rest'.[12]

Whitman was someone who was constantly awed by the wonder of life and always aware of the radiance and harmony of spirit-force pervading the world. He sensed that he was divine, that the whole world was divine and that there was no separateness between himself and other human beings, or himself and the world. As he writes in *Song of Myself,*

> Seeing, hearing, feeling, are miracles, and each part and tag of me is a miracle.

> Divine am I inside and out, and I make holy whatever I touch or am touch'd from...

> I see something of God each hour of the twenty-four, and each moment then,
> In the faces of men and women I see God, and in my own face in the glass...[13]

Bucke felt able to make such high claims for Whitman because he was a friend of his – or perhaps 'disciple' might be a better word – and had personally experienced the powerful radiance that he emanated. He first met Whitman in 1877, five years after his own experience of 'cosmic consciousness' (as reported at the end of Chapter 1). Writing of himself in the third person, Bucke noted that he and Whitman only spent an hour together and that the poet 'only spoke to him about a hundred words altogether, these quite ordinary and commonplace'. However, shortly afterwards a feeling of ecstasy filled him:

> *A state of mental exultation set in, which he could only describe by comparing to the slight intoxication by champagne, or to falling in love! And this exultation, he said, lasted at least six weeks in a clearly marked degree, so that, for at least that length of time, he was plainly different from his ordinary self. Neither did it then, or since, pass away. Though it ceased to be felt as something new and strange, but became a permanent element in his life, a strong and living force.*[14]

Perhaps, you might argue, this was just the result of Bucke's admiration of Whitman's poetry, the kind of intoxication a fan of a pop singer feels when they meet them in person. But significantly, other people were aware of a kind of 'radiance' or energy emanating from Whitman. The English author and poet Edward Carpenter visited him for the first time in 1877 and was immediately aware of a 'certain radiant power in him, a large benign effluence and inclusiveness, as of the sun, which filled out the place where he was'.[15]

PAUL BRUNTON AND RAMANA MAHARSHI

The English author and spiritual teacher Paul Brunton had an even more powerful experience of *satsang* when he visited the ashram of the great sage Ramana Maharshi in the early 1920s. Brunton had come to India in search of spiritual wisdom (as described in his book *A Search in Secret India*) and was aware that Ramana was a truly enlightened man the first time he met him, someone who had completely transcended his ego and become one with ultimate reality. He felt the spiritual effect of his *satsang* straight away. He sensed that 'a steady river of quietness seems to be flowing near me, that a great peace is penetrating the inner reaches of my being'. While sitting near him, he realized that his mind was becoming stiller, and suddenly all of the intellectual questions he'd had about spiritual matters no longer seemed important. The only question in his head now was: 'Does this man, the Maharishee, emanate the perfume of spiritual peace as the flower emanates fragrance from its petals?'[16]

Towards the end of his first visit to the ashram, Brunton was sitting quietly while the sage was meditating. A feeling of awe built up inside him and he could sense a powerful force filling the room, emanating from Ramana. The sage opened his eyes and gazed at him, and Brunton felt that he was aware of his every thought and feeling. He felt that a telepathic current was passing between them, that Ramana was transmitting his deep serenity to him, and began to feel a sense of euphoria and lightness. He felt that his own being had become one with the sage's and that he had transcended all problems and all desires.

After this, Brunton resumed his travels around India, meeting magicians, miracle workers and self-proclaimed gurus who were less enlightened than they claimed to be. Eventually he returned to the Maharashi's ashram and again experienced an 'ineffable tranquillity' when sitting close to him. Again he experienced revelations which he was sure were 'nothing else than a spreading ripple of telepathic radiation from this mysterious and imperturbable man'.[17] And finally, after a period of wrestling with his own thoughts and his intellect, he had the enlightenment experience that I quoted on pages 28–29.

ANDREW COHEN
AND H. W. L. POONJA

The American spiritual teacher Andrew Cohen had a similar experience when he first met the Indian teacher who became his guru, H. W. L. Poonja, who was, coincidentally (or perhaps not!), a direct disciple of Ramana. Cohen had had profound spiritual experiences before, but had spent many years feeling frustrated and disillusioned, yearning for spiritual liberation but being disappointed by a series of other teachers. He asked Poonja whether it was important to make an effort in spiritual practise and he replied, 'You don't have to make any effort to be free.' And at that moment Cohen experienced *moksha*, or freedom:

> *His words penetrated very deeply. I turned and looked*
> *out into the courtyard outside his room and inside myself*
> *all I saw was a river – in that instant I realized that I*
> *had always been Free. I saw clearly that I never could*
> *have been other than Free and that any idea or concept*
> *of bondage had always been and could only ever be*
> *completely illusory.*[18]

After this, Cohen spent three weeks with Poonja and found the liberation he'd been yearning for. He 'surrendered' to his guru and let go of his own identity and everything which made up his life. He became one with Poonja and began to experience 'waves of bliss and love that at times were so strong that I felt my body wouldn't be able to contain [them]'. And from that point on, although his initial euphoria faded a little, he had a constant sense of 'being always in the present with much contentment and calm. I feel no desire for other than what IS.'[19]

Once he had reached this state, Cohen realized that other people were affected by his presence in the same way that he had been by Poonja's. Friends who spent time with him found that they experienced a powerful sense of bliss and freedom too. He became a spiritual teacher, giving talks and holding retreats, and found that people were naturally drawn to him and that around him they would 'easily and often instantly ... have profound realizations, insights into their true nature and powerful feelings of love, joy and bliss'.[20] (Although at the same time Cohen laments that rather than becoming permanently enlightened, almost everybody would 'fall back again into a condition of confusion and unenlightenment'.)[21] In the last chapter, I used Elizabeth Debold's experience as an example of how retreats can generate spiritual states, but since she was on a retreat with Andrew Cohen, it's possible that the experience was partly the result of *satsang* too.

About ten years ago my wife and I went to one of Cohen's talks in Manchester and for days afterwards she felt like a different person. There was a feeling of freedom inside her, a sense that, in her words, 'Nothing mattered. I didn't have any problems. I didn't want anything because I was happy as I was. My life was quite stressful at that point, but suddenly none of the stress could affect me.' And she's sure that this wasn't so much down to what Cohen actually said but the effect of simply being there, in his presence.

Cohen has had some controversy in recent years, with ex-disciples reporting on financial irregularities, pettiness and coercion. I don't feel qualified to make a judgement on these matters, but even if he does have some questionable methods as a spiritual teacher, this doesn't necessarily mean he isn't awake. From my reading of his books and my experience of his presence, I would say that he certainly has had an experience of awakening and perhaps even experiences wakefulness as a normal state. But wakefulness does not necessarily make you a perfect person.

RUSSEL WILLIAMS AND ME

I was a little jealous of my wife's *satsang* experience with Andrew Cohen because I didn't have any of those feelings. At that time I was taking a more intellectual approach to spiritual matters and was so busy trying to understand what he was saying conceptually that I must have been shut off from the feeling dimension.

A couple of years before then I'd started to visit a spiritual teacher called Russel Williams and had also taken a largely conceptual approach to his teachings. Russel – whom I still visit regularly – is 88 years old and has been the president of the Manchester Buddhist Society for over 50 years, even though he's not specifically a Buddhist. He doesn't chant or meditate or read Buddhist scriptures and doesn't adhere to or promote any particular set of teachings. He's a humble self-realized man who talks about the most profound spiritual truths and the most intense spiritual states as if they're the simplest, most natural things.

In my first years of going along to Russel's meetings, I used to wonder why most people didn't seem to be paying attention to him. He was saying some of the most profound things I'd ever heard and people didn't seem to be listening – they were just staring into space or sitting with their eyes closed. They rarely asked questions, seeming content to let Russel be silent, when as far as I was concerned he was full of wisdom which I wanted to absorb.

But about five years ago I began to realize why this was. Perhaps I'd changed, become less interested in the conceptual side of spirituality, or perhaps I'd finally completed a long process of getting attuned to the atmosphere at the meetings, but when I went to see Russel I started to experience very strange, pleasurable states of consciousness. Even before then I'd often experienced feelings of peacefulness and well-being, which sometimes lasted for a couple of days. But this was something stronger. The first time it happened, I was staring at Russel while he was speaking to me and began to feel very relaxed and calm, as if the flow of my life-energy was becoming smoother and lighter. And then, all of a sudden, everything became unfamiliar – the light became brighter, the colours began to merge and the distinctions between people and objects began to fade away. My main feeling, however, was of a powerful sense of strangeness – the scene was completely alien, as if I was suddenly on a different planet. Even though it was accompanied by a sense of exhilaration, I was a little scared and pulled away from it.

Over the following months I had the same experience several times and I learned to relax and trust it. I would let the sense of strangeness overcome me and, as the light in the room became brighter, all the objects there would begin to shimmer and fade into one another. The room would be filled with a beautiful shimmering haze of golden light and I would experience a deep serenity, a glow of intense well-being filling my whole body. I would feel it flowing through my legs and my feet, as if I'd taken a powerful sedative of some kind. I'm sure that this golden light is the same radiance of pure consciousness that many people see in awakening experiences, and which – as we've just seen – is a feature of near-death experiences.

Even when I didn't have this particular experience at the meetings, I usually had a very powerful feeling of calmness and serenity inside me. I was often aware that my breathing had slowed down dramatically and when I left I found myself doing everything very slowly, with a natural mindfulness. My mind was still and quiet, and outside everything looked beautiful and alive.

After a few months I said to a member of the group, 'I've been having really very strange experiences here over the past few months.' I tried to describe them and he laughed and said, 'So now you know why we've all been coming here for so long! Now you're *really* a member of the society.'

I still have these experiences now and I'm certain that they're the result of *satsang*, of being in the presence of an enlightened person. The experience of the scene becoming unfamiliar and the light becoming brighter usually only happens when Russel is talking directly to me. In these moments I can almost feel spiritual power radiating from him and flowing into me, feel my own life-energy being affected by his.

THE SOURCES
OF *SATSANG*

So why do enlightened people have this strange ability to generate awakening experiences in others?

Satsang experiences suggest that the esoteric concept of an aura has some basis in fact. They suggest that our being or life-energy isn't just confined to our own mind or body – it radiates out from us, creating an atmosphere, or aura, which can affect the people we come into contact with. The auras of most people don't appear to be particularly strong, or at least don't have particularly strong negative or positive qualities, so that we don't usually feel anything palpable from them. But we've all met certain people whom we instinctively recoil from. We might not even exchange any words with them but they still fill us with a sense of unease or even fear or dread. These are people who have a strong 'bad aura' around them, perhaps because their life-energy is heavily poisoned with negative emotions and egotism.

But with enlightened people, of course, the exact opposite happens. Their life-energy is so intensified and stilled, and has such powerful positive qualities, that they 'transmit' waves of calm and bliss to everyone around them.

Perhaps more specifically, though, these experiences are another example of the connection between energy and awakening. There is a direct transmission of energy from the enlightened person – the 'current' or 'telepathic radiation' that Paul Brunton could sense passing from Ramana to him. The guru provides an extra input of energy which may intensify our life-energy to the point that we experience an ISLE state and therefore an awakening experience.

At the same time, the sheer power of an enlightened person's presence can halt our chattering thoughts and weaken our ego. Paul Brunton was aware of how naturally still his mind became when he was near Ramana and I'm often aware of this when I go to see Russel. His presence seems to expose normal thinking as the trivial and insignificant activity it is. The very idea of pondering over what's happened to me today or what I've got to do tomorrow in his presence seems ridiculous, like choosing to watch a TV commercial rather than look at an amazingly beautiful sunset. The radiance of his presence draws me in and seems to dissolve the boundaries of my ego. As a result, there is a meditative energy-conserving effect, intensifying the ISLE state created by the transmission of energy.

SCHIZOPHRENIA AND WAKEFULNESS

Since we've been looking at the connection between energy and awakening, this is perhaps a good point to look at the relationship between the condition of schizophrenia and spiritual awakening.

There is one sense in which schizophrenia resembles awakening experiences: an ability to perceive the is-ness of the world. According to psychologists, schizophrenia brings a 'heightened perceptual acuity' and a greater sensitivity to the 'the raw data of new experiences'.[22]

A friend of mine – the same person who had the awakening experience of becoming one with seabirds described on page 17 – experienced this when she had some psychiatric problems during a time of great stress in her life. When driving she found it difficult to concentrate on the road because 'I could see every single blade of grass in the fields, and every feather on every bird.' But rather than being exhilarating, she found that 'all that visual processing was exhausting'.[23]

Similarly, a lady named Norma McDonald says that when she developed schizophrenia it was as if her brain 'awoke' after being asleep for years. Her senses woke up to the is-ness of her surroundings and she became acutely aware of the behaviour and motivation of other people. After recovering and reflecting on her experience, she realized that potentially human beings are always able to 'hear every sound within earshot and see every object, line and colour within the field of vision'. But as this would make everyday life very difficult, 'the mind must have a filter which functions without our conscious thought, sorting stimuli and allowing only those which are relevant to the situation in hand to disturb consciousness'.[24]

This is practically identical to the 'reducing valve' theory described by Aldous Huxley that I mentioned in Chapter 4. This 'filter' is the desensitizing mechanism which switches our attention off to reality as a way of conserving energy for the ego. We've seen that in awakening experiences the perceptual intensity is due to the fact that the ego is no longer monopolizing our energy. Either through a meditative activity or *satsang,* the ego becomes quiet. As a result, there is a freeing up of energy, and this energy naturally begins to be used perceptually. The desensitizing mechanism is no longer needed and falls away, leaving us able to perceive the is-ness and beauty of our surroundings. Something similar happens in schizophrenia, with the important difference that in schizophrenia the ego does not just become quiet but *disintegrates* as a structure.

Strictly speaking, in awakening experiences – or in spiritual development in general – the ego does not disappear. It still exists as a structure but as a *different* structure. It's no longer a powerful, isolated entity which dominates the psyche and monopolizes our life-energy. Now it is much weaker and is *integrated* into our being. You could compare the ego to a country's government. In our normal state, the government is autocratic and authoritarian. It interferes with every aspect of our life and takes all our money in taxes. But in an awakened state, it's like a democratic and liberal government which regulates our life to some degree but doesn't place any demands on us and is almost invisible. In other words, in an awakened state the ego still exists as an organizing centre, allowing us think rationally and make decisions and plans, but it is no longer the centre of our being.

However, in schizophrenia the ego no longer functions in this way. To continue the same metaphor, the government crumbles away, leaving anarchy in its wake. It may not disappear completely, but it no longer functions cohesively. And this disintegration of the ego has some terrible effects: a loss of the sense of identity, disorganized thoughts and speech, the inability to concentrate, difficulty distinguishing mental images and thoughts from reality, etc. However, as with awakening experiences, now that the ego no longer functions, there's a massive freeing up of psychic energy, which begins to fuel perception. As a result, at the same time as suffering their other terrible symptoms, people with schizophrenia are often intensely awake to the is-ness of the world.

However, even this isn't necessarily a positive thing. Because they don't have a stable sense of self, people with schizophrenia can't order or control their perceptions. They can't switch off their intense perception when they need to focus or concentrate, which makes everyday life every difficult. For example, my friend recognized that 'For writing poetry or painting, such sensory hyperacuity could be a great advantage. But for driving to the supermarket it was just a nuisance.'[25] At the same time, a person with schizophrenia might find this intense reality threatening. In the words of the psychiatrist J. S. Sullivan, 'The schizophrenic is surrounded by animistically enlivened objects which are engaged in ominous performances which it is terribly necessary – and impossible – to understand.'[26]

This is why, although there is this one parallel between schizophrenia and mystic states, they are completely different. Far from being a mental disorder, the awakened state is one of optimum mental health – a higher state of mental health, you might say – which makes our normal mental state seemed limited and unsatisfactory.

SPIRITUAL CRISIS

One of the most puzzling aspects of awakening experiences is that they are often induced by states of despair or mental turmoil. Paradoxically, great suffering often gives rise to experiences of great joy and liberation. Here, for example, a man describes how he was severely depressed and became so desperate that he prayed for help. Immediately he experienced a shift in consciousness:

> *At a flash, the scene changed. All became alive – the trees, the houses, the very stones became animated with life – and all became vibrant with the life within them. All breathed effulgent light, vivid sparkling light, radiating out and in every direction; and not only that but everything seemed to be connected with everything else. Although all*

[were] separate forms, and all vibrating with their own
intensity of life, yet they all seemed to be connected by their
vibrations into one whole thing, as the different coloured
parts of a picture are yet of the same picture...[27]

Here, even more powerfully, a woman describes how her son was
close to dying from tuberculosis and how she felt impelled to pray
for his recovery, even though she wasn't religious. At that moment
she had a high-intensity awakening experience in which she
experienced oneness with the cosmos to such an extent that she
became all things:

I knew that a veil had been lifted. I was as God. I was
everywhere and everything. The only two things I now
remember being were a tree and a squirrel. I thought how
odd it was that anyone had difficulty accepting that God
was everywhere and everything. I was, and it seemed so
natural and obvious. Also I saw millions of jigsaw pieces
all floating into their correct position. All was well. All was
completed.[28]

These experiences don't seem to make any sense. How is it possible
to move from the deepest turmoil to the highest ecstasy in a moment?
Unlike awakening experiences induced by meditation or relaxation,
these experiences don't seem to be organic, to arise naturally from
particular activities or states of mind. Instead there's a very abrupt
shift to a completely different state of being, one which is almost the
polar opposite of what was originally being felt. Perhaps this is why
people are so ready to interpret these experiences as being given by
God, especially when they seem to come in response to prayer. The
shift from despair to joy and revelation seems so abrupt that it seems
logical to believe that a higher power has intervened and actively
caused the experience.

PERMANENT CHANGE

However, it's not simply a question of awakening *experiences* – even more importantly, psychological turmoil sometimes brings about a shift into *permanent* wakefulness. This is a massive subject and one that I'm not going to investigate in detail here – in fact, it's the subject of my next book. But it's significant that many spiritual teachers or gurus have become awakened – or enlightened – after periods of intense mental torment. This is true of my own teacher, Russel Williams, as well as other modern teachers such as Eckhart Tolle, Byron Katie and Catherine Ingram. Recently I've interviewed many other people who have undergone similar transformational experiences, including an alcoholic who reached rock bottom and lost everything but then became liberated; a woman who has lived in a state of wakefulness ever since being told she has breast cancer; a man who became paralysed after falling from a bridge onto a river bed, struggled for months with pain and despair, then underwent a spiritual rebirth and now lives in a state of permanent bliss. (I will discuss all of these cases in detail in my next book.)

Experiences such as these often occur when people have an intense encounter with their own death, either through an accident or sudden medical emergency or, most commonly, when they are told that they have a fatal illness. Paradoxically again, for some people, this can be a massively liberating experience. They emerge with a new appreciation of the wonder and beauty of life and no longer take anything for granted. They become centred in the present rather than looking towards the future and become less interested in possessions and status or success. They become less self-centred and more compassionate, more concerned about other people's problems (or world problems) than their own. They often develop a new spiritual outlook, leading to an interest in meditation and other spiritual practises. As one man who almost died of a heart attack told me, 'It's the best thing that's ever happened to me.'

DETACHMENT

The key to understanding these experiences is the concept of *attachment*. Normally, we're psychologically attached to a large number of constructs, such as hopes and ambitions for the future, beliefs and ideas concerning life and the world, the knowledge we have accumulated and our image of ourselves, including our sense of status, our appearance and accomplishments and achievements. These are *accoutrements* which become attached to the sense of self but are not actually a part of our true nature.

On the other hand, there are more tangible attachments in our life, such as our possessions, our jobs, and people whose approval and attention we crave. These provide food for the psychological construct of our self-image, since they help us to feel that we are significant and that our life has value. All of these attachments support our sense of identity like scaffolding and give us a sense of security. They are the building blocks of our sense of 'I'. We feel that we are 'someone' because we have hopes, beliefs, status, a job and possessions, and because other people give us approval.

The important point is that in states of despair and depression at least some of these psychological attachments are broken. This is the very *reason* why you are in despair – because the constructs you were depending on for your well-being and security have been destroyed, because the scaffolding which supported your ego has fallen away. Hopes and beliefs are revealed as illusions; you've lost your possessions, your job and your status; and the lovers or friends you were dependent upon have rejected you. As a result you feel naked and lost, as if your identity has been destroyed.

This effect is especially powerful when we encounter death. If you're told you're going to die soon, there can be no more hopes or ambitions for you. Your possessions, successes and status and the knowledge you've accumulated can have no more meaning now that you're going to be separated from them forever. The normal worries and concerns of daily life fade away for you too, as does your attachment to your job and to people whose approval you sought.

But at this point you are, paradoxically, close to a state of liberation. You're now in a state of *de*tachment; your self has been cut loose from all external things and is free and clear. You're in a state of inner *emptiness*. And so, in an instant, it's possible for you to shift from despair to freedom and joy. The pain of being naked and alone gives way to the joy of liberation.

This can also be interpreted in terms of life-energy. These psychological attachments consume our energy. On the one hand, they do so because they occupy our attention and thoughts. At the same time, they exist as psychological 'forms' within our mind which are present even if we aren't aware of them at a particular moment. Together, these forms constitute a whole network of attachment, and as a structure this network needs a continual input of energy to maintain itself, in the same way that there has to be a continual input of energy to maintain the physical structure of the body. And so when attachments dissolve, the energy they use up is released.

You might remember that I made same point earlier about the ego: that it needs a lot of psychic energy just to be maintained as a structure. And this makes sense when you consider that, to a large extent, these psychological attachments *constitute* the ego – as I've just mentioned, they are its 'building blocks'. Along with our constant thought-chatter, they create our sense of who we are. So, when attachments fade away, the superficial ego-self which they create fades away too. That's why many people who undergo transformation through intense turmoil feel that they have become a new person. This doesn't mean that there is *no* ego or self left, only that, in Eckhart Tolle's words, 'the self which live[s] through identifications'[29] fades away, leaving a much more integrated, less domineering and more fundamental sense of self.

It's a pity that we need encounters with death or other forms of turmoil to bring us to this point of liberation. Wouldn't it be wonderful if we could live in a state of wakefulness without coming close to death?

I believe that we can do this. One of the main purposes of this book is to show you that you have much more control over your own state of consciousness than you assume. Awakening experiences don't have to happen accidentally – if we know why and where they occur, then we can create those conditions consciously. And it's the same for a permanently awakened state – if we know what the psychological conditions of that state are, then we can make a conscious attempt to create them.

However, in order to reach this point, we need to examine ISLE states in a little more detail to find out exactly what it is about them that gives rise to awakening experiences.

8

ENERGY AND AWAKENING

We've spent the last four chapters investigating awakening experiences caused by ISLE states, but the question we haven't really answered yet is *why* do ISLE states generate awakening experiences? Or, to break it down further, how can an ISLE state account for all the different characteristics of awakening experiences that we looked at in Chapter 1 – the sense of the oneness of things, the inner well-being, the feeling of becoming a deeper and truer self, and so on? What is it about a state of intensified and stilled life-energy that gives rise to these characteristics?

We've already seen in Chapter 5 why ISLE states give rise to heightened awareness and a sense of the 'alive-ness' of the world. As Arthur Deikman and Philip Novak pointed out, when our normal ego-chatter is quieted, it results in 'a surplus of psychic energy' (in their term) which is naturally 'transferred' to perception. Our vision of the world ceases to be automatic (because there is no need for the psyche to conserve energy any more) and we experience a brighter and more vivid reality.

In fact, all of the 'perceptual' aspects of awakening experiences can be explained in terms of this 'deautomatization of perception' (in Deikman's phrase). As I described in Chapter 3, in a sense our 'normal' perception of the world is the vision that traditional indigenous peoples had: a vision of the life and sentience of all things, an awareness of the harmony, meaning and benevolence shining from the world around us and of the all-pervading spirit-force, or *brahman,* or Great Spirit, which *makes* everything alive and radiates this harmony and meaning. The only reason we don't see the world in this way all the time is because our powerful ego 'gobbles up' our life-energy, leaving none over for 'present-centred awareness'. In my terminology, this is because of the desensitizing mechanism in our psyche, whose purpose is to 'edit out' the reality of our surroundings so that we only use a bare minimum of our energy in perceiving our surroundings. This conserves energy, which is then used by the ego. But when the ego is quiet, this process stops. Our perception becomes 'energized' and we find ourselves in a new world, as different from our normal dreary shadow-reality as a black-and-white photograph is from an actual multi-coloured three-dimensional scene. We find ourselves in the *real* world – or at least a *much more* real one – rather than the dark cave we normally inhabit.

There are degrees of this, of course, corresponding to *how* intense, still and pure our life-energy becomes and how 'de-automatized' our perceptions become. With a mild de-automatization, you might only gain a sense of the is-ness and 'aliveness' of your surroundings; with a stronger de-automatization, you might become aware of a powerful harmony and benevolence radiating from the world; and at a higher level you might become aware of *brahman* pervading the world and making everything one. All of these characteristics are fundamental realities which are hidden from us by our normal automatic perception – and which therefore reveal themselves when our perceptions are de-automatized.

INNER WELL-BEING

In Chapter 4, I suggested that one important difference between ISLE and HD states was that the latter didn't give rise to the same *inner* changes as ISLE states. ISLE states bring a sense of inner well-being, which becomes more intense as the awakening experience itself intensifies. But higher states of consciousness induced by drugs, fasting or pain, or other methods of disrupting homoeostasis, are usually visual and perceptual experiences which don't often bring powerful inner feelings of bliss.

So where does the well-being of ISLE states stem from? It has two sources. On the one hand, ISLE states bring a sense of inner peacefulness for the simple reason that there *is* peacefulness inside us in these moments. 'The storm of inward thoughts' subsides; our mind is quiet and still rather than filled with the crazy thought-chatter of the ego. Our emotions are still too. So our being is free of disturbance, and to some extent the sense of peacefulness we feel is the direct experience of this stillness inside us.

At the same time, this well-being is a direct experience of the natural *blissful quality* of life energy. Hindu philosophy tells us the essence of reality is *Sat Chit Ananda* – 'being-consciousness-bliss'. Bliss is the nature of *brahman*, as is evident from many of the mystical experiences we've looked at, particularly the high-intensity void experiences. And the important point is that this universal energy is also our life-energy. We can, therefore, experience the blissful nature of this energy inside ourselves – which is what happens in ISLE states, when the energy becomes more intensified than usual. And the more intensified it becomes, the more bliss we experience.

However, this doesn't often happen in HD states. The 'storm of inward thoughts' may well become a little quieter than normal – since we'll mainly be focusing our attention on the beauty outside us, depriving it of some of the 'attention food' that fuels it – but it's unlikely to fade away completely. There's still likely to be some form of mental activity – after all, our mind only ever becomes completely quiet after long periods of intense meditation or concentration. As a result, we don't experience an inner peacefulness.

We're also less likely to experience the blissful quality of life-energy itself. Since our mind is still full of activity, our life-energy doesn't intensify. It's probably at the same low intensity during the HD state as it is in ordinary life – a level at which it's not concentrated enough to enable us to experience its natural joyfulness.

Of course, this doesn't mean that HD experiences aren't pleasurable, but their positive feelings don't usually come from our inner being but from more superficial sources – exhilaration at the new world of is-ness and beauty we have access to, or chemical changes such as the release of adrenaline or endorphins.

THE SENSE OF ONENESS AND COMPASSION

We've seen that another important characteristic of awakening experiences is the sense that *we* are a part of the ocean of oneness which pervades the world. There is no duality between us and our surroundings; we *are* the moon and the sun and the other people and the trees around us, and we can feel what they feel. *Atman* and *brahman* are one.

This sense of oneness also has two sources. Our normal sense of separateness from the world is caused by the strong boundaries of our normal ego. But in awakening experiences these boundaries dissolve. We've seen that to a large extent our normal ego is continually reinforced by thought-chatter and so when thought-chatter quiets, the ego becomes much weaker. This could happen through the dissolving of attachments too, since attachments are the building blocks of the ego. And as the normal ego becomes weaker, its boundaries become much softer. So the 'wall' between us and the world begins to melt away, and our sense of being stretches beyond our own body and brain, merging with the world as a whole or with other individual phenomena.

This is the reason why awakening experiences often bring a strong sense of compassion and love for other beings. As our sense of being merges with other human beings and other creatures, we 'feel with' them and feel compassion for their suffering. We love them because they *are* us, expressions of the same consciousness that constitutes our being.

Unlike the sense of inner well-being, this oneness can be a feature of HD states too, although for different reasons. Our normal ego structure is an integral part of the ordinary 'optimum' survival consciousness which homoeostasis partly serves to maintain. So when homoeostasis is disrupted, the ego structure may be disrupted too and this may include a melting away of its boundaries.

However, the second source of this sense of oneness only applies to ISLE states. And this is closely related to the second reason for the well-being ISLE states bring. In fact, it's extremely simple: we feel a sense of oneness because the life-energy that constitutes our being is one and the same as the spirit-energy that pervades the universe. It's the same energy in a different form; our own life-energy is a kind of 'influx' of spirit-force, 'canalized' into us. Or, to put it more simply, the spirit inside us is the same spirit that pervades the universe and everything in it. And when our life-energy becomes intensified, we begin to experience this oneness. We become aware that the spirit-energy that constitutes our own being is the same spirit-energy that constitutes all other things, so that we *are* the sea and the trees, animals and other people. We become immersed in the ocean of spirit.

Incidentally, the weakening of ego boundaries is the source of another characteristic of awakening experiences: the expansion and transcendence of time. As I have shown in my book *Making Time,* our normal linear perception of time is created by our ego. It develops in parallel with the ego from birth to adulthood and fades away in states of consciousness when our normal ego structure becomes weaker or dissolves away altogether. There is a wide variety of experiences which can bring an expanded sense of time: accident and emergency situations, 'zone' experiences, hypnotic trances, mental illnesses such as schizophrenia, psychedelic drug experiences – and, of course, awakening experiences. What all these experiences have in common is that in one sense or another they are all experiences of 'egolessness'. In accidents and emergencies the sheer shock and intensity of the situation seem to stun the ego into silence; in zone experiences it seems to fade away due to intense concentration; in schizophrenia the ego structure is damaged or disrupted, and so forth. And since the ego generates our sense of time, during these experiences time fades away too.

BECOMING THE REAL SELF

We've seen that another characteristic of ISLE states is an 'identity shift', a sense of 'becoming who we really are'. Our normal sense of identity is bound up with the ego and largely sustained by the endless thought-chatter that runs through our mind. And so when these thoughts stop, this 'I' fades away and we lose our normal sense of identity.

As this normal identity fades away, a new one emerges. As we've just noted, our essential being is life-energy. Our true identity seems to be *embedded* in this energy, so that when there is a high intensification of it we feel that we become who we really are. In our normal state, there's a low intensification of life-energy inside us, but when there's a build-up of life-energy inside us, which usually happens as thought-chatter becomes quieter and the ego begins to fade away, we begin to feel our connection to the energy of our being. Our essential identity grows stronger as our normal ego-identity grows weaker.

In terms of the Hindu concept of the *koshas,* as the outer 'sheaths' fade away, we become closer to our true identity. The energy bodies of the physical, etheric, mental and intellectual layers become quiescent and we no longer identify ourselves with them. We become one with the most subtle layer of being, the *ananda-maya-kosha,* the layer of bliss, or even one with *atman* itself, our essential spiritual self.

This is definitely how it *feels* subjectively. When I have a good meditation and manage to quiet my mind, I always feel this sense of becoming a new self. My life-energy intensifies and becomes stiller, filling me with a sense of calm and well-being, and at the same time I feel a new self emerging, like a clear blue sky behind the rushing clouds of the ego. As Patanjali put it, 'restricting the whirls of consciousness' enables my 'transcendental Self' to reveal itself.[1] I immediately feel that my normal self is false and limited in comparison with this new self. This self feels more stable and fundamental and has a much clearer awareness of the world. It also seems much more spacious – as if 'I' normally live in a cramped and claustrophobic part of my psyche, but now I'm in a much wider and more open space.

All of this makes sense, since our normal ego exists in a state of separateness, like an island – an I-land – in the middle of an ocean. But the new self we become when the ego's boundaries melt away is one which is part of the universal ocean of spirit.

HD states generally don't feature this sense of becoming a deeper self. They do sometimes bring about a dissolution of the ego, which means a loss of our normal sense of identity, but the ego self isn't replaced by a new self, as in ISLE states. There's no reason why it should be, since this new self comes from an intensification of life-energy, which doesn't take place in HD states. In fact, as we noted in Chapter 4, this is one of the reasons why HD states can be dangerous – because they can dissolve away the structures of the ego but don't replace them with anything else. You don't become a deeper and stronger self, just an *impaired* normal self. And eventually, if you disrupt homoeostasis too often, this may lead to psychosis – the permanent disruption of the ego structure.

DIFFERENT DEGREES OF AWAKENING

One final feature of awakening experiences which can be explained in terms of life-energy is the fact that there are different intensities of them.

Of course, there are different intensities of HD experiences too, probably related to the *degree* of homoeostasis disruption. The greater the change to the body's normal physiological functioning – for example, the more powerful the chemical you've ingested or the higher your body temperature, your blood pressure and your heart rate as a result of dancing – the more intense the experience is.

In a similar way, the intensity of ISLE awakening states depends on the *degree* to which our life-energy is intensified and stilled. If there's only a small degree of intensification, you'll have a low-intensity awakening experience. But if your ego-mind becomes silent and your life-energy is intensified to a high degree, you'll have a high-intensity one.

It's tempting to suggest that this is a finite process, that there is a point at which our life-energy becomes as intense and still as it can possibly be – *completely* intense and still, in other words – and this is the point where we reach the highest possible level of consciousness. Our ego-mind becomes completely silent, the ego itself fades away, our mind's senses are completely withdrawn from the world, there is no outflow of energy at all and no disturbance from thoughts and emotions. Our being is completely empty and completely pure. This is when the void experience occurs, when the material world dissolves away and we become one with the formless spiritual ocean which is the essence of reality.

This explains why low-intensity awakening experiences are so common, while high-intensity ones are so rare. It's quite easy to generate a mild ISLE state – all you have to do is conserve energy by quieting your ego a little, or by relaxing and withdrawing from external stimuli. But higher ISLE states are usually only accessible to people who have had some degree of spiritual training, like Paul Brunton or Ramakrishna, who have learned to control their thought-chatter and weakened their ego structure to some degree. It's obviously more difficult to build up the 'inner pressure' of energy that generates high-intensity awakening experiences in the same way that it's difficult to build up the physical energy to run a 100-metre sprint.

ENERGY AND NATURAL AWAKENING

The connection between energy and awakening helps to explain the natural wakefulness of indigenous peoples and children, as described in Chapter 3. Both indigenous peoples and young children are naturally awake to some degree because they have a naturally high intensity of life-energy inside them. Their egos are less active and less developed as a structure, and so don't use up as much psychic energy. At the same time, since their egos are less active, their beings are stiller than ours. In other words, both indigenous peoples and young children live in a constant ISLE state.

However, it's important to remember that, as I pointed out in Chapter 3, indigenous peoples appear to experience a *medium* intensity of awakening, while young children appear to experience a *low* intensity, which suggests that the ISLE state they experience is correspondingly medium or low. Since their egos are undeveloped and they're free of mental chatter, you might expect that young children would experience a higher intensity of wakefulness. However, the regular storms of emotion and desire which sweep through them – states of excitement, upset, anger and frustration when their desires aren't met – obviously create quite a significant outflow of energy and a large degree of disturbance. This is probably the reason why, as I mentioned earlier, children very rarely attain states of absolute wakefulness. It's almost impossible for them to attain the state of *complete* stillness and inner emptiness – and complete energy-intensification – that makes these experiences possible.

HD VERSUS ISLE STATES

So we have seen that there are two sources of awakening experiences: HD and ISLE states. Both of these enable us to wake up from the sleep of our ordinary consciousness and experience a more intense and complete reality. However, we've seen that the two sources give rise to two distinct types of experience: HD states usually give rise to wild, ecstatic experiences, while ISLE usually give rise to more sedate and blissful experiences. HD states can be generated by hunger, sleep deprivation, drugs, pain or breathing exercises. ISLE states can be generated by meditation, sports, sex, music, *kundalini* experiences, near-death experiences, *satsang* and detachment.

Admittedly, there isn't always a clear distinction between these two sources. In some situations, we might experience a combination of their effects – for example, when a long-distance runner experiences an ISLE state through the meditative effect of nature and the rhythm of their running and at the same time an HD state due to the physiological effects of intensive exercise; or when two lovers experience an ISLE state due to the meditative and ego-dissolving effects of sex and at the same time an HD state due to the effects of exertion and deep breathing.

In Chapter 4, we saw that HD states have some drawbacks: they can be dangerous to both body and mind, they are essentially artificial and they can't lead to a permanently awakened state. But none of these applies to ISLE states. They don't carry any physical or psychological risks – in fact, if anything, they *improve* our physical and mental health. We've already looked at the massive range of benefits of meditation – lower blood pressure and heart rate, stimulation of the immune system, reduced anxiety and stress, and so on. Presumably ISLE states in general have these benefits, since they're always deep states of relaxation and almost always involve a quieting of the chattering ego-mind which is the source of most of our stress and anxiety.

But perhaps the biggest advantage of ISLE states compared to HD states is that they *can* lead to a permanently awakened state. The 'peak' – or 'peek' – experiences they bring can lead to a plateau of permanent wakefulness. The temporary psychic change which causes them can become a permanent psychic change. In other words, our life energy can become *permanently* intensified and stilled. We've seen that the main cause of ISLE experiences is the quieting of the ego, and it's possible, by regularly meditating and following other spiritual practises and lifestyle guidelines, to permanently quiet the ego. In effect, this means reversing the psychological change I believe occurred several thousand years ago, when our ancestors' sense of ego intensified and we lost earlier human beings' naturally awakened state. (We'll look at this process of permanently 'waking up' in a lot more detail in the last part of this book.)

ISLE states are also more *complete* than HD states. As we have seen, they have a powerful inner, affective dimension (i.e. the sense of well-being or joy and of becoming a deeper, truer self) which HD states generally lack.

However, as I also pointed out in Chapter 4, this certainly doesn't mean that drug experiences and other HD states are not *genuine* mystical experiences. HD states clearly do transcend the limits of our normal consciousness. It's just that they are not as complete and as satisfactory as ISLE states.

THE TRUE MEANING OF SPIRIT

The word 'spiritual' is used in so many different ways that it's difficult to define. We say things like 'It gave me a very *spiritual* feeling,' 'He's such a *spiritual* person' or 'I'm interested in *spirituality,*' but are we really sure of what we mean? In everyday speech, a 'spiritual' person could be someone who goes to church or the mosque every week, or someone who goes to see crystal healers and astrologers, or more generally someone who is calm and humble, generous and compassionate, rather than materialistic or status-seeking. As Ken Wilber notes, 'The real difficulty ... is getting almost anyone to agree with what we call "spiritual". The term is virtually useless for any sort of coherent discussion.'[2] That's why I've used the term 'awakening experience' instead of the potentially confusing 'spiritual experience'.

However, if we think in terms of life-energy, we can come to a very precise definition of these terms. In the strictest sense of the term, 'spirit' refers to life-energy. The word comes originally from the Latin *spiritus*, which means 'breath'. We could therefore say that 'spirit' refers to the breath *of life*, the animating principle inside us, the life-energy that we expend as we live our life and that regenerates when we rest. And if 'spirit' is equivalent to life-energy, 'spiritual experiences' are states when our life-energy becomes more intensified and stilled than normal. (This is why, as I mentioned in Chapter 4, HD states shouldn't be considered spiritual experiences, even though they are awakening experiences.) 'Spiritual' people are people who have managed to permanently intensify and still their life-energy to a higher degree than normal and who, as a result, are permanently 'awake' to the world around them and have a permanent sense of connection to the cosmos and a sense of inner well-being.

Many of the characteristics popularly described as 'spiritual', such as humility, contentment and compassion, are secondary effects of ISLE states. People who live in a permanent ISLE state usually *are* content, calm, humble, compassionate, non-materialistic and non-status seeking. These characteristics come from their softer and less dominant ego structure. They are free from – or at least are less affected by – the crazy thought-chatter that fills our mind with worries and triggers negative emotions, and also the sense of ego isolation which gives us a basic sense of insignificance and anxiety. This means that there is a basic sense of contentment and completeness inside them. They don't need to try to complete themselves or to find compensation for psychological discord by accumulating money or chasing after status and success. They are humble because they are self-sufficient; they don't need to gain the attention and admiration of others. They are compassionate because their softer ego structure means that they're not 'walled off' from other people or creatures. They sense other people's suffering and feel the desire to alleviate it.

THE 'SPIRITUAL POTENTIAL' OF ACTIVITIES

When we say that a particular activity or experience has made us feel 'spiritual', what we mean – or at least should mean – is that it has had the effect of intensifying and stilling our life-energy. And this gives us a useful benchmark for judging how spiritual – or *un*spiritual – different activities are. Activities like meditation, yoga, walking in the countryside, fishing, long-distance running, listening to music, looking at paintings, reading poetry, etc. can all be called 'spiritual' activities because, as we saw in the last chapter, they lend themselves to intensifying and stilling life-energy. And by the same token, we can see activities like shopping, watching television or working in a busy office or restaurant as 'non-spiritual', because they're much less likely to bring about an intensification of our life-energy.

This isn't completely clear-cut, of course – walking in the countryside or listening to music certainly won't always (or even often) generate a spiritual state of being and in the right circumstances (maybe a quiet and empty 24-hour supermarket at four o'clock in the morning) shopping could generate an ISLE state. But we could say that every activity has a certain *spiritual potential,* and that while the spiritual potential of activities like meditation or yoga is high, the spiritual potential of shopping or watching TV is low.

Judged by these criteria, there are some activities that might claim to be spiritual but aren't really. For example, there's nothing spiritual about being a member of an esoteric study group and collecting arcane knowledge, or about being a religious authority and knowing more about rituals and sacred texts than other people. Knowledge in itself can never be spiritual. On its own it's more likely to be anti-spiritual, since it often creates a sense of self-importance and superiority.

Similarly, there's not necessarily anything spiritual about communicating with your guardian angel, seeing other people's auras, levitating, using hidden powers to 'hold' higher frequencies or vibrations that will keep your body young, and so on. No matter how mind-blowing and exhilarating some of these activities are, they're unlikely to have the effect of intensifying and stilling your life-energy, and so shouldn't be seen as spiritual.

The term 'spiritual' is often used in relation to religion, but this can be misleading too. As I suggested in the introduction, religion and spirituality are two different things. If you define religion as accepting certain beliefs, worshipping a particular god or messiah or prophet and living by the rules set out by that divine figure, then this has nothing to do with spirituality. However, it's true that religious people – particularly seriously religious people – may experience spiritual states sometimes, because of practises like prayer (which may bring about an ISLE state) and fasting (which may bring about an HD state). It's also true that some of the teachings of religious prophets emphasize spiritual qualities, such as empathy and tolerance and serving the less fortunate. I personally have met many religious people who embody these qualities and who are clearly spiritually developed. On the other hand, many – perhaps most – religious people and religious organizations have absolutely no spiritual aspect to them. Rather than being motivated by empathy and compassion, many 'born-again' or fundamentalist Christians and Muslims are driven by egotism and desire for dominance. Rather than experiencing the well-being and harmony of ISLE states, they just feel a smug sense of superiority at feeling that only they possess the Truth and will be saved.

We can interpret long-term spiritual development in terms of intensifying and stilling life-energy too. However, long-term spiritual development is such an important issue that we need to devote a whole chapter to it.

9

PERMANENT AWAKENING

So far in this book we've been looking at temporary states of awakening – moments in which we 'wake up' from the sleep of our normal consciousness. However, you could say that this actually doesn't help us very much. Awakening experiences usually don't last for very long – sometimes just a few seconds, sometimes a few minutes, sometimes a few hours. And what's the good of waking up for a few minutes every now and then if we keep falling back to sleep? you could argue.

What we really need to do is to *permanently* wake up, to *live* in a higher state of consciousness. We need to permanently alter the structure of our psyche so that the mould of our normal consciousness isn't able to reform. Our peak experiences need to become a plateau of permanent wakefulness.

This is what spiritual *development* is all about: the long-term effort to permanently transform our consciousness by following certain practises, exercises and lifestyles. This could just mean meditating twice a day or doing yoga *asanas* every morning. It could mean becoming a Buddhist and following the Buddha's lifestyle guidelines and the Eightfold Path. Or it could mean leaving the everyday world behind and going to live in a forest or a monastery, living a life of austerity in silence and solitude, meditating or praying for hours each day.

Often spiritual development is an incremental process. Through regular meditation and *asanas* you may gradually tame your ego-mind, so that your thoughts and emotions become more restful. You may become more mindful of your experience and gain access to a new source of well-being inside you. After several years you will probably be significantly more 'spiritual' than you were when you began, with an intensified vision of the world, a permanent sense of serenity and meaning, and a feeling of connectedness to the cosmos. Or this might happen through turmoil or trauma – you might go through a long period of suffering which has the gradual effect of dissolving psychological attachments and so weakening the ego. Slowly you transcend the negative side of suffering and begin to feel more whole and more connected to the cosmos.

At other times, however, spiritual development can be an explosive event, a sudden jump rather than a slow climb. You might follow a spiritual lifestyle for years without feeling that you've made any real progress. But without realizing it, you've gradually been setting up the conditions for awakening to occur, like an engineer slowly building a plane. At a certain point the plane is ready to take flight and there is a blinding flash of enlightenment which establishes itself permanently. As we noted in Chapter 7, this often happens after an intense episode of trauma, as happened with Russel Williams and Eckhart Tolle.

So what does 'spiritual development' actually mean? If, as we saw in the last chapter, spirit equals life-energy, then it could be defined as follows:

Spiritual development means trying to create a permanent ISLE state through following certain practises which have the effect of intensifying and stilling our life-energy on a permanent basis.

If you're following a path of spiritual development – maybe regularly doing meditation and yoga, following the self-development systems of Vedanta, Buddhism or Tantra, or living as a monk – this is one way of interpreting what you're trying to do. To some extent, the aim of these teachings – and the goal of your strivings – is to permanently intensify and still the energy of your being.

Just as temporary awakening experiences have different intensities, so there are different degrees of permanent awakening. One person might become 'stabilized' at a low degree of awakening in which they are continually struck by the beauty and is-ness of their surroundings and feel a strong sense of kinship with nature. Another person might be permanently stabilized at a medium degree, where they see the world as infused with spirit and feel a permanent sense of inner peace and joy. And some people might reach the highest point of spiritual development and always see the whole of the phenomenal world as a manifestation of the Divine Ground, the 'infinite shining ocean of consciousness' which is the essence of reality. As with temporary awakening experiences, the higher the state, the fewer people reach it. There are probably millions of long-term meditators and hatha yoga or *tai chi* practitioners who have attained a low-level awakened state. But it's likely that at this very moment there are no more than a few hundred mystics around the world who have reached the highest pinnacle of spiritual development.

Permanent awakening – not just at the higher levels, but the lower ones too – is potentially open to everyone. We all have the freedom to intensify and still the energy of our being if we so choose. This usually means permanently closing down – or at least reducing the outflow of – some of the channels through which our life-energy normally leaks away and permanently stilling some of the constant disturbances of thought, desire and emotion that take place inside us. This creates a new kind of psychic organization inside us and a new distribution of psychic energy. The redistribution which took place several thousand years ago, when the ego 'exploded' and became so powerful, is reversed. At the very least, we return to the naturally awakened state which we 'fell' away from several thousand years ago.

Throughout history a small number of people have been born with the instinctive feeling that their ordinary consciousness is incomplete and have devoted their lives to achieving a fuller and truer state of being. Whilst some of these people have tried – at least initially – to do this by disrupting homoeostasis, like Rimbaud and my friend Samuel, most have recognized that the only real way of attaining a permanent higher state of consciousness is through a long process of spiritual discipline and training. Many of these people have lived as ascetics, hermits or monks, rejecting the world of everyday life in order to give their complete attention to the effort to wake up.

In this chapter, we're going to look at how these spiritual seekers have gone about this and see how their efforts can be interpreted in terms of life-energy.

TAMING THE BODY

One practise which has been used by spiritual seekers from time immemorial and which is an integral part of many spiritual traditions is 'taming the body', or asceticism.

In Chapter 4 I suggested that it's wrong just to see asceticism as masochistic self-punishment. I mentioned then that to some extent ascetics used self-inflicted pain as a way of inducing awakening experiences through homoeostasis disruption. But in its moderate form, asceticism may have another genuinely spiritual purpose: it has been – and can be – used as part of the process of long-term awakening.

In the Christian mystical tradition, this is the rather severe-sounding process of 'mortification' or of subduing the 'body of desire'. Christian mystics like St Francis of Assisi, St Teresa, St Catherine of Siena and Walter Hilton denied themselves any kind of pleasure or gratification and purposely sought out unpleasant situations. They followed the advice of one of the most austere of Christian mystics, St John of the Cross, who wrote that in order to purify the soul the seeker has to 'strive always to prefer, not that which is easiest, but that which is most difficult; not that which is most delectable, but most unpleasing … not that which is restful, but that which is wearisome'.[1]

St Francis of Assisi gave up his life of wealth and privilege to live as a homeless beggar and do strenuous manual work, and forced himself to work in a leper colony. The Spanish mystic Ignatius Loyola was originally a vain nobleman who was obsessed with his appearance. But later, when he decided to follow a path of spiritual development, he stopped combing or cutting his hair and never cut his fingernails or toenails.

Outside the Christian tradition, the Persian mystic Al-Ghazali gave up all his possessions and spent two years in solitude, 'conquering my desires, struggling with my passions, striving to purify my soul',[2] while more recently, Mahatma Gandhi always slept on the floor, ate nothing but nuts and berries, drank nothing but hot water, wore only a loincloth. He was celibate from the age of 37 and had no possessions apart from a watch, food utensils and a copy of the *Bhagavad-Gita*.

Even though this isn't as extreme as the sadistic asceticism of St Simeon Stylites or Henry de Suso which we looked at in Chapter 4, it's still difficult to see anything redeeming in it. It seems perverse – why should we deny ourselves pleasures and repress our instincts? We could use the same criticism with which the third-century mystic and philosopher Plotinus famously rebuked the Gnostics. He scolded them for 'despising the world and all the beauties in it' when in reality there was no distinction between matter and spirit, since spirit 'penetrates and illumines' the world and makes it a 'living and blessed being'.[3] This is one of the important insights of the Tantric traditions of Buddhism and Hinduism too: the whole material world, including the human body and the natural world, is pervaded with spirit, and therefore divine and sacred. To abuse the body is therefore a crime against spirit. From this point of view, asceticism is actually *anti*-spiritual, since it means rejecting and despising spirit as it manifests itself in the world.

Asceticism also suggests an opposition between the 'spirit' and the 'flesh'. It seems to tell us that the 'flesh' is evil and corrupt and has to be 'tamed', and in order to become 'spiritual' we have to try to root out all of our 'lusts' and physical desires. Some spiritual traditions and teachers did take this extreme view, especially early Christian mystics like St Augustine and the Desert Fathers, and movements like Gnosticism and Manichaeanism. The ancient Indian spiritual tradition of Jainism comes close to this view too, suggesting that we can only find liberation by overcoming the desires of the body and so halting the flow of karma. Throughout history monks and ascetics from many different traditions have taken a similar attitude and done their utmost to punish themselves for the 'sinful lusts' of their 'corrupt and base' bodies.

However, there are milder forms of asceticism that don't take this attitude. The Indian traditions of Vedanta, Yoga and Buddhism take a much more measured stance, for example. They don't believe that the body is 'evil', but do tell us that one of the prerequisites of spiritual development is to control its appetites. Its desires for sex, food, alcohol, sensory stimulation, laziness, material comforts and luxury goods shouldn't be allowed to run riot. Instead we should be moderate, giving our body what it needs without being an inveterate pleasure-seeker. In Buddhist terms, this means following the Middle Way, a path of moderation midway between excess and extreme asceticism.

This isn't asceticism in the sense of punishing the body and rejecting and repressing our instincts and desires, it's asceticism in the sense of learning to *control* our instincts and desires. The body is accepted and valued, but needs to be tamed in the same way that you have to tame a wild horse in order to ride it.

It's also important to remember that even the ascetics who punished themselves most masochistically saw the process of mortification as a *temporary* one, a kind of training that they had to put themselves through in order to transform their being. In almost all cases, they only followed an ascetic and renunciate lifestyle for a certain number of years, until they were satisfied that they had tamed the 'body of desire' and were free to re-enter the world as new human beings in a permanently awakened state. They were not so much motivated by a hatred of their bodies as by a strong desire to transform themselves.

ASCETICISM AND ENERGY

The important thing about asceticism, and the reason why it has always been used as a technique of spiritual development, is that it has the long-term effect of intensifying life-energy. You can see the ascetic lifestyle as a way of trying to permanently close (or at least reduce) the channels through which life-energy normally leaks away, so that we can build up a permanently high energy concentration.

A degree of desire is natural, of course, especially on a physical level. It's completely natural to desire sex, food or physical comfort, for example. But it's easy for desires to become amplified beyond this biological level. The desire for sex, for certain kinds of food or drink, or for possessions and luxuries can completely take over our being. The same is true of psychological desires, such as for attention and love, or for status and success. For the spiritual seeker, part of the problem with these desires is that they are a distraction. You can't sit down to meditate when your mind's full of daydreams about sex or food or while you're imagining how wonderful it would be to be rich or famous. The path of spiritual development requires dedication and concentration, and you won't make any progress while you're busy trying to make sexual conquests or to become rich.

Closely related to this is the *disturbing* effect of desires. They disturb our inner being like a storm blowing across the calm surface of a lake. We've seen that our thought-chatter does this, but desires have a much bigger effect, because they affect us on a mental, emotional and physical level at the same time. For example, sexual desire might start on the mental level, as a daydream, but affects you physically straight away, as sexual energy awakens inside you, bringing biochemical changes. At the same time sexual daydreams may quickly trigger feelings of frustration, jealousy and anger. It's impossible for us to develop any inner peace or serenity with strong desires such as these rising up inside us.

But perhaps most importantly, the problem with desires is that when they're very active they use up a lot of life-energy. In the words of Evelyn Underhill, physical desires have 'usurped a place beyond their station; become the focus of energy, steadily drained the vitality of the self'. She notes that strong desires cause a 'wrong distribution of energy' and that 'no genius can afford to dissipate his energies: the mystic genius most of all.'[4] The mystic can't afford to dissipate the energies they need to intensify their life-energy in order to attain a permanent higher state of consciousness.

This is why asceticism is necessary: as a way of taming our desires so that they no longer create disturbance inside us and no longer consume as much energy. Taming the 'body of desire' can permanently close – or at least reduce – a major channel through which our life-energy drains away. Gandhi led an ascetic lifestyle because he believed that control of the body intensified what he called 'soul-force'. Similarly, Paul Brunton recognized that the ascetic discipline 'was given to beginners who had renounced the world, and who needed to economise all their forces, all their *vital life substance,* for this one purpose they had set themselves'.[5] (Here Brunton is also suggesting – as I have just done – that asceticism is only an introductory part of the spiritual path, which can be abandoned as soon as the 'body of desire' has been tamed and a new 'distribution of energy' has been achieved.)

Perhaps, however, this energy-intensifying effect of asceticism is best described by the early Catholic mystic Gregory of Nyssa, who uses the metaphor of water running upwards through a pipe:

We often see water, contained in a pipe, bursting upward through this constraining force, which will not let it leak, and this in spite of its natural gravitation; in the same way the mind of man, enclosed in the compact channel of an habitual continence, and not having any side issues, will be raised by nature of its natural powers of motion to an exalted love.[6]

This also shows the connection between a high level of life-energy and a state of awakening.

In the Indian traditions, this connection between asceticism and energy is even clearer. Even before the formulation of the path of Yoga, asceticism was used as a method of transforming consciousness in ancient India. It was called *tapas* (literally 'heat'), and usually meant being celibate, controlling your desires and instincts and avoiding pleasures. *Tapas* is mentioned in the *Rig-Veda*, India's oldest religious text (first written down around 1500 BCE), which describes how the practise generates 'an inner heat' that leads to states of ecstasy, visions of gods and psychic powers.

Indian yogis tell us that the purpose of this asceticism is to conserve and transmute energy. Frustrating the body's desires and instincts fills us with spiritual radiance and vitality and generates a numinous energy called *ojas* which pervades the whole of the body and mind. The twentieth-century yogi Swami Prabhavananda defined *tapas* as 'the practise of conserving energy and directing it toward the goal of yoga ... obviously, in order to do this, we must exercise self-discipline; we must control our physical appetites and passions'.[7]

After the tradition of Yoga developed (from around 500 BCE), *tapas* continued as a separate tradition, but was also incorporated into Yoga itself. (Incidentally, I should make it clear that Yoga in the sense I'm using the term here doesn't refer to the physical exercises of yoga, but to the ancient path of self-development of which *asanas* are just one part.) Yoga was first systematized by the ancient sage Patanjali, in his 'eight-limbed' path. He included *tapas* as an essential observance and recommended such practises as prolonged standing, fasting, bearing cold and heat, and prolonged silence. The purpose of this, as he states in his *Yoga Sutras*, is to generate vitality (*virya*).

However, Indian asceticism was rarely as severe as the Christian kind. *Tapas* certainly doesn't mean inflicting pain on yourself and injuring the body. The *Bhagavad-Gita* recommends the same path of moderation as Buddhism, stating that 'Yoga is not for the excessive eater, nor for one who avoids food too intently, not for one addicted to excessive sleep, nor to excessive wakefulness.'[8] Despite recommending some austere practises, Patanjali himself stresses that the purpose of *tapas* is not to harm the body, but to make it stronger and healthier: 'From *tapas*, with the decline of impurity, comes the powers of the body and the organs, and excellence of the body consists of correct form, beauty, strength, and very firm well-knittedness or great energy.'[9]

CELIBACY

The practise of celibacy is at the core of the ascetic tradition. Monastic traditions have always seen abstaining from sex and attempting to become free of sexual thoughts and desires as a prerequisite of spiritual development.

As with asceticism in general, it's easy to see this as an expression of aversion to the body, an unhealthy impulse to repress 'base' sexual instincts. After all, what could be more natural and healthy than sex? And what could be more neurotic than to suppress our sexual urges?

It's true, of course, that some religious teachers, such as St Augustine and many other early Christian teachers, did harbour disgust towards sex and the body and advocate celibacy as a way of avoiding the 'uncleanness' of our 'base animal instincts'. But again, celibacy doesn't *necessarily* entail a hostile attitude to the body. The main reason why the practise has always been so widespread is simply because, if practised in the right way, it can have a spiritual effect, helping to intensify and still life-energy. This is simply a matter of economics of energy. Sexual desire is the most powerful force that moves through us and so can consume a lot of our life-energy. And so if you can manage to conserve this energy, there will be a massive inner intensification of life-energy.

Indian spiritual traditions explicitly state that this is the purpose of *brahmacarya* – chastity or celibacy. In the words of the English scholar of Yoga Ernest Wood, celibacy 'leads to a sublimation of the bodily energy, which would otherwise have been expended wastefully, into the functions and powers of the higher mind'.[10] Or, as Swami Prabhavananda puts it, 'Sexual activity, and the thoughts and fantasies of sex, use up a great portion of our vital force. When that force is conserved through abstinence, it becomes subliminated as spiritual energy.'[11]

The problem is that this has to be done very carefully; it's not just a simple matter of taking a vow of celibacy and trying to distract yourself from sexual thoughts every time they occur. Sexual energy *has* to be transmuted, not repressed. One of the problems with celibacy in the Christian tradition is that monks and priests usually aren't offered any methods of containing or transforming their sexual energies. They're expected to remain celibate just through their own will-power or with the help of God. Practised in this way, celibacy doesn't make you more spiritual at all. Rather than being channelled into the 'higher mind', the energy remains latent as sexual energy inside us and has to express itself somehow – usually in unwholesome ways, as illustrated by the recent scandals involving paedophile Catholic priests. On the other hand, even if you do manage to contain your sexual desires, this repression is likely to generate hostility and aggression – towards other people in general, but particularly towards women and the human body itself. (This partly accounts for the hysterically anti-female and anti-physical attitude of many early Christian teachers.) In Indian traditions, however, there are recognized methods of transmuting sexual energy, including diet and certain yoga postures, to help ensure that this doesn't occur.

Again, it's important to emphasize that, like asceticism itself, celibacy doesn't have to be permanent. Indian traditions often see *brahmacarya* as a temporary energy-conserving measure, a phase of 'spiritual training' which is necessary at the beginning of the spiritual path or at times when the seeker needs to move to a new stage of development.

RENUNCIATION AND DETACHMENT

Another major feature of the spiritual paths that adepts have taken throughout history is *renunciation*. In every culture spiritual seekers have turned away from the everyday world of work and family and chosen to live in the forest, desert or monastery, ridding themselves of all possessions and relinquishing ambitions or interests of their own. In almost all spiritual traditions, adepts are expected to practise 'voluntary poverty', to have a bare minimum of possessions, not to own any property and to live without any unnecessary comforts and luxuries. They are expected to make spiritual development the only goal of their life and not to have 'worldly ambitions' for fame, success or power.

Many people find this renunciation as unnatural and repulsive as asceticism. After all, why should there be any distinction between the spiritual and the mundane? Surely every aspect of our life, including business, food and relationships, offers the opportunity for spiritual growth? Like asceticism, renunciation has been seen as part of the 'ascending' world-rejecting tradition which posits an artificial duality between matter and spirit. And, as the Integral Philosophy developed by Ken Wilber suggests, making spiritual development the only goal of our life surely means neglecting other aspects of our being. If you spend all your time in solitude in a forest, meditating 16 hours a day, you may reach a more spiritual state, but what good will it do you if you can't cook a meal or communicate with other people, or if your body is so weak that you can't run a few yards without getting out of breath?

Another problem is that it may not actually be possible to become stabilized at a permanent state of wakefulness while there are other areas of your being that are seriously underdeveloped and need attention. This mal-development is likely to lead to problems which work against the progress you've made on a spiritual level. For example, if you have poor social skills, at some point you'll experience embarrassment and isolation. And if you are emotionally immature, you'll have difficulties if you begin a sexual relationship. These situations will create emotional disturbances which will stop you developing any inner stillness and serenity.

Once again, however, there isn't *necessarily* anything life-denying about renunciation. It's simply another 'energy-conserving' measure to try to generate an intense concentration of life-energy. In the last chapter we saw how awakening experiences can occur when our attachment to psychological constructs and to external things, such as possessions and other people, dissolves away. And this is the basic principle of renunciation. By renouncing the world, adepts are trying to consciously cultivate a state of detachment in order to retain and intensify the 'powers of the soul'. We saw how a prolonged period of intense turmoil can permanently dissolve attachments and so lead to a state of permanent wakefulness. And, in a sense, adepts who practise renunciation are trying to follow the same process – with the important difference that they're making themselves suffer *consciously*.

This underlying purpose of detachment was noted by Evelyn Underhill, who describes it as a process of 'stripping or purging away of those superfluous, unreal, and harmful things which dissipate the precious energies of the self'.[12] The practise of 'voluntary poverty', for example, can be seen as a method of stopping our thoughts being occupied and our energies drained by possessions. Meister Eckhart's point (quoted in Chapter 8) that being attached to possessions dissipates 'the powers of the soul' applies here. Similarly, Underhill notes that possessions 'are a drain upon the energy of the self, preventing her from attaining that more intense life for which she was made'.[13] The same can be said for our attachment to success and status, ambitions or other people.

However, like asceticism, renunciation is ideally only a temporary measure. It's a training process by which the adept learns to free themselves from attachments, to exist without them, and eventually reaches a state of self-sufficient wholeness and well-being. In fact, it's difficult to separate asceticism and renunciation, since they're almost always undertaken together. They are processes directed to a particular end: a release from what Underhill calls 'the tyranny of selfhood' and from the dominance (and energy monopolization) of our lower, hedonistic impulses and our psychological attachments. As Underhill writes of detachment, 'It is a process, an education directed towards the production of a definite kind of efficiency... [These disciplines] do release the self from the pull of the lower nature, establish it on new levels of freedom and power.'[14]

In the Christian mystical tradition, detachment and asceticism – or 'purgation' – traditionally led to a stage of 'illumination', the point when the mystic first awakened to the divine reality. Illumination is roughly equivalent to a medium level of wakefulness, featuring a heightened awareness of the phenomenal world, awareness of spirit-force (or the radiance of God, as the Christian mystics would have termed it) and a constant sense of inner joy or ecstasy. Some mystics ended their development there, but for others illumination was followed by a terrible phase of desolation and depression, traditionally called 'the Dark Night of the Soul'. During this phase the mystic felt abandoned by the divine, as if, in Meister Eckhart's words, 'there were a wall erected between Him and us'.[15] They felt empty and arid inside, full of self-hatred and contempt for the world.

However, as Underhill points out, the Dark Night of the Soul is actually a process of *further* detachment, a 'last and drastic purgation of the spirit'.[16] The mystic has already broken his or her psychological attachment to external things and now they have to break their attachment to *themselves,* to their own individuality and ego. If they do this, they will reach the *final* stage of the mystical path: union, or deification, when they don't just *see* God in the world, but become one with Him.

NON-ATTACHMENT TO ACTIONS

Another aspect of renunciation is non-attachment to your actions or to the events of your life. Many spiritual teachers have told us that we shouldn't let ourselves be affected by external events, that we shouldn't be moved to joy or sorrow or anger or any other emotion by what's happening around us but instead attain a state of serenity which is constant and independent of the external world. For example, the *Bhagavad-Gita* tells us that the ideal person is 'the same in pleasure and pain; to whom gold or stones or earth are one, and what is pleasing or displeasing leaves him in peace; who is beyond both praise and blame, and whose mind is steady and quiet'.[17]

Many people find this mental detachment a little off-putting too. It seems a little cold and inhuman. Surely it's natural to be affected by events, to be happy when good things happen to you or to be sad when you get some bad news?

But there are two reasons for this detachment. One is that if we feel strong desires and emotions like anger and fear, it creates disturbance inside us and so makes it impossible to develop the inner stillness we need to experience wakefulness. We need to develop equanimity in order to maintain an ISLE state.

The other reason is that being affected by external events is a sign that we are psychologically attached to them. When we become angry or disappointed it usually means that we're depending on something external for our well-being, that we're attached to hopes for the future or to possessions or status, or the affection and attention of other people.

For example, if you feel disappointed when a publisher rejects your novel it means that you're attached to the hope of being a famous writer. Or if you feel angry because a colleague at work criticizes you, it means that you're dependent on the image other people have of you and need to feel respected. This works the other way round too — if you let yourself be too carried away when good things happen (for example, if your book is accepted by a publisher or if a colleague compliments you), it's also a sign that you're psychologically dependent on ambitions and other people.

From a spiritual point of view, it's more ideal to react with equanimity, to react to both negative and positive occurrences simply by smiling inwardly and telling yourself, 'Oh well, it would have been nice but...' or 'Oh well, that's good, but it's not such a big deal really.' This detachment doesn't mean being dead inside and feeling nothing – on the contrary, it means that your life-energy is always intensified and still so that you constantly experience its blissful quality and are filled with joy and serenity.

TAMING THE EGO THROUGH SERVICE

It's difficult to separate any of this from the effort to tame the *ego* as well. Of course, monks and spiritual seekers do this directly through long periods of meditation and prayer. But you could say that this is the indirect purpose of renunciation and asceticism too. As we saw in Chapter 7, our ego structure is largely made up of our attachments – our hopes, beliefs, knowledge, image of ourselves as belonging to a certain gender, class or culture, our achievements, possessions, and so on. And so when we detach ourselves from these *accoutrements*, we also slowly weaken the ego.

This is also probably true of asceticism to some extent. To a large degree, our desires are the result of a sense of lack and psychic disharmony caused by our strong ego structure. For example, the desire to acquire material possessions or to gain status and success can be seen as a way of trying to override the basic sense of insignificance and incompleteness generated by our ego isolation. We feel a basic sense of lack because our strong ego structures separate us from the cosmos, and so we use possessions and status to try to *complete* ourselves, to try to make ourselves significant and important. Our physical needs are often amplified by the ego as well. Sex and food are natural desires, but once they're channelled through the ego they become much more complex and usually much more intense. For example, a man who tries to make as many sexual conquests as he can may be trying to sustain a sense of power or status, while an attractive woman might use her beauty to flirt with as many men as possible, without necessarily having sex with them, to boost her self-esteem. It's also possible that someone might overeat or have a poor diet because they're using food as a source of hedonistic happiness to try to override their inner discontent. And so, since these desires largely stem from the ego, taming them may also have the indirect effect of weakening the ego.

Many spiritual traditions advise us to tame the ego through *service*. This may mean serving God, the poor, the sick, or even, in a more abstract sense, the world as a whole. In terms of taming the ego, service is important because it means subsuming our own desires to those of others. You put their needs before yours and so become less egocentric. At the same time, it weakens the ego because it transcends separation. It means reaching out beyond the walls of your ego and connecting with other people, empathizing with and even *becoming* them. In fact, as we saw at the beginning of Chapter 2, this connection isn't just with another person or other people, but with something greater than any individual. Once your ego boundaries have faded away through service, you may make contact with a dimension beyond human individuality, a shared network of being, where you feel a natural sense of empathy for *all* human beings. As Arthur Deikman writes, 'Service is probably the most effective activity for providing access to the connectedness of reality.'[18]

This is why the idea of service is an important part of Christian spirituality, including tending to the sick and feeling compassion for the oppressed and weak. This is also the aim of the Indian path of *Bhakti Yoga,* which emphasizes devotion and service to God or the Supreme. This devotion helps you to transcend your own desires, until the boundaries of your self fade away and you become one with the divine.

THE END OF THE SPIRITUAL PATH

And so, after years of spiritual training, the seeker may have engineered a permanent inner transformation, a new psychic organization with a new distribution of energy. At this point, in Evelyn Underhill's words, 'All the energy of a strong nature flows freely in the new channels.'[19] Or, as we would say, the life-energy of their being has become permanently intensified and stilled.

Renunciation and asceticism have served their purpose now; there's no need to continue with them in the same way that there's no need to carry on doing an apprenticeship once you've learned the skill properly and are qualified. At this point it's common for mystics to give up renunciation and return to the everyday world, where they're usually extremely active.

Henry de Suso, the German mystic whose ascetic practises I described in Chapter 4, reached this stage after 16 years of asceticism and renunciation. Quite suddenly, he gave up his ascetic lifestyle and never returned to it. He spent the rest of his life as a preacher, writer and reformer, travelling around central and northern Europe.

In a similar but less systematic way, St Teresa of Avila's 18-year-long spiritual struggle finally ended around the age of 39, when she had a 'second conversion' which gave her a constant mystical awareness. From that point on, she lived a life of frenetic activity. She founded 17 convents, wrote several books and thousands of letters, and almost single-handedly brought about a religious revival throughout Spain.

The spiritual training of Henry de Suso and St Teresa was unusually long compared to others, though. The fourteenth-century Italian mystic St Catherine of Siena, for example, only needed to spend three years living as a hermit and an ascetic before undergoing permanent transformation. At that point she abandoned her solitude and was active in society for the rest of her life, teaching, serving the poor and the sick and trying to bring peace to the warring states of Italy.

Similarly, her fifteenth-century compatriot and namesake Catherine of Genoa spent four years living as an ascetic, wearing a hair cloth, never eating fruit or meat and praying six hours a day. But after these four years, as her nineteenth-century biographer writes, 'Her mind became clear and free, and so filled with God that nothing else ever entered into it.'[20] From this point on, she was extremely active as a theologian and nurse, tending to the sick and the poor of Genoa and eventually becoming the manager and treasurer of the city hospital.

All of these mystics presumably reached a stage where they had tamed their desires and their ego and freed themselves from attachments and so created a permanent ISLE state.

THE PATHS OF YOGA AND TANTRA

Since spiritual development has always been a prominent part of Indian culture, it's not surprising that the spiritual paths from Indian traditions are the most detailed and systematic in the world. Perhaps the most systematic and detailed of all is the 'eight-limbed' path of Yoga developed by the sage Patanjali.

Patanjali, sometimes known as the 'father of Yoga', is an enigmatic figure. We know nothing about him apart from that he may have lived during the second century CE and was probably the head of a Yoga school. It's likely that, rather than actually devising the eight-limbed path himself, he simply recorded and explicated a tradition that was already established.

The eight-limbed path is a system of spiritual training with eight stages of practise and development which the *yogin* has to move through in order to reach a state of permanent *samadhi*. The stages are progressive, and it's impossible to move to a higher level without first having mastered a lower one. This path can be interpreted as a long-term effort to progressively still and intensify life-energy, leading to a permanent ISLE state.

The first two steps of the path of Yoga are *niyama* and *yama,* normally translated as 'restraint' and 'discipline'. *Niyama* involves renunciation, being celibate (or at least controlling your sexual desire to some degree) and being free of possessions. At the same time the *yogin* has to regulate their behaviour, refraining from violence, theft and dishonesty. *Yama* is the ascetic stage of the path, including *tapas*, also purity (in terms of bathing, diet and clothing), contentment and the study of sacred texts. The scholar of Yoga Georg Feuerstein hints at the energy-conserving purpose of these practises when he notes that they are 'intended to check the powerful survival instinct and rechannel it to serve a higher purpose'.[21]

Once the *yogin* has mastered these stages, he or she begins to practise *asanas*, which Patanjali recommends as a method of removing tension inside the body and quieting the mind, so leading to better powers of concentration. After this, they practise techniques of *pranayama*, or breath control, which, in Feuerstein's words, are a way of 'energizing the inner continuum'. The *yogin* slows down and deepens his or her breathing and also uses concentration exercises, and this leads to greater calmness and clarity and even stronger powers of concentration.

After these four levels, the *yogin* is ready to move within, to enter the world of their consciousness and practise 'sense-withdrawal'. They learn to rest comfortably within their own mind, without any sensory input. Then they begin the practise of concentration, training the mind to become so focused on an object that all thought ceases and their life-energy becomes completely still. This prepares them for the seventh stage, meditation proper, when they learn to completely empty their mind and yet at the same time remain highly alert and conscious. And finally, after progressing through these seven stages, they are ready to ascend to the peak of *samadhi,* a permanent higher state of consciousness in which they transcend duality and experience themselves as a part of the spiritual essence of the universe.

We could say, therefore, that the first three stages of Yoga deal mainly with conserving life-energy through self-discipline and renunciation and stilling the mind through controlling desires. The higher levels mainly deal with stilling the mind, or 'restricting the whirls of consciousness', in Patanjali's phrase, until life-energy becomes completely concentrated and stilled. At the end of the path, when every outflow of life-energy is closed and every disturbance has been stilled, a state of *samadhi* is attained.

In the Tantric traditions of Hinduism and Buddhism this relationship between spiritual development and energy is even more explicit. I've mentioned Tantra before, in connection with sex and *kundalini,* the powerful source of energy at the bottom of the spine. The concept of *kundalini* comes from Tantra, as does that of the *chakras.* Tantra began to flourish around the fourth century CE as a reaction against the world-denying attitude of traditional Yoga and Buddhism.[22] Its main principle is that there is no duality between matter and spirit or between the human body and the spirit. The whole world is infused with spiritual energy and is therefore sacred and divine. This applies to the human body too. All parts of the body and all physical process are sacred, including sex. Sexual union is a fusion of the male and female energies which created the universe, *shiva* and *shakti,* and so both partners – at least if they follow the correct sexual procedures – can experience the bliss of ultimate reality.

In Tantra, our own life-energy is seen as an inflow of the spiritual energy of the universe. Tantric practitioners try to harness and channel this divine energy in order to reach higher states of consciousness. They try to increase their 'bioenergetic volume' – *thigle* in Tibetan Buddhism – by undoing the 'knots' which block the flow of energy through their being. The goal is to raise as much energy as possible to the higher *chakras,* which are associated with higher states of consciousness. Tantric adepts practise visualization (of the different *chakras*), meditation techniques, fasting and *kundalini* yoga in order to accomplish this.

In other words, the goal of Tantra is to attain a permanent ISLE state. And significantly, one of the principles of Tantra is that every temporary higher state of consciousness gives us the opportunity to undergo permanent transformation. When our 'bioenergetic volume' becomes temporarily high – as a result of meditation, for example – we can practise certain techniques (certain Yoga postures or visualizations, for example) which permanently dissolve the knots that block our energy flow through the central channel of the *chakras.* As a result, energy flows through our being completely freely, through to the highest *chakras,* and we are permanently awake.[23]

Interestingly, the modern philosopher Michael Washburn's view of spiritual development has some parallels with these Tantric teachings and with my own views. Washburn also sees spiritual development in energetic terms. According to him, we normally experience ourselves as an isolated ego, separate from the world and from our own body, and alienated from the 'Dynamic Ground' – Washburn's term for the spiritual source of our being. This state comes about through what Washburn calls 'primal repression'. As we grow into adults, we repress the Dynamic Ground, lose touch with its rich and radiant energy, and become 'housed' in the cramped space of the ego.

As Washburn sees it, the aim of spiritual practise is to undo this repression, so that the dormant energy of the psyche can sweep through us again and we can regain contact with the Ground. In our normal state, the *nadis* (that is, the channels through which *prana* or life-energy flows) are blocked by repression, but as primal repression is undone, the blockages dissolve. Powerful currents of energy flow through us, filling us with well-being or bliss. This energy heightens our perceptions and feelings and, in Washburn's words, 'gradually reveals itself to be – or to be the access to – the Sacred Ground, the Fertile Void, the Formless Godhead'.[24]

THE MONASTIC LIFE

However, perhaps the most direct method of trying to generate a permanent ISLE state is not through any particular spiritual path but through the monastic lifestyle. Almost every aspect of the monastic life – whether Buddhist, Hindu, Christian or any other tradition – is expressly designed to bring about a permanent ISLE state. Monks usually live simply and austerely, with a bare minimum of pleasures. They renounce possessions and worldly ambitions, are celibate and spend long periods meditating or praying. And, perhaps just as importantly, they surround themselves with quietness and have long periods of silence and solitude.

Some monastic traditions are fairly moderate. For example, Catholic Benedictine monks, who live the way of life established by St Benedict 1,500 years ago, live a simple life of detachment without being at all ascetic. They have no personal possessions, are celibate and have designated periods for prayer, meditation, silence and study. However, they have a great deal of contact with each other and a degree of contact with the outside world. They do around six hours of manual work every day, have a healthy diet (they're even allowed to drink wine) and are free to sleep as much as they like. Buddhist monastic traditions are usually fairly moderate too, in keeping with the Buddha's teaching of the Middle Way. Monks often spend three or four hours a day in meditation (both alone and in groups) and have two communal services a day, where they chant or recite *sutras*. They also do several hours' manual work a day and have a simple but healthy diet.

It's easy to see how this way of life could have an energy-intensifying and stilling effect. On a temporary basis, the general quietness, the periods of silence and solitude and the prayer and meditation would certainly reduce the normal outflow of life-energy and its disturbance, and so generate an ongoing ISLE state. Renunciation would help too, by weakening – or perhaps even dissolving – psychological attachments. And at some point, the detachment, self-discipline, meditation and prayer could lead to a permanent ISLE state.

However, other monastic traditions are much more severe. For example, Carthusian monks spend most of the day alone in tiny cells in a cloister, only coming together three times a day at church. Even then they're not allowed to speak to each other; they can only talk twice a week, once on Sundays after lunch and once on Mondays during a communal walk. They don't do any manual work and have no contact with the outside world.

Again, this lifestyle would certainly generate both ongoing and permanent ISLE states. (As we saw in Chapter 6, the German film-maker Philip Groening was affected in this way when he lived in a Swiss Carthusian monastery for six months). However, it's also easy to see how the constant silence and solitude and the neglect of important human needs such as communication and relationships could cause serious psychological problems. The need for interaction with other human beings is even more fundamental than the need for sex – and perhaps even more important, in that sex is something we only need periodically, whereas we need interaction on an almost constant basis. And so the awakening effect of this lifestyle would very likely have a 'shadow' side of psychological deterioration.

In fact, this is true of any monastic tradition, and of renunciation and asceticism in general. It's difficult to see how you could live the life of a monk – even in a fairly integrated tradition such as the Benedictine – without neglecting other important areas of development. As I suggested above, a monk might be able to reach a permanent state of wakefulness, but find – especially if he leaves the monastery and re-enters the everyday world – that this can easily be offset by psychological or emotional problems.

This is why, as I've pointed out, it's important to think of the monastic lifestyle as a kind of spiritual training which should only be undertaken for a certain amount of time. In my view, monks shouldn't live apart from the world for their whole lives; once they've completed their spiritual training and hopefully attained a degree of permanent wakefulness, they should return to the everyday world, like St Teresa and the St Catherines. At best, monasteries and nunneries should be seen as 'spiritual universities' which people attend in order to try to transform their being and leave as soon as they have done so. At that point, they should immerse themselves in everyday life again and attend to the social, emotional, sexual and other needs they've neglected, to correct any imbalance in their development.

MY OWN PERSPECTIVE

I hope I've made it clear that I'm not advocating a retreat from the world, or implying that everyday life is opposed to spirituality. I hold the non-dualist view that there's no distinction between spirit and the world, and that in principle every act of our life – from eating to washing the dishes, sex and socializing – is sacred and spiritual. In my view the best arena for spiritual development isn't a monastery but the everyday world, so that you can avoid – at least to some degree – the danger of unbalanced development.

However, this doesn't change the fact that a period of detachment and self-discipline may be necessary for spiritual development. A person who wants to reach a permanent ISLE state may need to undergo a period of training, of 'taming' their ego and their appetites and desires and weakening their psychological attachments through renunciation. This doesn't mean going to the extremes of the ascetics – it may only mean following the Middle Way which Buddhism recommends, halfway between hedonism and asceticism. According to this, we should avoid excessive desires and excessive activity, but not go to the extreme of punishing the body or neglecting other areas of our development.

On a personal note, I should also say that I went through a period of asceticism and detachment myself. This started when I was 20 years old and at university. I felt a strong impulse to isolate myself from the people around me – so much so that I stopped going to lectures, cut myself off from people I'd become friendly with and spent almost all my time alone. After a few months in a shared flat, I moved into a bedsit on my own and hardly had any social contact. I stayed up late, usually until four o'clock in the morning, to enjoy the solitude and the quietness outside.

At the time I had no idea why I was doing this – it was just impulsive. I knew almost nothing about mysticism and spirituality. But in retrospect it's clear that I was going through a process of detachment, trying to make myself free of psychological dependencies. I tried to live without any attachments whatsoever. I lived without any possessions apart from clothes and books. Even though I loved playing and listening to music, I left my guitars at my parents' house 100 miles away and didn't have a record or tape player. I also left my portable TV at my parents' and never read newspapers or magazines. I often went days without speaking to anyone except shopkeepers. Sometimes I felt incredibly lonely and I began to lose my social skills, so that after a few months I found it impossible to hold a conversation with anyone I didn't know well.

I also felt a strong impulse to subject myself to pain and discomfort. In my shared flat we only had two beds for three rooms, but I didn't mind; I slept on the floor in my sleeping bag. It was winter, but I never had the heating on in my room. I slept with the windows wide open in November and December and often spent my time in the room with my top off. I had cold showers and cold baths, and sometimes in the middle of the night I'd force myself to go on long bike rides (on my flatmate's bike), pedalling as hard as I could until I was exhausted and almost fainted. On a few occasions I went further and put my fingers into candle flames for a second or two until the first sharp jolt of pain shot through me.

At the time I didn't know anything about the ascetic practises of Christian mystics. But looking back now I can see that I was trying to develop powers of self-control and self-discipline. I felt that there was a part of me that was lazy and weak and that I had to gain control over. My philosophy was 'If the weak part of me is afraid of doing something, then I'll make myself do it.' So, as well as subjecting myself to pain and discomfort, I did exactly as St John of the Cross recommended and forced myself to do a lot of things which disgusted me, such as drinking my own urine and allowing spiders to crawl over me. It seems absurd to me now, but I somehow felt that I had to do these things in order to make myself mentally stronger.

One purpose of this life of renunciation was, I believe, to strip myself down, to remove the influences I'd absorbed through my upbringing so that I could find out who I really was. I was trying to rid myself of external things so that I could find my own essence. My upbringing had turned me into a certain type of person, but I sensed that this wasn't the person I essentially was.

Even though I'd stopped going to lectures, I still went to the occasional seminar at university (at one point I was threatened with expulsion unless I started attending more) and somehow managed to finish the course with a degree. Then I returned to Manchester, my home city, and continued to follow a life of detachment and asceticism, although not as intensely. I took a series of low-paid menial jobs, working as a warehouse porter, in a chip shop and as a postman, lived in a bedsit with no electricity and cooked my meals on a camping stove. However, I no longer inflicted pain on myself, and although I spent most of my time alone, I had some contact with friends and family.

About a year after I'd left university, I started to move into a more optimistic and positive phase. I began to have regular awakening experiences (the first example in the introduction dates from this time), with strong feelings of euphoria and peace and serenity. I reached a plateau of fairly constant – if low-intensity – wakefulness. After working as a postman, I took my low-paid office job at the Social Security and despite its dreariness, I felt happier than ever before. Most mornings I cycled through the meadows to work and was amazed by the beauty of the fields and trees, the sun and the clouds and the sky. There was a cemetery on the way and I always felt inspired by the fact that I was alive at that moment when I could have been dead. I still loved to stay up late at night, and would sometimes go for walks in the early hours of the morning, when the streets were completely deserted. A feeling of serenity would fill me as I walked and still be inside me when I went to sleep.

This was the time when I discovered spirituality, after buying the wonderful anthology and study *Mysticism* by F. C. Happold. I also discovered the beautiful and serene spiritual music of Van Morrison's 1980s albums and the poetry of Walt Whitman and D. H. Lawrence. All of these inspired me and intensified the serenity and ecstasy I felt inside.

At the time I didn't make a connection between these experiences and my period of renunciation and detachment. It was only several years later – in fact, when I was writing my first (unpublished) book on spiritual development – that I realized that they were probably linked. These spiritual feelings were probably the fruits of my renunciation and asceticism. After about two years of that lifestyle – including about a year of following it intensely – it seems that I had broken some of my psychological attachments and developed a degree of control over my 'body of desire'. I had brought about a permanent psychological change. I had, it seems, reduced the outflow of my life-energy and developed an ongoing ISLE state.

I remained on this plateau of mild wakefulness for about three years, until other factors intervened. I became a musician and moved to Germany, as I described in the introduction. At first it was an exhilarating experience and I retained my inner well-being and sense of beauty and wonder, but I had a difficult relationship with my girlfriend which affected my self-esteem and filled my life with turbulence. I couldn't speak any German when I arrived, and although I learned quite quickly, I often felt isolated and unable to communicate my thoughts properly. I also felt a general sense of alienation because everything about the culture I was living in was so different from my own. It was eastern Germany, just a couple of years after the Wall had come down, and 44 years of communism had imprinted themselves everywhere. People knew nothing about the spiritual issues I was interested in. There were no meditation groups, no esoteric study groups and no mind, body, spirit sections in bookshops. As a result I lost touch with my true self and began to live a hedonistic lifestyle. I fell away from that plateau of wakefulness into frustration and discontent.

In retrospect, the problem was that my development wasn't 'integral' enough. I was experiencing the same problem that the monastic life can cause: I may have been well developed spiritually, but in other areas I was underdeveloped. I was lacking in self-confidence, had a deep-rooted sense of inferiority and insecurity, and was emotionally immature. When I was living in Germany, I began to experience problems in these areas which offset the wakefulness I'd developed.

However, five years later, after my return to England, I started to meditate regularly, got into a healthier and more fulfilling relationship (with the woman who is now my wife), and began to regain my confidence and my equilibrium. I began to work on the 'lines' of development – in Ken Wilber's phrase – that I'd neglected and this time my spiritual development moved in parallel with my overall development. I started to have regular awakening experiences again and to regain a fairly constant sense of well-being. And eventually I found myself moving towards a plateau of fairly constant low-intensity wakefulness again.

I still try to live as simply as possible and still enjoy spending time in solitude and quietness, but I've never returned to fully fledged renunciation or asceticism. There is no need to. I feel that time was a period of necessary spiritual training which transformed my being in such a way that I've been able to experience a degree of wakefulness ever since.

Ultimately, this is what any form of spiritual development is about: restructuring our own being by taming our desires and the ego and freeing ourselves from attachments so that we can intensify and still our life-energy. I've hopefully shown that all spiritual paths or all systems of spiritual training can be interpreted as an effort to create a permanent ISLE state. This state can be ongoing, when it's an effect of your lifestyle and environment. For example, if you decide to go to live in a monastery for two months you'll probably experience an ongoing state of wakefulness (as some of the participants in the TV programme *The Monastery* did). But once you return to the disturbances and energy-draining demands of everyday life this may quickly fade away.

On the other hand, an ISLE state can be truly permanent. This is when you undergo a real psychological shift, when the structures of your psyche permanently change and you remain awake, whatever the conditions around you are.

We're going to look at spiritual development in a more direct way in the last chapter of this book, examining what we should do as individuals to move towards a permanent state of wakefulness.

10

THE WAY TO
WAKEFULNESS

Now that we're moving towards the end of this book, it's probably a good idea to look back at some of the ground we've covered. In this section, I'd like to briefly state and summarize some of the most important points, adding a few explanatory notes.

The normal consciousness with which we experience this world does not give us an objective and reliable picture of the world. This normal consciousness is really a kind of 'sleep'.

We are in the cave, looking at the shadows on the wall. Our vision of an inanimate, separate and indifferent world isn't objective, in the same way that a blurred picture from a faulty camera isn't a true image. This vision is the product of our psyche, of the mechanisms and structures of our mind, in the same way that the type of picture a camera produces is the result of its inner mechanism. Our psyche is structured in such a way that it hides the is-ness and harmony of the world from us. It also creates an illusion of separation, when in reality we are part of a great ocean of being which transcends the boundaries of matter and pervades all space.

The biggest mistake we can make – which most of us do make – is to believe that the view of the world that our normal psyche creates is true. Unfortunately many of our leading scientists and intellectuals make this mistake, taking their perceptions at face value and so believing that the inanimate, separate and apparently mechanistic world we perceive is absolute reality. But this is really only an extreme form of 'naïve realism'.

It's also a kind of arrogance. The underlying assumption is that we human beings are completely conscious, that our awareness of reality is complete. But there must be levels of reality beyond our awareness, in the same way that there are levels of reality beyond the awareness of an insect or a sheep. We are aware of more reality than insects and animals, and in the same way in the future evolution will surely produce beings – perhaps even human beings – who are aware of more reality than we presently are.

Higher states of consciousness are a temporary awakening from this sleep.

In higher states of consciousness, or awakening experiences, we realize that our normal vision of the world is incomplete and delusory. The world around us comes to life and is filled with a sense of meaning and harmony, and we feel a powerful sense of inner well-being. We become aware that the whole world is pervaded with spirit-force (*brahman*), spilling over the boundaries between things and folding everything into oneness. We become one with this force and therefore one with all things. And at the highest intensity of awakening, absolute awakening, the whole material world melts away and there is nothing but an impossibly powerful and radiant and harmonious force which is the 'Ground' of the universe, the essential reality.

Indigenous peoples and possibly prehistoric peoples may have lived in a naturally awakened state.

Indigenous peoples seemed to possess many of the characteristics of low- to medium-intensity awakening experiences as their normal state (and in some cases still do today). To them nature was alive and they were aware of a 'Great Spirit' or 'soul-force' pervading the world, making all things sacred. We seem to have lost their naturally spiritual state due to the overdevelopment of our ego. In this sense, higher states of consciousness are normal and our 'normal' state of consciousness is really sub-normal.

In a similar way, we've seen that the low-intensity awakened state of young children is lost as the ego becomes overdeveloped in us as individuals.

Awakening experiences have two different sources. They can be caused by a disruption of homoeostasis or by an intensification and stilling of life-energy.

States of homoeostasis disruption (HD states) can be produced by fasting, sleep deprivation, drugs, pain and breathing exercises. Intensification and stilling of life-energy (ISLE) states can be produced intentionally through meditation, but also happen accidentally through contact with the natural world, sex, listening to music, sports and relaxation. *Kundalini, satsang* and near-death experiences can also give rise to ISLE states. In addition, they can occur when psychological attachments are dissolved as a result of suffering and turmoil.

HD and ISLE states are both valid as awakening experiences, although HD states have some disadvantages (for example, they are dangerous to the mind and body and can't lead to a permanently awakened state) and are not as complete as ISLE states.

Higher states of consciousness can occur accidentally but are usually triggered by certain conditions or activities. This means that they can be consciously generated.

This is one of the most important points of this book. *If we know why awakening experiences occur – both in terms of the external circumstances that give rise to them and the psychological changes that these circumstances cause – then we don't have to wait for them.* We can make a conscious effort to create those circumstances and produce those psychological changes. We can *choose* to be awake.

More precisely, since we know that that awakening experiences are produced by ISLE states, we simply need to generate ISLE states – by meditating, contact with nature, periods of inactivity and quietness, listening to music or watching a dance performance with complete attention and no thought-chatter, and so on.

Long-term spiritual development is a process of permanently intensifying and stilling life-energy.

Long-term spiritual development – traditionally including practises such as asceticism, renunciation and detachment, meditation and service – is a process of trying to reduce or close outflows of energy so that we can build up a permanently high level of life-energy. At the same time, it's a process of stilling the disturbance of thoughts, emotions and desires so that we can create a permanent state of inner stillness. In other words, it's a long-term effort to create a new psychic organization in which we don't give away all our energy in the maintenance of our strong ego structure through the constant thought-chatter in our mind, the storms of emotion that erupt inside us, the constant desires that surge through us and the psychological attachments we have. We may reach a point where we permanently shift to this state, where there is always a high concentration of life-energy inside us and our being is always essentially empty and still. At this point we are permanently awake.

TOWARDS PERMANENT WAKEFULNESS

A state of absolute wakefulness may seem unattainable, but it's important to remember that there are different intensities of permanent wakefulness, just as there are different intensities of awakening experiences. It's true that very few of us may be able to reach a permanent state of absolute wakefulness, as Ramakrishna or Walt Whitman did. However, it's certainly possible for all of us to reach a permanent state of lower-intensity awakening.

In this section I'm going to suggest a number of practises and lifestyle guidelines which will help you to move towards this state.

MEDITATE REGULARLY

The importance of meditation can't be overestimated as a way of training the chattering mind to be quiet and therefore reducing the largest energy leakage and the greatest disturbance to our being. Meditation also teaches us to dis-identify with the ego, to shift the centre of our identity from the ego to the self that remains when the ego is quiet, the *atman* or witnessing self. In meditation we learn to stand back and observe the thoughts and desires swirling through our mind and so they no longer have as much control over us. We can watch them arising and passing away without being affected by them. And this 'dis-identification' itself weakens the ego as a structure. It's no longer as powerful because it's no longer being reinforced by identity.

Meditation has both a temporary and long-term awakening effect. Every good meditation practise should produce a temporary ISLE state lasting for a few hours until the ego becomes active again and our energy is depleted and disturbed by information processing and concentration. But on a long-term basis meditation can bring about permanent changes to the structure and functioning of the psyche. Neuroscientists are now discovering that the structure of the brain isn't fixed but changes throughout life, hence the recently coined term 'neuroplasticity'. In a similar way, the psyche isn't fixed and permanent – it's pliable, and meditation is a tool for restructuring it.

Meditation tames the ego on a permanent basis, making its thought-chatter quieter and its boundaries less defined. It weakens it as a structure, so that it's no longer such a powerful presence in our being and no longer monopolizes our psychic energy, and the desensitizing mechanism becomes obsolete. As a result, there's energy freely available for us to devote to present awareness and so we wake up to the intense and harmonious reality that indigenous peoples and children are aware of, and perhaps even to a vision of spirit-force pervading the whole world and bringing everything into oneness.

Most meditation teachers recommend two sessions per day, for between 20 and 30 minutes. Some people find meditation difficult to begin with. They feel uncomfortable, find it hard to concentrate and are amazed at how crazy and chaotic their thoughts are. But if you can ride out this difficult phase you'll quickly begin to gain benefits and to move towards wakefulness, both temporarily and permanently.

PRACTISE MINDFULNESS

As J. Krishnamurti pointed out, one of the dangers of meditation is that it can be isolated from the rest of your life. You might think you only need to be 'spiritual' for those 20 minutes twice a day and that it doesn't matter what you do the rest of the time. In practise, if you're managing to meditate fairly well this shouldn't be such a problem – as we've just seen, the state of being that meditation creates usually lingers for a few hours afterwards. However, it's still a good idea – especially if your meditation *isn't* going that well – to integrate meditation into your daily life through the practise of *mindfulness*.

Mindfulness is really a form of meditation in itself, from the Buddhist tradition. It simply means paying conscious attention to your experience and to your surroundings. Normally we live in a state of 'not-there-ness' – our attention is either immersed in activities or distractions or focused on the thought-chatter inside our heads. It's quite rare that we stop thinking and stop doing and actually focus our attention on the present moment and where we actually are in that present moment. It's rare, for example, that we pay full attention to the taste and the sensation of food when we're eating, or to the sensations we feel when we're having a shower or brushing our teeth, or to our surroundings when we're walking down the street or travelling on a train or a bus. In all these cases, our attention is usually focused on our thought-chatter or on newspapers, radio, TV or other external 'attention-absorbers'. All you need to do to be mindful is to make a conscious effort to bring your attention away from thoughts and out of distractions, and focus it on the sensations you can feel or on your surroundings.

Being mindful in this way has many of the benefits of meditation. On a temporary basis, it brings a sense of inner well-being and an awareness of the is-ness and beauty of the world. Even the most mundane experiences, such as washing up or brushing your teeth, can become pleasurable when they're done mindfully. Even the most mundane surroundings can become fascinating when you look at them mindfully. And in the long term, mindfulness helps to quiet our thought-chatter and soften our ego structure.

MODERATION

Another important way of conserving and stilling life-energy is by controlling our instinctive being – the 'body of desire' which craves sex, food, drugs, alcohol, sensory stimulation, material comforts and luxury goods – as well as our psychological cravings for status, power or success. Physical desires are completely healthy and there's nothing wrong with a degree of stimulation or material comfort. But all too often these desires become too dominant and take over our whole being – they 'usurp their station', as Evelyn Underhill put it.[1] In terms of the Tantric theory of the *chakras,* you could say that when we live hedonistically or materialistically, the lower *chakras* – where our instincts are rooted – become too active and monopolize too much *prana,* preventing energy from reaching the highest chakra at the crown of the head, which is associated with higher states of consciousness. We need to 'tame' our desires to stop them consuming life-energy and disturbing our being in the same way that we need to tame our wild, chattering ego.

However, I've already suggested that it's not advisable – or even necessary – to go the extreme lengths of the ascetics in order to do this. Rather than inflicting pain on ourselves and treating the body as if it were an enemy to be punished, we should follow the life of moderation that Buddhism recommends, giving our body what it needs but not much more. Instead of starving ourselves or eating extravagant rich food, we should eat enough food to keep ourselves healthy. Instead of living in abject poverty or living in a luxurious big house full of expensive ornaments, we should live in a simple house with just enough space and shelter and a minimum of possessions. Instead of buying things for the 'fix' of pleasure it gives us, we should simply buy what we need. Instead of being promiscuous or completely celibate, we should have sex with our partner as often as feels comfortable, treating sex as a spiritual and emotional act rather than a hedonistic one.

Of course, we're bound to desire more than we need at some point – we're bound to want to have a few glasses of wine or to eat ice cream sometimes, or to daydream about winning the lottery or having sex with other people. There's nothing wrong with any of this, but it's important to have some control over these impulses, to have enough self-discipline to stop them 'usurping their station'.

If we do live this life of moderation and simplicity, then the body of desire – or the lower *chakras* – will consume little life-energy and create little disturbance, making it easier for us to live in a state of wakefulness. And, as the ascetics did, we should eventually reach a point where our body of desire becomes permanently tamed.

Probably the most miserable time of my life was the period when I was living as a musician in eastern Germany and felt an almost constant sense of anxiety and frustration. As I mentioned, this was partly because I'd lost touch with the spiritual side of my nature, but it was also, I believe, partly the result of the hedonistic life I was living. Like almost everyone else I knew, I smoked endless cigarettes and hung around in bars almost every night, chatting and listening to music and drinking. I often drank at home too and smoked about 30 roll-up cigarettes a day. I often had the feeling that this wasn't really 'me', but didn't feel sufficiently in control of my life to stop it. I don't think I was an alcoholic, but I was certainly living an unhealthy lifestyle.

I don't want to moralize about this lifestyle – I don't think there's anything wrong with drinking *per se*. I still like a glass of wine and the occasional chocolate bar, and I can't resist spicy Indian food. But back then it was as if the hedonistic part of my being had become too strong and that was partly why I stopped experiencing the spiritual feelings I'd had before. (Although, ironically, it was during this period that I had the most powerful awakening experience of my life, as described in the introduction.)

DETACHMENT

We've seen that states of awakening are generated when psychological attachments are broken, whether it's attachment to other people, to hopes, ambitions or beliefs, to wealth and status, to a socially constructed identity, or even to drugs. We've also seen that many monks and spiritual seekers have made a conscious effort to generate wakefulness by living lives of detachment, with no possessions or property, no family responsibilities, no worldly ambitions, and so on. There's no doubt that detachment is an important part of spiritual development, but again, it's perhaps not necessary – or indeed advisable – for us to go these extremes. There's no reason why we should try to live without a partner, a family, possessions, ambitions and a career, as long as we don't look to them for fulfilment and expect them to sustain our sense of well-being. We should develop an inner self-sufficiency and contentment which mean we don't depend on these things, even if we have them, so that we don't feel deprived if they are taken away.

This kind of detachment should occur naturally if we practise regular meditation and mindfulness. As your mind becomes more still, you should begin to feel more at home inside yourself and develop an inner well-being which means you no longer need to seek compensation for discontent from external sources of happiness. But we can also confront the problem directly and make a conscious effort to break our psychological attachments. Many of our attachments aren't deep-rooted, just habitual. This applies to substances like cigarettes, alcohol or chocolate, or activities like watching TV or surfing the internet – we've become attached to them simply through habit. Their hold over us is so great that we feel a sense of lack when we can't have them. Other attachments are circumstantial – they've been a part of our life for a long time and as a result they've also become part of our *self*, and we develop a fear of what life would be like without them. This can happen with your partner, friends, family, even your job – you become so accustomed to them that you feel as though you need them to sustain your well-being, even that you couldn't live without them. You might be attached to a particular place, such as the town where you grew up, and feel afraid of leaving. Or perhaps you're dependent on the security and status you feel your job gives you, even though you'd really like to do something more interesting and challenging. Or maybe you're dependent on your partner and don't feel as though you can leave them, even though they treat you badly.

To break these attachments you usually only need to force yourself to go without them for a while, to withdraw yourself from them until the habit pattern starts to fade away and you begin to adjust to life without them. You only need to expose yourself to the situation you're afraid of until you adjust and realize that you're capable of dealing with it. The sense of lack or insecurity may be painful at first, but after a certain amount of time your being starts to heal over. The hole that the attachment left begins to fill with new strength. You should feel a sense of inner freedom and openness, as if you've somehow reclaimed the part of your being that you gave away.

I remember feeling this when I gave up smoking 12 years ago, for example. It was very difficult for the first three weeks or so, but then the habit pattern started to die down until I reached a point where I felt it had disappeared altogether. As that happened I started to feel much stronger and more whole inside, almost like a new person.

A friend and colleague of mine described overcoming his alcoholism in similar terms. After years of heavy drinking, he had lost everything: his wife, his job, his house and all of his possessions. He wanted to commit suicide, but as he'd been brought up to believe in the afterlife (his father was a psychic healer), he knew that that wouldn't solve anything. So he realized that he had no option but to give up drinking and started going to Alcoholics Anonymous meetings. He admitted to himself that he had a problem he couldn't deal with and followed the AA procedure of 'handing over' that problem to a higher power. And as soon as he did that he felt an amazing sense of liberation:

I actually physically sat down that night and handed it over. I did the process and said, 'OK, I can't do it by myself but if you're a higher power, this is within your ability.' So I did and it went. And I would class it as a miracle. I felt so content, so at peace. It was quite unbelievable.

Another friend had a similar experience when she split up with her long-term boyfriend. The separation was very painful and at first she fell into depression, sleeping a lot and finding it difficult to face the world. But after a few weeks, as she describes it, 'I felt as though I was coming back to myself. I felt as though I really knew who I was again, as if I was regaining something that I had lost. I started to feel a sense of inner strength. I began to do things that I had never done before and felt that I was capable of anything.'

These descriptions of feeling 'more whole' and 'coming back to myself' are very apt, because in these situations our being literally *does* become more whole. The life-energy that we gave away to the attachment is returned to us, and our being is less disturbed and occluded by attachments.

We do need to take some care with this, though – if there's a large degree of psychological discord inside us, we may detach ourselves from one substance or activity and just replace it with another. This is why some people are serial addicts, switching from being alcoholics to drug addicts to sex addicts to workaholics and so forth. The discord inside them forces them to make new attachments as soon as they're broken old ones. However, if it's done in conjunction with meditation and mindfulness, there's no reason why 'conscious detachment' shouldn't be effective. As long as there is a degree of inner contentment and self-sufficiency, psychological attachments can be dissolved without any negative effects.

At the same time, it's important to be realistic about this. Until we reach enlightenment, we will never be completely free of psychological attachments. There will always be moments of discontent and discord when we cling to other people, to hopes and ambitions. But it's certainly possible for us to 'prune away' unnecessary attachments and so generate a higher concentration and a greater stillness and purity of life-energy.

SILENCE, SOLITUDE AND INACTIVITY

The power of silence, solitude and inactivity to generate states of wakefulness is illustrated by the following story, which was given me by a correspondent. At the age of 17, he was left alone in his house when his parents' marriage broke up and his mother moved to London. At first, he found the silence and darkness frightening, and actually ran out of the house in fear on two occasions. However, after a while he felt himself begin to adjust and to become calm and serene. As he puts it, 'I began to get used to the silence and my state of consciousness became quieter and quieter.' His health and his relationships improved and he felt that people were drawn to him. And then he began to experience powerful feelings of well-being and love. As he describes it,

> When I lay down to go to bed at night I began to be aware
> of waves of bliss travelling through my body. The bliss
> was only just bearable. I started to feel a deep love for
> everything around me. I would lie in bed and think of my
> neighbours, my friends and my mother particularly. I had
> an insight that everything was connected… Time expanded
> in such a way so that the value of a week of living like this
> would be worth a year of living any other way.

After a few months he moved to London to be with his family and soon afterwards – partly because of his difficult relationship with his mother – this state of bliss began to fade. Its passing away was painful and, as he writes, 'My life since then has been about trying to get back to that state.'

This is, of course, why silence, solitude and inactivity are such an important part of the monastic way of life – and why they're very important if you want to generate an ongoing and possibly permanent spiritual state.

In our culture, however, silence, solitude and inactivity are often seen as enemies. Silence often makes us feel uncomfortable, inactivity often makes us feel bored and frustrated, and solitude makes us feel anxious and uneasy. This is mainly because of our normal psychological discord. We normally use activity and distractions to try to avoid facing this discord, but when we're alone, inactive and in silence we come face to face with it. To a large extent, the anxiety and unease we feel *are* this psychological discord. But once this discord fades away to some degree, we can begin to enjoy silence, solitude and inactivity. And in order to attain an ongoing or permanent ISLE state, it's important that we make space for them in our life in order to concentrate, still and purify our life-energy.

SERVICE AND THE INTEGRAL LIFE

Quietness and inactivity are difficult for me to find at the moment, with three small children (including one young baby), but I don't see having children as detrimental to my spiritual life, because they have given me the opportunity to devote myself to *service*. That is, rather than devoting my time to following my own desires and my own interests, I now devote a large part of it to caring for them. (At the moment I'm a part-time house-husband, looking after the children on my own two days a week.) Hopefully, in the long run, this service is teaching me to become less concerned with my own desires and ambitions and to be more empathic and less self-centred. It's enabling me to *connect,* not just to my children but to the shared human consciousness that lies beyond all of our individual selves. As a result, I hope, the boundaries of my ego are becoming softer and I'm intensifying my sense of connection to the cosmos.

In this way, any path of spiritual development should, I believe, include an element of service, whether it's bringing up children, working for charity or in a caring profession, or doing some form of community or voluntary work. As Gandhi famously said, 'The best way to find yourself is to lose yourself in the service of others.'[2]

It's also important not to forget the connection between life-energy and physical activity. We've seen that exercises like hatha yoga and *tai chi* can remove energy blockages and intensify the flow of energy through our body, and so they can help to generate ISLE states too.

Both service and physical exercise are also important from an 'integral' perspective. As we've seen, the danger with the ascetic and monastic ways of life is that they focus too severely upon spiritual development and neglect other important aspects of our being. One of the problems with this is that even if you do reach a plateau of wakefulness, you'll probably be dislodged from it by emotional and psychological difficulties (as I believe happened to me). Spiritual development should not entail a neglect of other forms of development, such as intellectual, social, physical and emotional. We need to keep developing in these areas at the same time as developing spiritually. For example, at the same time as following a lifestyle of moderation, detachment and quietness, you should still give yourself scope to develop through creativity, relationships, intellectual stimulation, and so on. Spiritual development should not mean dropping out of college, giving up sex, exercise and reading books, or stopping painting or writing. It does not mean *ending* your relationship with the world – it means *enhancing* that relationship. Service is important in this way because it means that your spiritual development is never a purely individual affair. It means that you're always connected to others and participating in their lives.

All of these activities and methods – meditation, mindfulness, moderation, detachment and quietness – are ways of conserving, stilling and purifying life-energy and of emptying our being. Following them certainly isn't easy; it may take months of self-discipline and struggle before you see any benefit from them. But if you persevere, they will, by the laws of energy conservation, help to generate a spiritual state.

Meditation is the most important single practise, because it prepares the ground for the other practises. By taming our mind and reducing our psychic disharmony, it makes it more feasible for us to live a life of moderation and detachment and to enjoy quietness and solitude.

And, like meditation itself, the practises as a whole have both temporary and long-term effects. They produce temporary (or ongoing) wakefulness because they create an ISLE state at that particular moment, through conserving and stilling energy. This state will last for as long as the energy conservation continues. But long-term change will occur at the same time. The ego structure will become softer and less dominant, the psyche will be gradually restructured and eventually a shift will occur and this restructuring will be complete. The mould of ordinary consciousness will dissolve, so that you no longer have to return to your normal limited view of reality. You will no longer need to do any spiritual training, to consciously follow a life of moderation or detachment. At this point the ego will have been completely tamed, your being will be free from the disturbances of thought-chatter and emotions and desires, and there will be a permanently high concentration of life-energy inside you. In other words, you will have become enlightened.

WAKING UP

Waking up isn't a question of going back, either to our childhood state or to indigenous peoples' state of being. Going back would mean sacrificing the benefits our strong ego has brought, such as our powers of logic, self-control and organization. We need to move forward, to a new state of being which has the positive effects of the ego but heals its pathological overdevelopment. We need to retain the amazing *conceptual* knowledge the ego has produced and combine that with the *perceptual* knowledge that indigenous peoples possess. Perceptual knowledge without conceptual leads to superstition and confusion, but conceptual knowledge without perceptual leads to alienation and discontent.

To wake up is the single most important thing we can do in our life. We need to wake up for our own sake, to become free of the illusion of separation and of the psychological discord which fills our life with suffering. We need to wake up so that we can stop squandering our life and our potential in discontent, anxiety and conflict. Spiritual development is the ultimate form of therapy, healing the underlying discontent and disharmony of the human psyche.

We need to wake up for the sake of the human race as a whole, in order to free ourselves from the social chaos and conflict that have blighted the last few thousand years of history. The only possibility the human race has of living in harmony – without warfare, inequality and the oppression of women and different ethnic and social groups – is through transcending the overdeveloped ego. Only then will the impulse to accumulate wealth and gain power over other people disappear. Only then will we gain the ability to empathize with other people rather than mistrust or exploit them, to sense the shared essence which lies beneath the superficial differences of race or nationality.

We also need to wake up for the sake of the Earth. Indigenous peoples' wakefulness meant that they revered and respected the natural world, but our state of sleep has meant that we've seen nature as nothing more than a supply of resources. We have lost native peoples' awareness of the sacredness of nature and their sense of bondedness to it. As a result, we're in the process of abusing the planet's life-support systems beyond repair. The only sure way to avoid this catastrophe and learn to live in harmony with nature is to transcend our sense of separation from it and sense that it is alive and sacred.

And finally, we need to wake up on behalf of the universe. As the teachings of Tantra and other traditions tell us, the energy of our own being, our life-energy, is an influx of the essential energy of the universe. As philosophers such as David Chalmers and Galen Strawson suggest, consciousness may not be something produced by the brain, but a fundamental universal force, a quality which is 'woven' into the very fabric of reality',[3] and the main purpose of our brain may be to channel this universal consciousness into our individual being. Consciousness exists prior to and beyond the brain; our brain receives and transmits it, so that universal consciousness becomes our own individual consciousness.

There are two ways of looking at evolution, an inner and an outer. From the outer point of view, evolution is the process of living beings becoming physically more complex and better organized. But from the inner point of view, it's the process of living beings becoming more conscious and alive. These inner and outer aspects can't be separated – as living beings become more complex and better organized, they also become more conscious and alive. And from the perspective of the 'receiver' theory, this makes sense: living beings become more complex so that they are able to receive more consciousness, or 'spirit-force', and as a result they become more conscious and alive.

In this way, you can see evolution as a process by which beings become progressively more infused with life-energy. From amoeba to jellyfish to insects to fish and reptiles and birds and apes and human beings, living beings have become progressively more complex and so more infused with life-energy, more conscious of their surroundings, more autonomous and more self-aware.

And so when we practise spiritual development we're trying to do exactly what evolution has been doing for millions of years: to intensify life-energy and make ourselves more conscious and alive. In this way, we become *agents* of evolution. We carry the evolutionary process forward and help to make the universe more conscious of itself.

In higher states of consciousness, we glimpse the future of evolution. In a sense, natural-born mystics like Walt Whitman, Ramana Maharshi or Meister Eckhart are evolutionary 'throw forwards'. They just happened to be infused with a greater intensity of life-energy and so experienced the higher levels of consciousness that lie in wait for us as a species (or perhaps for another species). They were more alive and more conscious than normal human beings in the same way that normal human beings are more alive and conscious than other apes.

This is the direction we are heading in. The danger is that the pathology of our overdeveloped ego may not allow us to move much further along it. As I've said, if we do not wake up collectively, at least to a degree – perhaps to the point where we regain the natural wakefulness of indigenous peoples – then we may not survive as a species. If we don't, presumably another species will eventually develop which will evolve to these higher levels.

At the moment evolution seems to be *impelling* us to wake up. For a vast and ever-growing number of people nowadays, spiritual development is not a conscious choice but an *impulse* from the deepest part of their being. These people – including you, no doubt, since you're reading this book – have an instinctive sense that ordinary consciousness is limited and an instinct to expand and intensify it by following spiritual paths or practising spiritual technologies such as meditation or Yoga. This is as instinctive for them as the instinct to have sex or to find a life partner.

At root, this is an *evolutionary* impulse. The impulse that we feel to intensify our life-energy is the *élan vital* itself, the same drive towards greater complexity and consciousness that has taken life from the first single-celled amoeba to human beings. It's the process of evolution manifesting itself inside us and impelling us to become more conscious and alive on its behalf.

But why should evolution be doing this? Why does it seem to be pushing us forward to a greater intensity of consciousness with so much urgency?

Perhaps this is because we are so close to destroying ourselves as a species and destroying millions of other species too. Perhaps evolution is urging us to wake up as a kind of natural check to stop this catastrophe occurring. It's impelling us to intensify our life-energy at least to the point where we can regain indigenous peoples' intense vision of reality and their sense of connection to nature.

And perhaps it's urging us further, to higher intensities of awakening, perhaps even to the point of absolute wakefulness. It may be that in absolute wakefulness we reach the culmination of the evolutionary process, when living beings become pure life and pure light and life itself becomes one with the unmanifest ocean of pure spirit from which it emerged. Life returns to its source, the universal spiritual essence which was canalized into individual life forms hundreds of millions of years ago.

But of course, we were always one with this universal spirit anyway. It was just that we fell asleep and forgot who we were.

NOTES

INTRODUCTION

1. Heald, 2000.
2. Greeley, 1974. Even more strikingly, a survey by the National Opinion Research Centre at the University of Chicago found that two-thirds of Americans had had at least one mystical experience and that 5 per cent had had them often (in Fenwick, 1995, p.335).
3. I believe that, to some degree, the study of mystical experiences has been distorted by being associated with religion. Many of the well-known scholars of mysticism, such as Evelyn Underhill, R. C. Zaehner and F. C. Happold, had strong Christian beliefs and saw 'deity mysticism' – in which the mystic attains union with 'God' – as the highest form of mystical experience. They saw other types of awakening experiences, such as what Hindu philosophy calls *samadhi*, nature-mysticism or drug-induced experiences, as either inferior or – in the case of drug experiences – false. The author Frithjof Schuon even stated that genuine spiritual experiences couldn't occur outside what he called 'the great orthodox traditions'. If they did, they would be 'inoperative, and even dangerous' (in Brown, p.240)

   These authors' beliefs prejudiced them against non-theistic forms of mysticism. As another scholar of mysticism, Ninian Smart, points out, the only difference between the experience of Indian mystics and Christian mystics is interpretation: '[The theist] already considers that there is evidence of a personal God and Creator; in the silent brightness of inner contemplative ecstasy it is natural (or supernatural) to identify what is found within with the Lord who is worshipped without.' (Smart, 1971, p.87.) Rather than conceiving of a personal God, the Indian sages of the Upanishads only spoke in terms of *brahman*, an impersonal spirit-force which pervades the world and which is the essence of our being too. There's no question of higher or lower about these experiences – they are the same. (If anything, the interpretation of the Upanishads is more 'pure', since you could accuse the Christian mystics of moulding their experience to fit their religious concepts.)

In particular, these authors' religious beliefs prejudiced them against drug-induced mystical experiences. Their association of mysticism with God meant that they couldn't accept that mystical experience might be produced 'artificially' by man-made chemicals (i.e. completely without the help of God). The Catholic scholar R. C. Zaehner, for example, was hostile to Aldous Huxley's claim that mescaline and LSD could give a person access to the same divine reality that Christian mystics were aware of. However, we'll see in Chapter 4 that although drug-induced awakening experiences are not as complete or as satisfactory as other types, they are certainly valid and genuine.

One of my secondary aims in this book is to try to free mystical or spiritual experiences from their association from religion, so that they can be interpreted from a purely psychological – or 'spiritual' in the true sense of the term – point of view.

CHAPTER 1

1. Diamond, 1974, p.170
2. Berman, 2000, p.30
3. Ibid., p.188
4. Gopnik, 2006, p.211
5. In Deikman, 1980, p.249
6. Ibid.
7. Ibid.
8. Hardy, 1979, p.35
9. Stace, 1964, pp.71–2
10. In Vardey, 1995, p.88
11. Thoreau, 2009
12. In Hardy, 1979, p.62, p.35, p.20
13. Ibid., p.53
14. In May, 1991, p.314
15. In Hay, p.143
16. In Hardy, op. cit., p.64
17. Wordsworth, 1950, p.71
18. In Mascaro, 1990, p.117

19. In Happold, 1986, p.146
20. In Spencer, p.238
21. In Hoffman, 1992, pp.94–5
22. In Hardy, 1979, p.98
23. Ibid., p.70
24. Hay, op. cit
25. In Hardy, op. cit., p.62
26. In Johnson, 1960, pp.84–5

CHAPTER 2

1. Gallup survey, 1987, in http://www.christianuniversalist.org/articles/mysticalexperiences.html
2. In Deikman, 2000, p.88
3. Ibid.
4. Ibid.
5. Another example of a 'communal' awakening experience is the *satsang* experience, which we will examine later. This is when a person or a group of people has an awakening experience through being in contact with an 'enlightened' person, absorbing the powerful spiritual energy which radiates from them. A further example is group meditation, when a number of people may have awakening experiences at the same time, partly as a result of building up a powerful group dynamic.
6. Huxley, *The Doors of Perception*, p.27
7. Taylor, 2007, pp.129–30
8. Lawrence, 'Pax', 1994, p.700
9. In Hardy, 1979, p.85
10. Hay and Heald, 1987
11. In Happold, 1986, p.147
12. Ibid.
13. Ibid., p.64
14. Ibid.
15. Brunton, 1972, pp.304–5
16. Underhill, 1911, p.304
17. In Isherwood, 1965, p.65
18. In James, 1985, p.339
19. In Wilber, 1996a, p.311

CHAPTER 3
1. Persinger, 1983; Ramachandran and Blakesee, 1998
2. In LaMermin, 1990, p.119
3. In Gebser, 1970, pp.12–13.
4. McTaggart, 2003
5. Boyer, 1969; Puthoff, 1988, 1989
6. Nadeau and Kafatos, 2001, p.216
7. In Scharfstein, 1973, p.28
8. In Johnson, 1960, p.24
9. James, 1985, p.380
10. In Hardy, p.39
11. Ibid., p.72
12. Ibid., p.109
13. In O'Brian, 1949, pp.223–4
14. In Merkur, 1999, p.51
15. Werner, 1957, p.152
16. Ingold, 2000, p.67
17. Adamson, 2008, p.34
18. Lawlor, 1991, p.166
19. In Swain, 1992, p.134
20. In Levy-Bruhl, 1965, p.17
21. Munro, 1962
22. In Eliade, 1967, p.13
23. In Wright, 1992, p.311
24. In Versluis, 1994, p.34
25. Thomas, 1987, p.90
26. Magesa, 1997, p.59
27. Deloria, 1973, p.299
28. In Magesa, op. cit., p.52
29. Ingold, 2000, p.43
30. Lyons, 2008, p.60
31. Ravuva, 1983, p.7
32. In Warshall, 1976, p.66
33. In Griffiths, 2005, p.64
34. Turnbull, 1993, p.29
35. Service, 1978, p.83
36. In Tolle, 1999, p.62
37. Diamond, 1974, p.17

38. Silberbauer, 1981, p.131

39. Boydell, 2001, p.21

40. Roberts, 1993, p.95

41. Wordsworth, 1950, p.71

42. In Jacobs, 2002, p.173

43. Schachtel, 1959

44. Loevinger, 1976, p.147

45. Gopnik, 2006, p.211. Further evidence for young children's perceptual intensity was provided by the psychologist D. Shapiro's (1960) study of children's responses to Rorschach images. This showed that as they grow older, children are less attentive to the sensory aspects of the cards (such as colour and texture) but more attentive to meaning, shape and size.

46. Robinson, 1977

47. In ibid., p.43

48. Ibid., p.42

49. Ibid., p.56

50. In Hoffman, 1992, p.33

51. Ibid., p.24

52. Washburn, 1995, p.24

53. In Robinson, op. cit., p.49

54. Ibid., p.114

55. In Hoffman, op. cit., p.101

56. Ibid, p.53

57. For a fuller discussion of childhood spiritual experiences, see Taylor (2009b). Incidentally, the awakening experiences of children are one of the strongest arguments against the 'deconstructionist' view of mystical experiences put forward by scholars such as Stephen Katz. According to Katz, the experiences are always largely formed and determined by religious traditions. The experiences of a Buddhist or a Jewish mystic will always be fundamentally dissimilar, so that there is no such thing as a 'mystical experience' *per se*, and no such thing as a 'perennial philosophy' (in the term popularized by Aldous Huxley). The experiences can't occur outside the religious tradition the mystic has been brought up in, as they are a product of this tradition. However, the fact that mystical experiences can happen to very young children who have not absorbed *any* religious teaching – and would be too young to understand it even if they had – argues strongly against this. This suggests that the experience must be much more fundamental and innate to human beings, beyond culture and tradition.

Another argument against the 'constructionist' view is that – as we saw in Chapters 2 and 3 – mystical experiences often happen to people who haven't been brought up in any religion. In addition, at the highest level of mystical experiences – absolute awakening – there is no conceptual content at all. You can't speak of *nirvikalpa samadhi* in terms of context or content from a religious tradition, because it is a state of complete emptiness and formlessness.

And finally, of course, there are many similarities between mystical experiences across different traditions, which suggest that they're talking about essentially the same experience, moulded into slightly different shapes by different traditions and cultures. For example, as we've seen, the mystical states described by Ramakrishna or Ramana Maharishi are essentially the same as those described by Plotinus or Meister Eckhart. This is, of course, why Huxley used the term 'perennial philosophy'.

58. Wordsworth, 1950, p.71
59. Becker, 1973, p.50

CHAPTER 4
1. Gopnik, 2006, p.211
2. James, 1985, p.387
3. Ramachandran and Blakeslee, 1998
4. Persinger, 1983
5. Newberg and D'Aqulli, 2000
6. Winston, 2005
7. In Chopra, 2006, p.43
8. *See* Radin, 2006; Sheldrake, 2004
9. McGinn, 1993, p.60
10. Strawson, 2006
11. Chalmers, 1995, p.209
12. Strawson, op. cit.
13. In Merkur, 1999, p.51
14. Leuba, 1925
15. Group for the Advancement of Psychiatry, 1976
16. Tart, 1983

17. Ludwig, 1966
18. Fischer, 1971
19. Rimbaud, 2009
20. Ibid.
21. Ibid.
22. Ibid.
23. Eliade, 1961; Krippner, 2000; Brown, 1980
24. In Spencer, 1950, p.157
25. Ibid., p.125
26. Ezra 8:21–3; Daniel 10:3; 1 Kings 19:8
27. Oswald, 1970
28. In Gynn and Wright, 2007, p.26
29. Huxleyli, 1977, p.121
30. Rudgley, 1993; McKenna, 1993; Smith, 1964
31. Weil, Metzner and Leary, 1965
32. Griffiths *et al.*, 2006
33. In Ornstein, 1969, p.46
34. James, 1985, p.388
35. Ouspensky, 1984, p.316
36. Ibid. Another description of drug-induced timelessness is given by R. H. Ward in his book *A Drug Taker's Notes* (1957). He describes his experience of inhaling ether. After a few inhalations of the gas he felt that he was experiencing a state of heightened awareness which was 'already far more complete than the fullest degree of ordinary waking consciousness'. He had a vision of the white radiance which often reveals itself during awakening experiences, which had 'an utterly indescribable purity and lucency'. And he felt that in this state time had no meaning whatsoever: 'In one sense it lasted far longer than the short periods between inhaling the gas and "coming round", lasted indeed for an eternity, and in another sense it took no time at all' (p.26).

There is another example in Thomas de Quincey's *Confessions of an English Opium-Eater* (1956). De Quincey writes that under the influence of opium, 'Sometimes I seemed to have lived for seventy or a hundred years in one night; nay, sometimes had feelings representative of a duration far beyond the limits of any human experience' (p.314).
37. Shukman, 2005

38. Shanon, 2001, p.42

39. In Grey, 1985, p.154

40. Jilek, 1989

41. Metzner, 1987

42. Eliade, 1967

43. In Peake, 2006, p.309

44. Armstrong, 2004, pp.205–6

45. In Smith, 2000, pp.109–10

46. Foote-Smith and Bayne, 1991, p.811

47. Ibid.

48. Bolte-Taylor, 2008

49. Prince, 1982

50. In Smith, op. cit., p.108

51. Julian of Norwich, 1982, p.68, p.80 and p.86

52. Walsh, 2003, p.2

53. Zaehner, 1961

54. In ibid., p.79

55. Huxley, 1977, p.45

56. Doblin, 1991, p.14

57. Smith, 1964, pp.528–9

CHAPTER 5

1. Happold, 1986, p.220

2. *The Cloud of Unknowing*, 1997, pp.22–3

3. In Bulatao, 1992, p.101

4. Jamison, 2006, p.57

5. In Deikman, 2009

6. Ibid. As another example, the fourteenth-century Greek mystic St Gregory describes how spiritual experience comes from a state in which the soul has become empty of all 'phantasmata of earthly and heavenly images' and is able 'to reject and spurn whatever sense impressions present themselves to its thoughts' (in Butler, 1967, p.70).

7. Andresen, 2000

8. Tang *et al.*, 2007

9. Flanagan, 2003. Similarly, in a 2003 study at the University of Wisconsin, people were given an eight-week training course in mindfulness meditation, which they practised for an hour a day. At the end of the course, brain scans showed an unusually high level of activity – compared to a control group – in the left side of their frontal lobes, the area which is linked to positive emotion and low anxiety levels. This study also showed that these people had stronger-than-normal immune systems. At the end of the course they and members of the control group were injected with a flu vaccine. Tests four to eight weeks later showed that the meditators had produced a significantly higher number of antibodies (Davidson *et al*., 2003).

10. Underhill, 1911, pp.301–2
11. Deikman, 2009
12. In James, 1985, p.384
13. Novak, 1996, p.277
14. Deikman, op. cit.
15. Horne, 1997
16. Ibid.
17. Marchetti, 2004
18. Csikszentmihalyi, 1992
19. Washburn, 2002
20. Freud, 1962
21. Jung, 1988, p.15
22. James, 2009
23. White *et al*., 2004; Linde *et al*., 2005
24. Munro, 1962, p.8
25. Hildebrand, 1988
26. Previously I used the term 'consciousness-energy' (e.g. Taylor, 2005a/b). However, I decided that this was slightly misleading too, partly because, like the term 'psychic energy', it implies that this energy is only related to consciousness, ignoring its emotional, sexual and somatic aspects. 'Consciousness-energy' is also slightly misleading in that it could be construed as suggesting that consciousness *is* nothing more than energy. As the philosopher Christian de Quincey (2002) points out in his book *Radical Nature*, consciousness exists independently of energy. Consciousness is the 'witness' which stands apart from our thoughts and from the flow of energy through our beings.

However, it's perhaps more helpful to think of consciousness as *both* an energy and a witness. I would suggest that there are three different functions – or aspects – of consciousness: *consciousness as witness, consciousness as cognition* and *consciousness as energy*.

All three aspects are valid and may be emphasized to a different degree in different traditions and cultures. Most spiritual traditions deal with consciousness in the first sense. In the Vedantic tradition, this is the *atman*, the pure, essential self which lies behind the disturbance of thought and desire. In contrast, the Tantric traditions emphasize consciousness as energy – as we have seen, rather than dis-indentifying with the ego and becoming the *atman*, their aim is to raise or intensify their *prana* or life-energy. Western philosophers, however, tend to deal exclusively with consciousness as *cognition*. They see consciousness as the activity of the mind, the 'I' which thinks and feels, oblivious to the fact that consciousness is also the self with which they are observing those thoughts and feelings.

27. Feuerstein, 1990
28. Meister Eckhart, 1979, p.7, my italics
29. Ibid., p.20
30. In Happold, 1986, p.223
31. In Forman, 1997, p.102
32. Mascaro, 1988, p.84
33. In O'Neal, 1996, p.52

CHAPTER 6
1. Laski, 1961
2. Hoffman, 1992, pp.38–9
3. Shelley, 'Hymn to Intellectual Beauty'
4. Hopkins, 'God's Grandeur'
5. Tolle, 2005, p.4
6. Watts, 2007
7. In Holroyd, 1991, p.138
8. In James, 1985, p.339
9. Roberts, 1993, p.32
10. Debold, 2005, p.56
11. 'Tony's Story', http://www.worthabbey.net/bbc/tony5.htm
12. In Duguid, 2007, p.15
13. In Hardy, 1979, p.85
14. In Laski, 1961, p.390
15. In Happold, 1986, p.133
16. In Murphy and Whyte, 1995, p.66
17. Ibid., p.103

18. Ibid., p.87
19. Bannister, 1955, pp.11–12
20. Hughes, 1967, p.72
21. Byrd, 1938, p.85
22. Lawrence, 1973, p.54
23. Ibid.
24. Ibid.
25. In Wade, 2004, p.30. This description is strikingly similar to D. H. Lawrence's poem 'Pax', which begins: 'All that matters is to be at one with the living God / to be a creature in the house of the God of Life. / Like a cat asleep on a chair / at peace, in peace / and at one with the master of the house, with the mistress, at home, at home in the house of the living, / sleeping on the hearth, and yawning before the fire.'
26. Ibid., p.55
27. Ibid., p.8
28. Ibid., p.27
29. Ibid., p.28

CHAPTER 7

1. Kason and Degler, 1994, pp.51–2
2. In Wilson, 1985, p.576. In fact, since *kundalini* experiences are so well documented, they can be seen as further evidence for the existence of a non-physical energy inside us. In ordinary life we may not always be aware of the life-energy ebbing and flowing inside us, but in *kundalini* experiences it becomes powerfully evident.
3. Fenwick, 1995; Fontana, 2005
4. Fenwick, op. cit.
5. In Fontana, op. cit., p.387
6. In Fenwick, op. cit., p.99
7. In Lorimer, 1990, p.86
8. In Grey, pp.xiii–xiv, p.33, p.51
9. Lawrence, 1994, p.676
10. Whitman, 1980, p.64
11. Coleman and Thupten, 2008
12. In May, 1991, p.52
13. Whitman, op. cit. p.68
14. In May, op. cit., pp.8–9
15. Carpenter, 2009

16. Brunton, 1972, p.141

17. Ibid., p.280

18. Cohen, 1992, p.30

19. Ibid., pp.34–5

20. Ibid., p.55

21. Ibid., p.56

22. Cutting and Dunne, 1989, p.400; Epstein, 1979, p.318

23. In Hartley, 2002, p.22

24. In Peake, 2006, p.224; McDonald, 1979

25. In Hartley, op. cit.

26. Sullivan, 1953, pp.151–2

27. Johnson, 1960, p.64

28. In Maxwell and Tschudin, 1990, pp.127–8

29. In Cohen, 2000, p.53

CHAPTER 8

1. In Feuerstein, 1990, p.171

2. Wilber, 1997, p.221

CHAPTER 9

1. In Happold, 1986, p.360

2. In Underhill, 1911, p.226

3. In Wilber, 1996a, p.352

4. Underhill, op. cit., p.220

5. Brunton, 1970, p.126, my italics

6. In Walker, 1987, p.64

7. Prabhavananda and Isherwood, 1969, p.102

8. In Wood, 1959, p.41

9. Ibid., p.42

10. Ibid., pp.49–50

11. Prabhavananda and Isherwood, op.cit., p.72

12. Underhill, 1911, p.205

13. Ibid., p.212

14. Ibid., p.178

15. Ibid., p.389

16. Ibid., p.396

17. Mascaro, 1988, p.68

18. Deikman, 2000, p.88

19. Underhill, op. cit., p.220
20. In ibid.
21. Feuerstein, 1990, p.185
22. Some scholars believe that Tantra is actually India's oldest spiritual tradition and was originally developed by the Dravidians – India's original inhabitants – before they were overrun by Indo-European invaders around 2000 BCE. It's possible that this spirituality merged with the ritualistic practises of the Indo-Europeans, as described in the Vedas, to produce the mystical philosophy of Vedanta, as described in the Upanishads.
23. Capriles, 2006
24. Washburn, 2002, p.5

CHAPTER 10
1. Underhill, 1911, p.220
2. http://quotations.about.com/od/gandhiquotes/tp/10_gandhi_quote. htm
3. Chalmers, 1995; Strawson, 2006

BIBLIOGRAPHY

Adamson, R. (2008). 'First Nations' Survival and the Future of the Earth' in M. K. Nelson (ed.), *Original Instructions: Indigenous Teachings for a Sustainable Future*, 27–35. Rochester: Bear & Company.

Allison, W. A. *et al.* (eds) (1984). *The Norton Anthology of Poetry* (third edition). New York: W. W. Norton & Company.

Andresen, J. (2000). 'Meditation meets behavioural medicine.' *The Journal of Consciousness Studies* 7 (11–12), 17–73.

Andresen, J., and Forman, R. (2000). 'Methodological pluralism in the study of religion.' *Journal of Consciousness Studies* 7 (11–12), 7–16.

Armstrong, K. (2004). *The Spiral Staircase: A Memoir*. London: HarperCollins.

Armstrong, T. (1984). 'Transpersonal experience in childhood.' *Journal of Transpersonal Psychology* 16, 207–30.

Attar, F. A. (1990). *Muslim Saints and Mystics*. London: Arkana.

Baggini, J. (2007). 'Spirituality for atheists.' *Psychologies*. October, 114–16.

Bannister, R. (1955). *The First Four Minutes*. London: Corgi.

Becker, E. (1973). *The Denial of Death*. New York: Free Press.

Berman, M. (2000). *Wandering God: A Study in Nomadic Spirituality*. Albany, NY: SUNY Press.

Bindl, M. (1965). *Religious Experience Mirrored in Pictures: A Developmental Psychological Investigation*. Freiburg: Herder.

Bolte-Taylor, J. (2008). 'Jill Bolte-Taylor's powerful stroke of insight.' http://www.ted.com/talks/jill_bolte_taylor_s_powerful_stroke_of_insight.html.

Boydell, S. (2001). 'Philosophical perception of Pacific property: land as a communal asset in Fiji'. *Pacific Rim Real Estate Society*, Jan. 2001, 21–4.

Boyer, T. H. (1969). 'Cutoff: independent character of electromagnetic zero-point forces.' *Physical Review* 185, 2039–40.

Brown, J. E. (1980). 'The Question of "Mysticism" within Native American Traditions' in R. Woods (ed.), *Understanding Mysticism*, 240–60. New York: Image Books.

Brunton, P. (1934/1972). *A Search in Secret India*. London: Rider.

— (1970). *The Inner Reality*. New York: Rider.

Bucke, R. M. (1991). *Cosmic Consciousness*. London: Penguin.

Bulatao, J. C. (1992). *Phenomena and their Interpretation*. Manila: Ateneo de Manila University Press.

Burkert, W. (1987). *Ancient Mystery Cults*. Cambridge, MA: Harvard University Press.

Butler, D. C. (1967). *Western Mysticism*. London: Constable.

Byrd, R. (1938). *Alone*. New York: Puttman.

Capriles, E. (2006). 'Beyond mind II: further steps to a metatranspersonal philosophy and psychology.' *International Journal of Transpersonal Studies* 25, 1–44.

Carpenter, E. (2009). 'Some friends of Walt Whitman: a study in sex psychology.' Retrieved from http://www.edwardcarpenterforum.org/index.php?option=com_content&task=view&id=51&Itemid=59.

Chalmers, D. (1996). *The Conscious Mind: In Search of a Fundamental Theory*. Oxford: Oxford University Press.

Chalmers, D. J. (1995). 'Facing up to the problem of consciousness.' *Journal of Consciousness Studies* 2 (3), 200–19.

Chopra, D. (2006). *Life After Death: The Book of Answers*. London: Rider.

Cohen, A. (1992). *Autobiography of an Awakening*. Corte Madera, CA: Moksha Foundation.

— (2000). 'Ripples of the surface of being: an interview with Eckhart Tolle.' *What is Enlightenment?* 18, Fall/Winter 2000, 53.

Coleman, G., and Thupten, J. (2008). *The Tibetan Book of the Dead: First Complete Translation*. London: Penguin.

Cope, S. (1999). *Yoga and the Quest for the True Self*. New York: Doubleday.

Csikszentmihalyi, M. (1992). *Flow: The Psychology of Happiness*. London: Rider.

Cutting, J., and Dunne, F. (1989). 'Subjective experience of schizophrenia.' *Schizophrenia Bulletin* 11, 397–408

Davidson, R. J., Kabat-Zinn, J., Schumacher J. *et al.* (2003). 'Alterations in brain and immune function produced by mindfulness meditation.' *Psychosomatic Medicine* 65, 564–70.

De Quincey, C. (2002). *Radical Nature*. Montpelier, Vermont: Invisible Cities Press.

— (2003). 'Consciousness and conquest.' Retrieved from www.scimednet.org/library/articlesN73+/N73deQuincey_conquest.htm - 19k, accessed 10/12/07.

De Quincey, T. (1821/1956). *Confessions of an English Opium-Eater*. London: MacDonald.

Debold, E. (2005). 'Spiritual but not religious: moving beyond postmodern spirituality.' *What is Enlightenment?* December 2005, 56–9.

Deikman, A. (1980). 'Deautomatization and the Mystic Experience' in R. Woods (ed.), *Understanding Mysticism*, 240–60. London: The Athlone Press.

— (2000). 'A functional approach to mysticism.' *The Journal of Consciousness Studies* 7 (11–12), 75–93.

— (2009). 'Experimental meditation.' Retrieved on 11/2/09 from http:// www.deikman.com/experimental.html.

— (2009). 'Implications of experimentally induced meditation.' Retrieved on 11/2/09 from http://www.deikman.com/experimental.html.

Deloria, V. (1973). *God is Red*. Golder, CO: Fulcrum Publishing.

Dennett, D. (1992). *Consciousness Explained*. Boston: Back Bay Books.

Diamond, S. (1974). *In Search of the Primitive*. New Brunswick: Transaction Books.

Ditman, K. S., Hayman, M., and Whittlesey, J. R. B. (1965). 'The Subjective After-effects of Psychedelic Experiences: A Summary of Four Recent Questionnaire Studies' in G. M. Weil, R. Metzner and T. Leary (eds), *The Psychedelic Reader*. New York: University Books.

Doblin, R. (1991). 'Pahnke's "Good Friday Experiment": a long-term follow-up and methodological critique.' *The Journal of Transpersonal Psychology* 23, 1–28.

Duguid, H. (2007). 'The chant show.' *The Independent Extra*, 13/6/07, 15.

Eliade, M. (1961). *The Sacred and the Profane: The Nature of Religion*. New York: Harper.

— (1967). *From Primitives to Zen*. London: Collins.

Epstein, A. (1979). 'Natural healing processes of the mind: 1. Acute schizophrenic disorganization.' *Schizophrenia Bulletin* 5, 313–20.

Evans-Pritchard, E. E. (1967). *Nuer Religion*. London: Oxford University Press.

Fenwick, P. and E. (1995). *The Truth in the Light*. London: Headline.

Ferrer, J. (2001). *Revisioning Transpersonal Theory*. New York: State University of New York Press.

Feuerstein, G. (1990). *Yoga: The Technology of Ecstasy*. Wellingborough: The Aquarian Press.

Fischer, R. (1971). 'A cartography of the ecstatic and meditative states.' *Science* 174, 897–904.

Flanagan, O. (2003). 'The colour of happiness.' *New Scientist*, 24 May 2003.

Fontana, D. (2005). *Is There an Afterlife?* Winchester: O Books.

Foote-Smith, E., and Bayne, L. (1991). 'Joan of Arc.' *Epilepsia* 32 (6), 810–15.

Forman, R. (1997). *The Problem of Pure Consciousness: Mysticism and Philosophy*.Oxford: Oxford University Press.

— (1998). 'What does mysticism have to teach us about consciousness?' *Journal of Consciousness Studies* 5 (2), 185–201.

Freud, S. (1923/1962). *The Ego and the Id*. New York: W. W. Norton & Company.

— (1930).*Civilization and its Discontents*. The Standard Edition of the Complete Psychological Works of Sigmund Freud, 24 vols. Ed. James Strachey. 21, 64–145. London: Hogarth Press.

Gebser, J. (1970). 'The invisible origin: evolution as a supplementary process.' Retrieved from www.unca.edu/-combs/integralage, 1/2/2009.

Gopnik, A. (2006). 'Babies are more conscious than we are.' Retrieved 17/4/06 from http://www.edge.org/q2005/q05_9.html#gopnik.

Gopnik, A., Meltzoff, A., and Kuhl, P. (1999). *How Babies Think*. London: Weidenfield & Nicholson.

Goswami, A. (1993). *The Self-Aware Universe*. London and New York: Simon Schuster.

Greeley, A. (1974). *Ecstasy: A Way of Knowing*. Englewood Cliffs, NJ: Prentice-Hall.

Green, S. (1987). *Physiological Psychology: An Introduction*. London: Routledge & Kegan Paul.

Grey, M. (1985). *Return from Death*. London: Arkana.

Griffiths, J. (1999). *Pip Pip: A Sideways Look at Time*. London: Flamingo.

— (2005). 'Living Time' in T. Aldrich (ed.), *About Time: Speed, Society, People and the Environment*, 53–67. Sheffield: Greenleaf Publishing.

Griffiths, R. R., Richards, W. A., McCann, U., and Jesse, R. (2006). 'Psilocybin can occasion mystical-type experiences having substantial and sustained personal meaning and spiritual significance.' *Psychopharmacology* (online edition), July 11, 2006.

Grof, C. and S. (1993). 'Addiction as Spiritual Emergency' in R. Walsh and F. Vaughan (eds), *Paths Beyond Ego*, 144–6. New York: Tarcher..

Grof, S. (1990). *The Psychology of the Future*. Albany, NY: SUNY Press.

Gross. R. (1996). *Psychology: The Science of Mind and Behaviour*. London: Hodder & Stoughton.

Group for the Advancement of Psychiatry (1976). *Mysticism: Spiritual Quest or Psychic Disorder?* New York: GAP.

Gynn. G., and Wright, T. (2007). *Left in the Dark: The Biological Origins of the Fall from Grace*. Lulu.

Happold, F. C. (1986). *Mysticism*. London: Pelican.

Hardy, A. (1979). *The Spiritual Nature of Man*. Oxford: Oxford University Press.

Hartley, J. (2002). 'Psychosis: the ultimate reality.' *Asylum* 13 (1), 21–2.

Hay, D. (1987). *Exploring Inner Space*. Oxford: Mowbray.

Hay, D., and Heald, G. (1987). 'Religion is good for you.' *New Society*, 17 April.

Hay, D., and Nye, R. (1998). *The Spirit of the Child.* London: HarperCollins.

Heald, D. (2000). 'BBC "Soul of Britain" questionnaire.' Fieldwork conducted 25 April–7 May 2000 by the Opinion Research Business (ORB), London.

Hildebrand, M. von (1988), 'An Amazonian Tribe's View of Cosmology' in P. Bunyard and E. Goldsmith (eds), *Gaia: The Thesis, the Mechanisms and the Implications*. Camelford, Cornwall: Wadebridge Ecological Centre.

Hoffman, E. (1992). *Visions of Innocence*. Boston: Shambhala.

Holroyd, S. (1991). *Krishnamurti: The Man, the Mystery and the Message*. Shaftesbury: Element Books.

Horne, J. (1997). 'Sleep.' *Karger Gazette* 61, 1–5.

Horton, P. C. (1974). 'The mystical experience: substance of an illusion.' *Journal of the American Psychoanalytical Association* 22, 364–80

Hughes, T. (1967). *Poetry in the Making*. London: Faber and Faber.

Huxley, A. (1977). *The Doors of Perception and Heaven and Hell*. London: Grafton.

Ingold, T. (2000). *The Perception of the Environment*. London: Routledge.

Isherwood, C. *(1980)*. Ramakrishna and His Disciples. *Hollywood, CA: Vedanta Press.*

Jacobs, A. (ed.) (2002). *Poetry of the Spirit*. London: Watkins.

James, W. (1902/1985). *The Varieties of Religious Experience.* London: Penguin.

— (2009). 'The Energies of Man' http://psychclassics.yorku.ca/James/energies.htm

Jamison, C. (2006). *Finding Sanctuary: Monastic Steps for Everyday Life*. London: Weidenfeld & Nicholson.

Jilek, W. (1989). 'Therapeutic Use of Altered States of Consciousness in Contemporary North American Indian Dance Ceremonials' in C. Ward (ed.), *Altered States of Consciousness and Mental Health: A Cross-Cultural Perspective*, 167–85. London: Sage.

Johnson, R. C. (1960/1988). *Watcher on the Hills*. New York: Harper.

Johnston, W. (1988). *Silent Music*. London: Fontana.

Joseph, R. (2000) *The Transmitter to God: The Limbic System, the Soul and Spirituality.* San José: The University Press California Press.

Julian of Norwich (1982). *Revelations of Divine Love*. London: Penguin.

Jung, C. G. (1928/1988). 'On Psychic Energy' in *On the Nature of the Psyche*, 3–66. London: Arkana.

Kahneman, D. (1973). *Attention and Effort*. Englewood Cliffs, NJ: Prentice Hall.

Kason, Y., and Degler, T. (1994). *A Farther Shore: How Near-Death and Other Extraordinary Experiences Can Change Ordinary Lives*. Toronto: HarperCollins.

Katz, S. (ed.) (1983). *Mysticism and Religious Traditions*. New York: Oxford University Press.

Kostrulaba, T. (1976). *The Joy of Running*. Philadelphia: Lippencott.

Krippner, S. (2000). 'The epistemology and technologies of shamanic states of consciousness.' *Journal of Consciousness Studies* 7 (11–12), 93–118.

LaMermin, N. D. (1990). *Boojums all the Way: Communicating Science in a Prosaic Age*. Cambridge: Cambridge University Press.

Lamy, L. (1981). *Egyptian Mysteries*. London: Thames & Hudson.

Lancaster, B. L. (2004). *Approaches to Consciousness: The Marriage of Science and Mysticism*. Basingstoke, UK: Palgrave Macmillan.

Laski, M. (1961). *Ecstasy.* London: The Cresset Press.

Lawlor, R. (1991). *Voices of the First Day: Awakening in the Aboriginal Dreamtime*. Rochester, Vermont: Inner Traditions.

Lawrence, D. H. (1973). *John Thomas and Lady Jane*. London: Penguin.
— (1994). *Complete Poems*. London; Penguin.

Lee, R. B., and DeVore, I. (eds) (1968). *Man the Hunter*. Chicago: Aldine.

Leuba, J. H. (1925). *The Psychology of Religious Mysticism.* New York: Harcourt, Brace.

Levy-Bruhl, L. (1965). *The Soul of the Primitive*. London: Allen & Unwin.

***Life** of Ramakrishna* (Anonymous, 1929). Madras: Ramakrishna Math.

Linde, K. *et al.* (2005). 'Acupuncture for patients with migraine: a randomized controlled trial.' *Journal of the American Medical Association* 17, 2118–25.

Loevinger, J. (1976). *Ego Development: Conception and Theories*. San Francisco: Jossey-Bass.

Lorimer, D. (1990). *Whole in One*. London: Arkana.

Ludwig, A. M. (1966). 'Altered states of consciousness.' *Archives of General Psychiatry* 15, 225–34.

Lyons, Chief Oren (2008). 'Listening to Natural Law' in M. K. Nelson (ed.), *Original Instructions: Indigenous Teachings for a Sustainable Future*, 22–6. Rochester: Bear & Company.

McDonald, N. (1979). 'Living with Schizophrenia' in D. Goleman and R. J. Davidson (eds), *Consciousness, Brain, States of Awareness and Mysticism*. New York: Harper Row.

McGinn, C. (1993). 'Consciousness and Cosmology: Hyperdualism Ventilated' in M. Davies and G. W. Humphreys (eds), *Consciousness*, 155–77. Oxford: Blackwell.

McKenna, T. (1993). *The Food of the Gods*. New York: Bantam.

McTaggart, L. (2003). *The Field*. London: Thorsons.

Magesa, L. (1997). *African Religion*. New York: Orbis.

Marchetti, G. (2004). 'The role attention plays in building our subjective experiences.' *Journal of Non-Locality and Remote Mental Interactions* 1 (2), retrieved 11/10/04 from www.emergentmind.org/marchettiI2.htm.

Marshall, P. (2006). *Mystical Encounters with the Natural World*. Oxford: Oxford University Press.

Masters, R. E. L., and Houston, J. (1966). *The Varieties of Psychedelic Experience*. New York: Delta.

May, R. (1991). *Cosmic Consciousness Revisited*. Shaftesbury, Dorset: Element.

Maxwell, M., and Tschudin, V. (eds) (1990). *Seeing the Invisible: Modern Religious and other Transcendent Experiences*. London: Penguin.

Meister Eckhart (1979). *German Sermons and Treatises*, vol. 1. Trans. M. Walshe. London: Watkins.

Meister Eckhart: From Whom God Hid Nothing (1996). Ed. D. O'Neal. Boston: Shambhala.

Merkur, D. (1999). *Mystical Moments and Unitive Thinking*. Albany, NY: State University of New York Press.

Metzner, R. (1987). 'Shamanism, alchemy & yoga: traditional techniques

of transformation.' Retrieved 17/08/06 from www.rmetzner-greenearth.org/
research-articles.

Moxon, C. (1920). 'Mystical ecstasy and hysterical dream states.' *Journal of Abnormal Psychology* 15, 329–34.

Munro, N. G. (1962). *Ainu Creed and Cult*. New York: Columbia University Press.

Murphy, M., and White, R. A. (1995). *In the Zone: Transcendent Experience in Sports*. London: Arkana.

Nadeau, R., and Kafatos, M. (2001). *The Non-Local Universe: The New Physics and Matters of the Mind*. Oxford: Oxford University Press.

Naranjo, C., and Ornstein, R. (1971). *On the Psychobiology of Meditation*. London: Allen.

Newberg, A., and D'Aqulli, E. (2000). 'Neurospsychology of religious and spiritual experience.' *The Journal of Consciousness Studies* 7 (11–12), 111–22.

Novak, P. (1996). 'Buddhist meditation and the consciousness of time.' *Journal of Consciousness Studies* 3 (3), 267–77.

O'Brian, J. (ed.) (1949). *The Road to Damascus: The Spiritual Pilgrimage of Fifteen Converts to Catholicism*. Oxford: Oxford University Press.

Ornstein, R. (1969). *On the Experience of Time*. London: Penguin.

Oswald, I. (1970). *Sleep*. Harmondsworth: Penguin.

Ouspensky, P. D. (1984). *A New Model of the Universe*. London: Arkana.

Pafford, M. (1973). *Inglorious Wordsworths: A Study of Some Transcendental Experiences in Childhood and Adolescence*. London: Hodder & Stoughton.

Pascal, B. (1966). *Pensées*. London: Penguin.

Peake, A. (2006). *Is There Life After Death?* London: Arcturus.

Persinger, M. A. (1983). 'Religious and mystical experiences as artefacts of temporal lobe function: a general hypothesis.' *Perceptual and Motor Skills* 57 (3), 1255–62.

— (1987). *Neuropyschological Bases of God Beliefs*. New York: Praeger.

Pickover, C. (1999). 'Transcendent experience and temporal lobe epilepsy.' Retrieved 27/7/08 from http://www.meta-religion.com/Psychiatry/The_Paranormal/trascendent_experiences.htm

Piechowski, M. (2001). 'Childhood spirituality.' *Journal of Transpersonal Psychology* 33, 1–15.

Plato (2007). *The Republic*. Trans. D. Lee. London: Penguin.

Prabhavananda, Swami, and Isherwood, C. (1969). *How to Know God: The Yoga Aphorisms of Patanjali*. New York: Mentor.

Prince, R. (1982). 'Shamans and endorphins.' *Ethos* 10, 409–23.

Puthoff, H. E. (1988). 'Zero-point fluctuations of the vacuum as the source of atomic stability and the gravitational interaction.' *Proceedings of the British Society for the Philosophy of Science International Conference.*

— (1989). 'Gravity as a zero-point-fluctuation force.' *Physical Review A*, 39 (5), 2333–42.

Radin, D. (2006). *Entangled Minds*. London: Pocket Books.

Ramachandran, V. S., and Blakesee, S. (1998). *Phantoms in the Brain*. London: Fourth Estate.

Ravuva, A. (1983). *Vaka I Taukei: The Fijian Way of Life*. Java: Institute of Pacific Studies, the University of the South Pacific.

Rimbaud, A., and Varese, L. (2009). *Une Saison en Enfer* and *Le Bateau Ivre: A Season in Hell* and *The Drunken Boat.* http://books.google.co.uk/books?id=orcRB8ncjCgC&printsec=frontcover&dq=the+drunken+boat+rimbaud#v=onepage&q=&f=false.

Roberts, B. (1993). *The Experience of No-Self*. Albany, NY: SUNY.

Robinson, E. (1977). *The Original Vision: A Study of Religious Experience of Childhood.* RERU: Manchester College, Oxford.

Rousseau, J-J. (1979). *Emile*, or *On Education*. Trans. A. Bloom. New York: Basic Books.

Rudgley, R. (1993). *The Alchemy of Culture*. London: British Museum Press.

— (1998). *Lost Civilisations of the Stone Age*. London: Century.

Rudmin, F. W. (1994). 'Property' in W. J. Lonner and R. Malpass (eds). *Psychology and Culture*, 55–9. Boston: Allyn and Bacon.

Sandbach, F. H. (1975). *The Stoics*. London: Chatto & Windus.

Schachtel, E. G. (1959). *Metamorphosis.* New York: Basic Books.

Scharfstein, B. (1973). *Mystical Experience*. Oxford: Basil Blackwell.

Selman, R. (1971). 'The relation of role-taking to the development of moral judgment in children.' *Child Development* 42, 79–92.

Service, E. R. (1978). *Profiles in Ethnology*. New York: Harper and Row.

Shanon, B. (2001). 'Altered temporality'. *The Journal of Consciousness Studies* 8 (1), 35–58.

Shapiro, D. (1960). 'A Perceptual Understanding of Color Response' in M. Richers-Ovisiankina (ed.), *Rorschach Psychology*. New York: Wiley.

Sheingold, K., and Tenney, Y. (1982). 'Memory from a Salient Childhood' in U. Neisser (ed.), *Memory Observed*, 201–12. New York: W. H. Freeman.

Sheldrake, R. (2004). *The Sense of Being Stared at*. London: Arrow.

Shukman, H. (2005). 'Stirred and Shaken.' *The Guardian Review*, 12/3/05.

Silberbauer, G. (1981). 'Hunter Gatherers of the Central Kalahari' in R. Harding and G. Teleki (eds), *Omnivorous Primates: Gathering and Hunting in Human Evolution*, 455–98. New York: Columbia University Press.

Smart, N. (1971). *The Religious Experience of Mankind*. London: Fontana.

Smith, H. (1964). 'Do drugs have religious import?' *Journal of Philosophy* LXI, 517–30.

— (2000). *Cleansing the Doors of Perception*. New York: Tarcher, Penguin.

Spencer, S. (1950). *Mysticism in World Religion*. London: Penguin.

Stace, W. (1964/1988). *Mysticism and Philosophy*. Los Angeles: J. P. Tarcher.

Strawson, G. (2006). *Consciousness and its Place in Nature: Does Physicalism Entail Panpsychism?* Exeter: Imprint Academic.

Sullivan, J. S. (1953). *Conceptions of Modern Psychiatry.* New York: Norton.

Swain, T. (1992). 'Reinventing the Eternal: Aboriginal Spirituality and Modernity' in N. Habel (ed.), *Religion and Multiculturalism in Australia*, 122–36. Adelaide: Australian Society for the Study of Religions.

Talukder, G. (2009). 'Researchers examine the effects of sleep deprivation on the brain.' Retrieved 11/7/08 from brain connection.com/topics.

Tamminen, K. (1994). 'Religious experiences in childhood and adolescence: a viewpoint of religious development between the ages of 7 and 20.' *International Journal for the Psychology of Religion* 4.

Tang, Y. Y., Ma, Y., Wang, J., Fan, Y., Feng, S., Lu, Q., Yu, Q., Sui, D., Rothbart, M. K., Fan, M., and Posner, M. I. (2007). 'Short-term meditation training improves attention and self-regulation.' *Proceedings of the National Academy of Sciences* 104, 17152–6.

Tart, C. (1983). *States of Consciousness*. El Cerrito, CA: Psychological Processes.

— (1991), 'Influence of previous psychedelic drug experience on students of Tibetan Buddhism.' *Journal of Transpersonal Psychology* 23, 139–74.

Taylor, S. (2001). 'From the unreal to the real: the reality of higher states of consciousness.' *New Renaissance* 10 (1), 12–14.

— (2002). 'Spirituality: the hidden side of sports.' *New Renaissance* 10 (4), 6–9.

— (2003). 'Primal spirituality and the onto/phylo fallacy: a critique of the claim that indigenous peoples were/are less spiritually and socially developed than modern humans.' *International Journal of Transpersonal Studies* 22, 61–76.

— (2005a). 'The sources of higher states of consciousness.'
International Journal of Transpersonal Studies 24, 48–60.

— (2005b). *The Fall: The Insanity of the Ego in Human History and the Dawning of a New Era*. Winchester: O Books.

— (2009a). 'Beyond the pre/trans fallacy: the validity of pre-egoic spiritual Experience.' *Journal of Transpersonal Psychology* 41, 22–43.

— (2009b). 'Spiritual emergencies: when despair and desolation trigger spiritual experiences.' *ReSource* 16, January.

The Bhagavad-Gita (1988). Ed. J. Mascaro. London: Penguin.

The Cloud of Unknowing (1997). Ed. W. Johnston. London: Fount.

The Upanishads (1990). Ed. J. Mascaro. London: Penguin.

Thomas, G. T. (1987). 'The Land is Sacred: Renewing the Dreaming in Modern Australia' in G. W. Trompf (ed.), *The Gospel is not Western: Black Theologies from the Southwest Pacific*, 90–94. Maryknoll, NY: Orbis Books.

Thoreau, H. D. (2009). *On Walden Pond*. Retrieved 9/8/09 from http://xroads.virginia.edu/~hyper/WALDEN/hdt05.html

Tolle, E. (1999). *The Power of Now*. London: Hodder and Staughton.

— (2005). *A New Earth*. London: Penguin.

'Tony's Story.' http://www.worthabbey.net/bbc/tony5.htm (from *The Monastery* TV programme).

Turnbull, C. (1993). *The Forest People*. London: Pimlico.

Underhill, E. (1911/1960). *Mysticism*. London: Methuen.

Vardey, L. (1995). *God in all Worlds*. London: Pantheon.

Versluis, A. (1994). *Indigenous American Traditions*. Shaftesbury: Element.

Vincent, K. R. (2009). 'Mystical religious experiences and Christina Universalism.' Retrieved 11/1/09 from http://www.near-death.com/experiences/origen021.html

Wade, J. (2000). 'Mapping the course of heavenly bodies: the varieties of transcendent sexual experiences.' *Journal of Transpersonal Psychology* 32, 103–22.

— (2004). *Transcendent Sex*. New York: Paraview.

Walker, B. (1987). *The Women's Encylopedia of Myths and Secrets*. San Francisco: Harper.

Walsh, R. (2003). 'Entheogens: true or false?' *International Journal of Transpersonal Studies* 22, 1–6.

Ward, R. H. (1957). *A Drug-Taker's Notes*. London: Gollancz.

Warshall, P. (1976). 'The voices of Black Lake.' *Co-Evolution Quarterly* 39, 64–9.

Washburn, M. (1980/1995). *The Ego and the Dynamic Ground*. Albany, NY: SUNY Press.

— (2002). 'Psychic energy, libido & spirit: three energies or one?' Retrieved from www.personaltransformation.com, 12/11/07.

— (2003). *Embodied Spirituality*. Albany, NY: SUNY Press.

Watts, A. (2007). *In My Own Way*. Novato CA: New World Library.

Werner, H. (1957). *The Comparative Psychology of Mental Development*. New York: International Universities Press.

White, J. (ed.) (1972). *The Highest State of Consciousness*. Garden City, NY: Anchor/Doubleday.

White, P., Lewith, G., Prescott, P., and Conway, J. (2004). 'Acupuncture versus placebo for the treatment of chronic mechanical neck pain: a randomized controlled trial.' *Annals of Internal Medicine* 141 (12), 911–19.

Whitman, W. (1980). *Leaves of Grass*. New York: Penguin.

Wilber, K. (1996a). *Sex, Ecology and Spirituality*. Boston: Shambhala.

— (1996b). *The Atman Project*. Wheaton, IL; Quest Books.

— (1997). *The Eye of Spirit: An Integral Vision for a World Gone Slightly Mad*. Boston: Shambhala.

— (2000a). *One Taste*. Boston: Shambhala

— (2000b). *Integral Psychology*. Boston: Shambhala.

— (2000c). 'Waves, streams, states and self: further considerations for an integral theory of consciousness.' *Journal of Consciousness Studies* 7, 11–12.

Wilson, C. (1985). *Mysteries*. London: Grafton.

Winston, R. (2005). *The Story of God*. London: Transworld.

Wood, E. (1959). *Yoga*. London: Penguin.

Wordsworth, W. (1950). *Poems*. London: Penguin.

Wright, R. (1992). *Stolen Continents*. Boston: Houghton Mifflin.

Wulff, D. M. (2000). 'Mystical Experience' in E. Cardeña, S. J. Lynn and S. Krippner (eds), *Varieties of Anomalous Experience: Examining the Scientific Evidence,* 397–440. Washington, DC: American Psychological Association.

Zaehner, R. C. (1961). *Mysticism Sacred and Profane*. Oxford: Oxford University Press.

INDEX

Mind Map of *Waking from Sleep*

by Paul Jones (author of *How to Live in the Here and Now*)

MEDITATION
MINDFULNESS
MODERATION
DETACHMENT
SERVICE
INTEGRAL LIFE

MOVING TOWARDS PERMANENT WAKEFULNESS

AWAKE

OUR EVERYDAY CONSCIOUSNESS

LIMITED SHADOWY–VISION OF REALITY

INANIMATE WORLD

DUALITY SEPARATION

EGO ISOLATION

MEANINGLESS WORLD

TAKING FOR GRANTED — SYNDROME

ONENESS OF THINGS
AWARENESS OF SPIRIT FORCE
TIME EXPANSION
BENEVOLENCE + HARMONY
ISNESS + ALIVENESS
LOW INTENSITY EXPERIENCES

INCREASE IN WELLBEING

H.D.

OF HOMEOSTASIS

DISRUPTION

- INCOMPLETE
- TEMPORARY
- QUICK
- RISKY

- EGO — DISSOLVES OR OPERATES

SLEEP DEPRIVATION

DRUGS

ASCETISM — SENSORY DEPRIVATION — DISCOMFORT — PAIN

FASTING

TEMPERATURE

ILLNESS — INFECTIONS — BRAIN CONDITIONS

DANCING

BREATHING — HYPER O² VENTILATION — HYPO CO²

EXPERIENCES

NING

UNITY
SLOW
POTENTIAL-PERMANENCE
WELL BEING
HARMONY
SEE LIFE FORCE

EGO REDUCTION — REAL SELF — BLISSFULL LIFE-ENERGY — STILLNESS IN SELF

INTENSIFICATION OF LIFE ENERGY

I.S.L.E.

+ θ −

ART
MUSIC
SEX
} SPONTANEOUS

POETRY
MEDITATION
CELIBACY
STILLNESS
SATSANG
RENUNCIATION + DETACHMENT
} CONSCIOUS SPIRITUAL PRACTICE

N.D.E.
SPIRITUAL CRISIS
} EXTREME

HIGH INTENSITY EXPERIENCES
ABSOLUTE WAKEFULNESS
TIMELESS TRANSCENDENCE
ONENESS OF SELF WITH — ALL THINGS
COMPASSION + LOVE

SERENITY, BLISS, EUPHORIA

269

Steve Taylor is an author and researcher whose main interests are spirituality, psychology and anthropology. He has been a lecturer in psychology at The University of Manchester and Leeds Metropolitan University, and is now a researcher in Transpersonal Psychology at Liverpool John Moores University and a lecturer at Salford City College. Earlier in his life he was a postman, a warehouse porter, a busker and professional musician, and an English teacher in Germany and Singapore. He has meditated since the age of 19, and taught yoga and meditation classes.

Steve has published two previous books, *The Fall* (O Books) and *Making Time* (Icon). His articles have been published in over 30 academic journals, magazines and newspapers including *The Journal of Transpersonal Psychology*, *The Journal of Consciousness Studies*, *Kindred Spirit*, *Resurgence* and *The Daily Express*. His work has been featured widely in the media in the UK, including on BBC Breakfast, BBC World TV, Radio 5, Radio 4 and *The Guardian*. His books have been translated into ten other languages, including German, Spanish, Japanese and Korean. Eckhart Tolle has described his work as 'imbued at all times with the higher faculty of spiritual awareness'.

As Steve says of his own work: 'My writings cover a wide range – spiritual experiences, history, anthropology, the psychology of time perception and of human well-being – but I see them as an attempt to explore and explain different varieties of human experience, in particular experience which stems from what the psychologist Abraham Maslow called "the farther reaches of human nature". I see normal human consciousness as a kind of aberration, which results in discord and turmoil both in the individual and the world. Ultimately, the aim of my work is to help human beings – and the human race as a whole – to transcend this aberrational state and shift into a higher state of being, a permanently spiritual state in which we can live harmoniously with ourselves and each other.'

Steve lives in Manchester with his wife and three children, including a young baby. He is a part-time house husband and regularly runs workshops and gives talks based on his books. His website is **www.stevenmtaylor.com**.

NOTES

NOTES

NOTES

NOTES

NOTES

NOTES

NOTES

NOTES

We hope you enjoyed this Hay House book. If you'd like
to receive our online catalog featuring additional information
on Hay House books and products, or if you'd like to find
out more about the Hay Foundation, please contact:

Hay House, Inc., P.O. Box 5100, Carlsbad, CA 92018-5100

(760) 431-7695 or **(800) 654-5126**
(760) 431-6948 (fax) or **(800) 650-5115 (fax)**
www.hayhouse.com® • **www.hayfoundation.org**

***

Published and distributed in Australia by:
Hay House Australia Pty. Ltd., 18/36 Ralph St., Alexandria NSW 2015
Phone: 612-9669-4299 • *Fax:* 612-9669-4144 • www.hayhouse.com.au

Published and distributed in the United Kingdom by:
Hay House UK, Ltd., 292B Kensal Rd., London W10 5BE • *Phone:*
44-20-8962-1230 • *Fax:* 44-20-8962-1239 • www.hayhouse.co.uk

Published and distributed in the Republic of South Africa by:
Hay House SA (Pty), Ltd., P.O. Box 990, Witkoppen 2068 • *Phone/Fax:*
27-11-467-8904 • info@hayhouse.co.za • www.hayhouse.co.za

Published in India by: Hay House Publishers India,
Muskaan Complex, Plot No. 3, B-2, Vasant Kunj, New Delhi 110 070
Phone: 91-11-4176-1620 • *Fax:* 91-11-4176-1630 • www.hayhouse.co.in

Distributed in Canada by:
Raincoast, 9050 Shaughnessy St., Vancouver, B.C. V6P 6E5
Phone: (604) 323-7100 • *Fax:* (604) 323-2600 • www.raincoast.com

***

Take Your Soul on a Vacation

Visit **www.HealYourLife.com**® to regroup, recharge,
and reconnect with your own magnificence.
Featuring blogs, mind-body-spirit news, and life-changing wisdom from
Louise Hay and friends.

Visit **www.HealYourLife.com** today!